PHENOMENOLOGY
OF EROS

———

SÖDERTÖRN
PHILOSOPHICAL STUDIES 10
2012

Phenomenology of Eros

Jonna Bornemark
& Marcia Sá Cavalcante Schuback (eds.)

SÖDERTÖRN
PHILOSOPHICAL STUDIES
10

Other titles in this series

Rethinking Time (2009)
Hans Ruin & Andrus Ers (eds.)

Phenomenology and Religion: New Frontiers (2010)
Jonna Bornemark and Hans Ruin (eds.)

Ambiguity of the Sacred (2012)
Jonna Bornemark & Hans Ruin (eds.)

Foucault, Biopolitics and Governmentality (2013)
Jakob Nilsson & Sven-Olov Wallentein (eds.)

Translating Hegel (2013)
Brian Manning Delaney & Sven-Olov Wallenstein (eds.)

———————————

Södertörn University

2012

Södertörn Philosophical Studies 10
ISSN 1651-6834
Södertörn Academic Studies 48
ISSN 1650-433X
ISBN 978-91-86069-46-9
© The authors
Graphic design: Johan Laserna
Print: E-print
Cover painting: Anders Widoff, untitled 04.02.04 (05) 2004.
From "anecdotes between faith and evening"
English proofreading: David Payne
Distribution: Södertörns högskola, Biblioteket
S-141 89 Huddinge
Phone: + 46 (0)8 608 40 00
E-mail: publications@sh.se

Table of Contents

Introduction
– Toward a Phenomenology of Eros

JONNA BORNEMARK
AND MARCIA SÁ CAVALCANTE SCHUBACK

The expression "phenomenology of eros" is ambiguous. On the one hand, it includes the erotic as a region or domain for phenomenological description; on the other hand, one might identify an "eros" internal to phenomenology such that phenomenology demands an eros. As a region for phenomenological description the erotic is one among many possibilities, with phenomenology being only a neutral method describing phenomena. But if it is considered that phenomenology has an "eros," then one must grant it a centrality in such philosophizing, not only in terms of its thematic coverage but also the constitutive role it plays in phenomenology. It is therefore possible to speak about a philosophical eros. This foregoing dichotomy can be exposed as false, allowing us to refuse to choose between these two approaches. Instead if we understand phenomenology as a continuous self-grounding of philosophy, insofar as each "region" or "domain" redefines phenomenology as such – or better expressed, co-constitutes phenomenology in the moment phenomenological research grounds its thematic field – then, in this sense, there cannot exist *a* phenomenology, but rather, phenomenologies.

Phenomenology both departs from and grounds a fundamental philosophical insight, namely that "being" is nothing but "appearing." This is the fundamental implication of the phenomenological motto "back to things themselves." And this is also the fundamental starting point to understand why phenomenology cannot be defined simply as a method of inquiry and description, but as a movement "back" to things such as they show themselves in themselves and not to something that lies hidden behind their way of appearing. Defined as a movement "back to things themselves," phenomenology assumes that at the same time as things show themselves in themselves, the finitude of consciousness covers them with partial views; things are sensed, glimpsed from the corner of our eye, without being fully known. This also implies that phenomenology must be specifically critical of itself: phenomenology is an infinite thinking task. In this way, phenomenology is only possible as an infinite transformation of finitude.

Since the first discussions about philosophical eros in Plato's *Symposium*, eros has been said to be generated by, and thus placed between, richness and poverty (Poros and Penia). It involves the striving toward the infinite by a finite being, or, as Bataille formulated it, eros entails the play between continuity and discontinuity. Eros is deeply involved in the human discovery of its own finitude and thus also to its need to relate to infinity. It is also in this context that the relation to the body is complexified. In the Western tradition human finitude has been defined in terms of the body, with the erotic journey often described as a journey away from one's own body towards the infinite and the One. At the same time the relation between body and transcendence has been understood in a more complex and interdependent way. Such is the case with Plato, who writes that Eros could not come into existence through Poros alone. Penia is required insofar as eros occupies a place within the tension-field between finitude and infinity.

Finitude involves the phenomenological assumption that every view *on* something is necessarily a view issued from a "living wellspring of experience," to recall an expression of the Czech phenomenologist Jan Patočka.[1] This explains why the viewing cannot be separated from the viewed; what is viewed is necessarily always envisaged from within a view. The dream of pure objectivism, according to which a world without man could be described and assumed independently from the existence of human understanding, is still and always a human dream, it is itself an embodied point of view. At the same time,

---

1. Jan Patočka, *Body, Community, Language, World*, transl. by Erazim Kohák (Chicago and la Salle, Illinois: Open Court, 1998), 3.

the counter concept of objectivism, namely, subjectivism, cannot be confounded with the idea of an isolated "I" or subject. The idea of an isolated and worldless "I" or "ego" is as constructed and therefore is equally as partial as the idea of an objective and external world. As the double movement of winning things' phenomenality and grounding its phenomenology, phenomenology puts in brackets the thesis about the external objectivity of the world as well as an internal subjectivism of the subject. Man *and* world, consciousness *and* things, the "I" *and* the "other," each reciprocally constitutes the other out of the living wellspring of experience. This reciprocality and its in-betweeness can be considered the core of the erotic. That is why the erotic experience as an "in-between" must in one way or another always be taken into consideration in such an investigation.

In the attempts to pursue this task, a related problematic crops up: the erotic is not only an object for investigation but it is as much the source of investigation. To start out from "the living well-spring of experience" means in fact to set out from this springing stream as erotically structured. This is also why the grounding of philosophy in ancient Greece as the questioning of "what is being?" (*ti to on*) gains its point of articulation between eros and thinking (*noein*).[2] This articulation is, in a certain sense, already engraved in philosophy's own name as *philia tou sofou* – the love of wisdom, a determination that involves both experiences of love's wisdom and wisdom's love. Considering that the non-evidence and questionability of both the *meaning of being*, as a dualistic psycho-physic conception of the world, and of the exclusivity of the subject-object relationship, remain central questions for phenomenology's self-grounding and constitution, they become even more urgent with respect to a "phenomenology of eros." This is because "eros" pushes the questions regarding both the "meaning of being" and the "subject-object relationship" to their outer most limits, in terms of both a radicality and a mutual reciprocity. This touches upon the erotic experience, because the erotic is intimately personal at the same time as it constitutes a time-space in which the personal dissolves. It is for this reason that every attempt made either to objectify – that is, to universalize – the erotic or to leave it to

---

2. Aristotle, *Metaphysics*, book XII, 1072b 3–4.

purely subjective formulations, both loses and covers up the phenomenon.

Above all, it is in relation to the non-evidence of the subject-object relationship that different contributions toward a phenomenology of eros or of the erotic have been developed. As far as "the erotic" is considered as one central dimension of intersubjective relations, and intersubjectivity is assumed as a phenomenological ground for the constitution of meaning, we may say that every phenomenology of intersubjectivity has either explicitly discussed "erotic phenomenon" and tried to develop extensive phenomenologies of eros or implicitly presented elements that may contribute toward a phenomenology of eros. Such is the case with Max Scheler, whose discussions on love, sympathy and empathy are known;[3] in his *Studios sobre el Amor*,[4] Ortega y Gasset develops a phenomenology of love, where eros and eroticism are discussed; while Eugen Fink discusses "Eros und Selbstverständigung – Seinssinn des Eros" in *Grundphänomene des menschlichen Daseins*,[5] not forgetting the contributions of Simone de Beauvoir in *Le deuxième Sexe*,[6] and Ludwig Binswanger's *Grundformen und Erkenntnis menschlichen Daseins*[7] Yet at the same time as we find germs of a phenomenology of eros in different phenomenologists and phenomenological research, there are few explicit attempts to ground a regional phenomenology of erotic phenomenon. The most explicit treatments, in that they bare in their titles the terms "phenomenology" and "eros" ("erotic" or "eroticism") are to be found in Emmanuel Levinas' "Phénoménologie de l'Eros" in *Totalité et Infini*,[8] and in Jean-Luc Marion's *Le phénomène*

3. He discusses eros and eroticism explicitly in texts as *Zur Phänomenologie und Theorie der Sympathiegefühl und von Liebe und Haß* (Halle: Verlag von Max Niemeyer, 1913), *Liebe und Erkenntnis* (Bern: Francke Verlag, 1955), "Ordo amoris" in *Schriften aus dem Nachlass, Band I, Zur Ethik und Erkenntnislehre* (Bern: Der neue Geist Verlag, 1933), and in different texts in *Schriften aus dem Nachlass, Band III, Philosophische Anthropologie* (Bonn: Bouvier Verlag Herbert Grundmann, 1987).
4. (Madrid: Salvat, 1971), see for the English version, *On Love: Aspects of a Single Theme*
5. (Freiburg:Karl Alber Verlag, 1995)
6. (Paris: Gallimard, 1949)
7. (Zürich: Max Niehans, 1942)
8. (Paris: Kluwer, 1971)

érotique.[9] We could also include Georges Bataille, in particular his *Eroticism: Death and Sensuality*, as a close relative to the phenomenological tradition.[10]

The amplitude of the multifaceted erotic phenomenon makes it very difficult to construct strict distinctions between eroticism and sexuality, eroticism and desire and furthermore between eroticism and love. This is why different phenomenologies of love, desire, seduction, passions, sexuality and sexual difference are phenomenologies of eros and vice-versa. The title "eros" and "erotic phenomenon" is often used to show the variable interconnection between those meanings and to evoke the platonic and neo-platonic basis for the philosophical treatment of eros and the "erotic" wisdom of philosophy (Lucy Irigaray, among others). From out of different attempts toward a phenomenology of eros, at least one common basis can be affirmed. In its numerous faces and traces, (sexuality, desire, passion, love, friendship, etc), the "erotic phenomenon" appears and becomes central in every attempt to grasp the condition of possibility for oneness and otherness, for selfhood and alterity, finitude and infinity.

As such it challenges what could be called the "logical tendency" of various phenomenologies of intersubjectivity. As with every logic, this logical tendency is a moment of lack of criticism or even dogmatism within thinking itself; thought tries to "solve" contradictions instead of throwing itself in them and asking about their "origin." The "tendential logic" of various phenomenologies of intersubjectivity – and arguably the "tendential logic" of the dominant idea of phenomenology in general – is the *logic of difference.* The phenomenological "logic of difference" can be defined as the search for solving the "paradox of subjectivity," whereby the other is admitted as a self that I myself am not but whose "absolute difference" can only be sustained if I admit it in *analogy* with my own self. One of the main criticisms addressed by different philosophical and even cultural traditions to those different but still very close phenomenologies of intersubjectivity is the danger of what can be called existential solipsism.[11] Husserl's notion

---

9. (Paris: Bernard Grasset, 2003)
10. (San Francisco: City Lights Books, 1986 [1962])
11. See Hannah Arendt's essay "What is Existenz Philosophy?" in *The Phenomenology*

of *transcendental ego* and Heidegger's concept of *Jemeinigkeit* have operated as centers around which such criticisms have cohered; by some
critics each has been taken as an extreme case of the danger existing
within the phenomenological tradition.[12] In a very general way, it can
be said that, in whatever face eros may assume, a phenomenology of
eroticism touches and deals with the fundamental philosophical questions of identity and difference, of sameness and otherness, of mutual
dependency and independence, and of the double meaning of limit (as
separating and as a meeting-point).

The phenomenology of eros was the theme of a workshop held 2006
at Södertörn University. Most of the contributions to this anthology
were first written for this occasion but other texts have subsequently
been added. The anthology has been divided into two parts. The first
discusses eros in relation to antique philosophy and religion, while the
second part thematizes the erotic in light of modern phenomenology.

The first contribution in the anthology, "Tragic or Philosophic Eros
in Sophocles and Plato," written by Peter Trawny, takes us back to the
beginning of philosophy. While it can be said that philosophy created
reason, eros is that which philosophy receives, rather than something
it creates. This leads us back to tragedy where eros is exposed as tyrannical, as attacking social boundaries and human individuality. There
is no one to hold responsible and as a consequence the human being
experiences him- or her-self as exposed. Eros is a placeless force controlling the lives of human beings. Trawny then shows how Plato's
philosophy changes this tyrannical tragic eros into an eros that takes
place as the desire of the soul. But through this changed position of
eros an important shift becomes possible: the lover is no longer passively locked up in one beautiful object, rather he or she transcends to
the idea of beauty as such. Philosophical eros now becomes the overcoming of the body in desiring the supersensible. As an alternative to

Reader, ed. Dermot Moran and Timothy Mooney (London and New York: Routledge, 2002).
12. See for example Toru Tani's discussions in Transzendentales Ich und Gewalt
in *Phänomenologie und Gewalt*, edited by Harun Maye and Hans Rainer Sepp
(Würzburg: Königshausen and Neumann, 2005) and the paper "Das ich, der
Andere und die Urtatsache" held at the Annual Meeting of the Nordic Society for
Phenomnology 2007 in Copenhagen.

a philosophical life as overcoming the embodied eros in search of knowledge, Trawny offers us a poetic life: in poetry the ecstatic temporality of eros becomes a gathering of intensity, the opening of a world that will soon be lost.

If the poetic constitutes the end-point in Trawny's contribution, in "Dionysian *Dankbarheit*: Friedrich Hölderlin's Poetics of Sacrifice" Elizabeth B. Sikes takes the poetic eros of Hölderlin as her starting-point. Here the expectation of a new religion of celebration and gratitude, and a love for the earth binds Eros and Thanatos (love and death) closely together. This Dionysian philosophy of love – just as with Socrates' discussion on Poros and Penia – shows the paradox of human life: a life at once striving for infinity and transcendence at the same time as it is determined and receiving. Eros here becomes the symbol for this ambiguous nature of the mortal. Love thus only takes place in time. On the one hand, the striving for love means to go towards the future; on the other, there is always an overflow of the present that takes place as a holy memory. This memory organizes civilization, but at the same time it always risks reducing the infinite feeling of life into a dead figure. The infinite is not possible to present, instead it is only through another temporal figure that infinity is granted an indirect presentation: *das Augenblick*, the momentary. The poetic songs are born out of the holy memory in which what escapes rational memory and reflection is remembered. Sikes even states that representational thinking cripples our ability to love. What is left is instead a song of gratitude in which an excessive intimacy might take place.

The relation between eros and poetry is examined further in Anna-Lena Renqvist's contribution, "Eros and poíesis." But this time it is the wider meaning of *poiesis* as production that stands at the center while eros is characterized as the kind of love that produces offspring. Eros is first of all responsible for difference as such and has the power to liberate forces by splitting them up. Only through such differentiation can they once again re-encounter one another. Eros is thus also on the border between mythology and philosophy. In mythology it is the Alpha and Omega of cosmos, while in Plato's philosophy eros is responsible for becoming in general, as well as for knowledge and wisdom as specific kinds of philosophical becoming. Eros binds the lover to what he does not have and it is in contemplation that the highest love is supposed to be fulfilled. Through this move towards theory, philosophy is separated from both praxis and poeisis. But theory is not the object of philosophical love; it is only a means. The true object of philosophical eros is instead immortality and the overcoming of a condition. But this overcoming continues to give birth to new separations.

Eros as the movement between one and the many is something that is investigated further in "The Nature and Origin of the Eros of the Human Soul in Plotinus" by Agnès Pigler. She contrasts the erotic philosophy of Plotinus with the erotic philosophy of Plato. As we have seen in Trawny's contribution, the seat of love in Plato is in the soul. Love is never a goal in itself but a means to reach the highest idea. Platonic intellectualism thus surpasses the erotic. Pigler shows that in Plotinus it is the other way around. Here love is life itself in its dynamic power, a power that constitutes the overflow of the One. Pigler distinguishes between love as a metaphysical and a mystical experience. The mystic experience originates in a divine initiative, but in Plotinus the One can never take any initiative and therefore can have no love for its creation. Love is instead always present and structures the relation of dependence and difference between the One and the many. In this structure love is the imprint and memory of the absolute origin, and it is through love, not reason, that the human being can transcend the manifold. But this only takes place through the abandonment of the multiplicity of possible loves and from their bodies. Only in this way is there a uniting with the One and a touching of the inexpressible.

The inexpressibility of eros is also discussed by Jason Wirth in "The Undesirable Object of Desire: Towards a Phenomenology of Eroticism." Wirth states that any clarity of desire is kitsch, preferring to understand love as the force of the life of life. Such an understanding places him in proximity with neo-platonic discussants. But, in contrast to neo-platonism, Wirth does not want to understand eros as a flight into mythic obscurity, rather it serves to define the search for the clear and undiscovered, and as such both binds together and lives on the periphery of art, science and philosophy. In accordance with a tragic understanding of eros, eroticism is neither an activity initiated by an individual nor is it a force that would throw an individual into passivity. The erotic is here above all a welcoming of the other to the table of philosophy for a discussion on death and philosophical life. Both Bataille and Schelling are presented here as providing a possibility to develop a non-philosophy of the erotic from which a self-critical standpoint in regard to self-possessed activity of philosophy could be unfolded. Only such non-philosophy can know death, chaos and the earth, and accordingly relate to the discontinuity of continuity and the continuity of discontinuity.

With Wirth's discussion on Bataille and Schelling we are already on our way to the second part of the volume that discusses eroticism by taking its point of anchorage in modern phenomenology. Sá Cavalcante Schuback opens this second part with an analysis of Heidegger's philosophy of love in "Heideggerian Love." Heidegger has been largely criticized for not having taken love into account, assuming *Dasein* to be a neutral being without desires. But Sá Cavalcante Schuback argues otherwise. She claims that the main reason for why Heidegger so rarely talks about love is that he departs from the limits of philosophy and from the impossibility to speak philosophically of love without losing love. However, precisely because Heidegger has brought philosophy to its limits, his thought constitutes a privileged place to think of love while losing it: at the moment where the Gods and thereby eros have abandoned earth. Heidegger does not thematize love but makes love come into play. Heidegger defines *Dasein* as care and as transcending, and thus, Sá Cavalcante Schuback adds, as love or eros. Heidegger's whole philosophy wishes to radically question the subject. Through his deconstruction of the autonomous self, just as in love, the oppositions between inside and outside, interior and exterior, selfhood and otherness are dissolved. *Dasein* is no longer a question of identity or of unity, but a question rather of being entire in the own finitude, i.e. of an intense entirety. Love is neither a feeling nor a knowledge, but rather an overwhelming transformation of both feeling and knowledge.

In "The Phenomenological Question of the Relation with the Other: Love, Seduction and Care" Françoise Dastur broadens the Heideggerian discussion with an analysis of love and seduction through a phenomenological analysis involving, among others, Sartre, Levinas,

Merleau-Ponty, Husserl and Arendt. In contrast to a traditional understanding of seduction, Dastur does not understand the seducer as
active, on the one hand, and, on the other, the seduced as passive; the
game is rather more nuanced. Neither does Dastur give us a strict division between love as connected to truth and being on the one side and
seduction as related to deception and appearance on the other. Instead, both love and seduction should be understood as ontological
phenomena, having to do with concern and solicitude. Dastur contrasts Sartre's and Levinas' understanding of the loving relation as full
of conflicts with Merleau-Ponty's and Husserl's "community of love"
where subjects are completely intertwined. It is with a background in
such a community of concern that seduction can take place. Seduction
as an inauthentic concern of the other takes place through the desire
to be seen and loved. And the authentic relation (if at all possible) will
always take place with this as its background.

As we have seen temporality is deeply connected to the theme of
eros. Eros is connected to the mortal and its striving beyond itself. In
"The Temporality of Sexual Life in Husserl and Freud" Nicholas
Smith investigates the temporality of the freudian unconscious and
how this temporality is connected to sexuality. The unconscious in
Freud is supposedly timeless and an unsurpassable limit for husserlian
phenomenology with its act-intentionality. But Smith shows how the
freudian concept of the unconscious and the husserlian analysis of
inner time-consciousness converge in the concept of *Nachträglichkeit*
('coming after'). Through a temporal delay consciousness is in communication with the unconscious, and it is also through this concept
that Husserl shows the limits of act-intentionality. In his later writings
Husserl shows another side to his otherwise slightly dry analyses when
the primordial stream of experiences turnout to be a system of drives.
In this way Smith claims that eros is found at the most basic structure
of inner time-consciousness and sexuality is thus understood as part
of a temporal *Urstruktur*.

Eros in the philosophy of Sartre is investigated further in Helena
Dahlberg's contribution "On Flesh and Eros in Sartre's *Being and
Nothingness.*" At stake here is the relation between eros and flesh. Sartre
claims that to be seen is always to be closed up in oneself, turning
oneself into a thing, and that the desire of the other has to relate to

this "thingness," continuing to transform the other into an object. Sartre thus understands the erotic relation and the relation between bodies by finding the starting-point in such an objectifying mode. He describes how caressing reveals the flesh of the other by stripping the body of its action, an act that also transforms the self that strikes into flesh. The body is no longer understood as full of possibilities, but as a purely "being there" instead of being for... or being on its way to.... If the enchantment of desire suddenly disappears then the "being there" of the flesh becomes obscene, stripped of meaning, with the living body coagulating into flesh. Here flesh plays on the difference of being-for-itself and being-for-others and Dahlberg points out the similarity of Sartre's concept of the flesh with the one Merleau-Ponty would develop twenty years later. She also argues that the combination of flesh and desire in Sartre becomes one of the very few ways to relate to what is present.

In "Accusing the Erotic Subject," Carl Cederberg points out that philosophy as predominantly a universal and neutral description of phenomena, has had problems relating to the erotic, since it is linked to sexual and gendered specificity and singularity. At worst the philosopher starts from a personal experience, claiming it to be universal. Levinas has received such criticism from, among others, Luce Irigaray. In defense of Levinas, Cederberg states the necessity of starting out from a male perspective in Levinas' phenomenological analyses. When later in *Otherwise than being* Levinas leaves this gendered position he also takes leave of the erotic. Even if claims for universality are to be disregarded, Cederberg argues, there are nonetheless some important points raised by Levinas. In *Totality and Infinity* eros is the copula between enjoyment and ethics. Enjoyment is described as our primary relation to life – before both every objectivation and the ethical as a rupture of this enjoyment, which calls us to responsibility and mutual enjoyment. Here the erotic is a dimension of subjectivity opened up to transcendence and the interpersonal, but where the borders of the ethical are crossed in a violence that plays between unity and difference, continuity and discontinuity.

In "Erotic Perception: Operative Intentionality as Exposure" Lisa Käll discusses the role of the erotic in Merleau-Ponty's philosophy and deepens our understanding through a discussion on Luchino Visconti's movie *Death in Venice* (based on the novel by Thomas Mann). Merleau-Ponty argues that intentionality at first does not show itself as a cogitatio aiming at a cogitatum. Rather things exist for us to the extent that we have an embodied desire towards them and our bodies are powers of transcendence toward the world. The erotic experience is the most manifest way in which this bond between the world and the self shows itself. As the self reaches out of itself it also becomes vulnerable and exposed to the world. Without being seen by the loved one, as well as seeing the object of one's desire, one could not exist – just as in *Death in Venice* where the main character, Aschenbach, follows his beloved Tadzio's every move, as if his whole existence depended on his exposure to Tadzio's presence. One can only come into existence by risking that very same existence. In this way existence shows itself as the ambiguity between autonomy and dependence, connectedness and distance, between being perceived as subject and being perceived as object.

In the last contribution, "The Erotic as Limit-Experience: A Sexual Fantasy," Jonna Bornemark discusses the ambiguity of the erotic as concerning limits. Following up to a certain point the thought of Jean-Luc Marion, Bornemark gives the phenomenological discussion of sexual relations an ontological weight: it points toward both the basic structure of life and the limits of object-intentionality. But, Bornemark claims, in trying to come to terms with a non-objectifying intentional structure, both Michel Henry's and Jen-Luc Marion's attempts tend to end up in a sharp division between immanence and transcendence, self-affection and object-intentionality, flesh and body. In Marion's case this also contributes to a chauvinistic understanding of the sexual relation where the female counterpart is described as passive and welcoming, and as "making room" for his transcending experience – an experience which cannot be shared afterwards. Through her own analysis of a sexual encounter, Bornemark wants instead to give objectness of the body and fantasy significant roles. Orgasm here does not lead beyond the world, but into an act of "limit-drawing" where the limits of the world shows themselves. After the orgasm there is thus everything to say, constituting the world anew.

Tragic or Philosophic Eros
in Sophocles and Plato

PETER TRAWNY

La poésie mène au même point que chaque forme de l'éroticisme à
l'indistinction, à la confusion des objets distincts. [Poetry leads to the
same place as all forms of eroticism – to the blending and fusion of
separate objects.]

Georges Bataille

1. *Introduction*

We find ourselves still involved in a decision between a *tragic* and a
philosophic Eros.[1] Only one who is willing to "crucify his flesh" (Gal.
5.24) or to shackle it in some way (1. Kor. 7.2) is confronted with a
decision other than this one. And yet, perhaps the question is whether
there is a "decision" at stake here at all, whether Eros, the erotic, or
even eroticism do not tend to indicate the end of "decision" itself.

Is it then possible that there is a decision for non-decision, for
necessity, for an unmitigated contingency? Decision for non-decision
would be abandon, wilful exposure, denudation. In any case, Eros and
the erotic are among those "things" in human life that eminently

---

1. This text is part of a larger work investigating Eros, the erotic, and erotics, on
which I have I been working for the last two years. I intend for this larger project
to examine Eros as it manifests itself in various cultural forms (poetry, literature,
music, film, etc.). Georges Bataille uses the term of "tragic eroticism" in his *The
tears of Eros* (San Francisco: City Lights Books 1989). But what he unfolds there
is more or less only a kind of draft. He approaches the phenomenon by discussing
the "religion" of Dionysios. Cf. also Georges Bataille, *Erotism: Death and Sensuality*
(San Francisco: City Lights Books 1986).

withdraw themselves from any rational organization, from ordering. At the same time, the erotic is located so deeply at the very center of our lives that its marginalization or expulsion must be recognized as an impossibility. Therefore, philosophy, too, cannot and has not been able to ignore its significance, but it has surely interpreted Eros in a certain way.

It can be shown that philosophy has received Eros, that it has not generated Eros out of itself as it has, for example, reason. Indeed, the origin of Eros leads us back to tragic poetry, which itself may have its own origin in Eros. Because Eros still is and remains what it was then, an intensive consideration is still and will be inevitable.

2. Tragic Eros

Tragic Eros is the Eros of Pre-Socratic, tragic poetry. The philosophical concept of Eros can be found in its interpretation by Plato and Socrates, which emerges out of a confrontation with the presentation of Eros in tragedy. Perhaps this confrontation could be characterized otherwise, as a confrontation between an *exposed* and a *sheltered life*.

The charter of Eros is expressed in poetry. I refer to a relatively late one, namely to the third stasimon in Sophocles' tragedy *Antigone*, which addresses itself to Eros. It reads (v. 781–800):

> Eros, undefeated in battle,
> Eros, who falls upon possessions,
> who, in the soft cheeks of a young girl,
> stays the night vigil,
> who traverses over seas
> and among pastoral dwellings,
> you none of the immortals can escape,
> none of the day-long mortals, and
> he who has you is maddened.
>
> You wrest the minds of even the just
> aside to injustice, to their destruction.
> You have incited this quarrel
> among blood kin.
> Desire radiant from the eyelids

of a well-bedded bride prevails,
companion in rule with the gods' great
ordinances. She against whom none may battle,
the goddess Aphrodite, plays her games.

(Translation by William Blake Tyrrell and Larry J. Bennett)

This stasimon is situated between Haimon's struggle with his father
Creon and Antigone's lamentation over her imminent execution and,
thus, her being destined not to marry her betrothed, Haimon, but
Acheron instead. Some readers have claimed that this stasimon contains a "misjudgment," an "error,"[2] because Haimon in his discussion
with Creon is presented not as one driven by Eros, but as one who
argues clearly and with reason. Such a view seems to misunderstand
poetry. It is obvious that the stasimon and its contents are not intended to represent or summarize the tragedy in general. Neither Haimon nor Antigone are "maddened" by Eros, in fact the atmosphere of
the whole drama is rather sober. Therefore, the stasimon must have as
its aim something other than simply commenting on the plot.

The direct link of the stasimon to the struggle between Haimon and
Creon is the statement that their blood bond is not strong enough to
effectuate Haimon's obedience. "Blood" or "blood relation" has a
manifestly special importance, not only in *Antigone*, but in Greek
tragedy in general. Here, already in her opening exchange with Ismene,
Antigone refers to their common body, their common blood, i.e. to
family. Eros and the charm of the goddess Aphrodite modify the
meaning of that blood, they undermine the meaning of the family.

Of course – *the* tragedy of Eros is Euripides' *Hippolytus*, the story of
the impossible love of Phaedra, in this tragedy blood bond is also
relevant. Hippolytus is Phaedra's stepson, her love concerns the family,
even if direct incest is not at stake. The tragic conflict appears from
semnótēs (already v. 93/94), i.e. from an ambivalent virtue in the
character of Hippolytos as well as Phaedra. Semnós is at first a
signification for a quite honorable person, but at the same time it

---

2. Cf. Ursula Bittrich, *Eros und Aphrodite in der antiken Tragödie. Mit Ausblicken auf
motivgeschichtlich verwandte Dichtungen* (Berlin: De Gryuter, 2005), 30–34.

fosters hybrid pride. Thus Hippolytos and Phaedra are both unable to cope with the problematic situation. Hippolytos with his relation to Artemis and his ignorance concerning Aphrodite, who appears at the beginning of the tragedy by announcing her revenge on the young man, and Phaedra with her stubborn refusal to obey her desire.

The most influential stasimon of the tragedy depicts Eros as a "tyrant" (v. 525–544):

> Eros, Eros, you who drip desire
> down into the eyes as you lead sweet delight
> into the souls of those you war against,
> never may you appear to me with harm
> or come out of measure.
> For the shaft neither of fire nor of the stars is superior
> to Aphrodite's, which Eros, the son of Zeus,
> sends forth form his hands.
>
> In vain, in vain along the Alpheus
> and in the Pythian home of Phoebus
> the [land] of Hellas slaughters more and more oxen,
> but Eros, the tyrant of men,
> the holder of the keys to Aphrodite's
> dearest inner chambers, we do not venerate,
> although he destroys mortals and sends them through every
> misfortune whenever he comes.
>
> (Translation Michael R. Halleran)

The mortal wish for measurement in relation to Eros is in vain. Eros can not be limited. The end of the second stanza is surprising. Eros, who is "the tyrant of men" (Plato later in the *Republic* will refer to this characterization (573b), hence assuming a tragic *topos*), can open "Aphrodite's / dearest inner chambers." For this he should be venerated – even if he causes the deepest pains.

What both songs have to say about Eros and Aphrodite is far-reaching. The first feature presented is already essential. Eros is an invincible power. If he announces himself, he descends on that which is ours, which has importance for us. He appears and withdraws wherever and whenever he wants. He is the *event of a specific temporality*, which transforms those who were formerly strangers into lovers. These participants in the event are not consulted, their intentions and customs are not taken into consideration. Eros or the erotic is a "tyrannical" emerging and happening.

In the erotic event, the human being experiences him- or herself as *exposed*. He or she is barely able to find shelter, being struck by a certain violence. A moment of this erotic exposure also seems to be a necessary denudation. Exposure is nakedness, a release for tenderness and excess, a compelled release at least in the eye of the poet.

Another element of the erotic event is that it can happen anywhere. Eros is always moving, it cannot be located. Nobody, not even a God, can escape his power. This omnipresent possibility of the erotic event, this exposedness of the human being, is therefore in itself a *delocalization*. The erotic, as a-topic, dislocates. Eros descends on the exposed no matter where he or she is. By doing so, it necessitates the institution of special places. It is one of the consequences of the primary place-lessness of the erotic that there are institutions for the service of Eros. Because Eros is principally without places, we have to create them.

In this sense the stasimon from Sophocles' *Antigone* and from Euripides' *Hippolytos* emphasizes erotic violence.[3] For the erotic there is no law and order. Plato calls this tyrannical Eros anarchic and anomic (Res pub., 575a). He knows neither written nor unwritten laws. Indeed, the Trojan war has an erotic cause. If Homer poetizes that Zeus takes and loves Hera, not first in their marital bed, but on the ground, on the soil (390c), such a poem has to be censured, barred from the ideal city. Insofar as the erotic attacks normal habits, attacks boundaries between certain social elements, for instance by causing adultery, it has a political significance. It is for this reason that both Plato's and Aristotle's writings on the constitution of the *polis* must take up the theme of Eros.

Attacking every social boundary, Eros can disintegrate the blood bond, be it that of the family (cf. even still Shakespeare's *Romeo and Juliet*) or that of the entire race. The concept of "racial defilement" refers to this eventuality. "Racial laws" are always a defensive means

---

3. Cf. not only Racine's *Phèdre*, but also Sarah Kane's *Phaedra's Love*. in *Complete Plays* (London: Methuen Publishing Ltd, 2001), 63–104.

established to hinder erotic delimitations and their disturbances of order. The tragic character of Eros lies for Sophocles most of all in the fact that a stable order has to fight erotic disintegration and exposure. Eros is not peaceful, even if at its center there may appear a powerful peace.

Exposure, delocalization, disintegration – without a doubt Eros attacks the integrity of the "individual" or of the "subject." This integrity seems to organize itself necessarily in moral and legal orders. The life of the subject demands a specific security, a being-sheltered, to realize itself in a social form. A functional structure, for instance that of the world of labor, requires regularity, and normalcy, which can then be shattered and disintegrated by the erotic event. In this sense the erotic event is also a *desubjectivation*. Important features of that security of the subject can be annihilated: responsibility or guilt cease to exist for the erotic, they cannot exist because there is no "personality" to hold responsible or feel guilty. Hölderlin translates one verse of the stasimon: "Whoever has it, [is] not himself." Eros is ecstasis and excess, a (desired) loss of the self. Nietzsche's emphasis on Dionysus, who is also evoked in the last stasimon of *Antigone* (1120), recollects just this effect of desubjectivation. And Levinas continues to speak of an "impersonnalité de la volupté."[4]

Tragic Eros exposes, dislocates, disintegrates and desubjectifies like a wholly anchorless event. For Sophocles this *exteriority* is almost total. Plato also speaks in his *Republic* of an erotic necessity (458d). He nevertheless distrusts such a tragic emphasis on a pure exteriority. And in fact we have to ask whether Eros can be understood as mere contingency, as a mere irruption of the human being's exposed openness. Certainly, as regards Sophocles' stasimon, Eros sleeps on the cheeks of a desired young girl – it is beauty, showing itself as skin and flesh, i.e. as a body. But are we able to renounce the possibility of thinking a *desire of the human being*, of thinking a desire that arises out of human *interiority*, however this is to be understood?

---

4. Emmanuel Levinas, *Totalité et Infini. Essai sur l'extériorité* (The Hague: Martinus Nijhoff, 1961), 243.

3. Philosophic Eros

The Eros of tragedy seems to overcome individuals, penetrating them and dragooning them, compelling their surrender. If Eros withdraws, this surrender ceases to be in effect. As mentioned above, in his description of the tyrannical man and the tyrant himself in the ninth book of the *Republic*, Plato remarks that Eros is called from ancient times a tyrant. One could think that the genesis of the tyrant presupposes a wholly exposed human being or, in other words, that it represents mere exteriority. Thus, the citizens could be exposed to the domination of the tyrant like he himself is exposed to Eros.

That this topic is not only a minor matter for Plato is shown in the beginning of the whole *Republic*. Socrates is going to the Piraeus to pray to the Goddess Bendis in respect of a festive procession. There he meets Polemarchos, who invites Socrates into his father's, i.e. Cephalos, house. Now we see Socrates asking the old man about his life advanced in years. At once Cephalos refers to a short conversation with Sophocles. He once asked him the same question in his (Sophocles') advanced age. And the poet ascertains that he is quite happy, because he does not have to live any more in the influence of the despot Eros (329a–c). What a remarkable introduction to a magnum opus of political philosophy in general. Considering that Homer, who is critically represented as the educator of Hellas (606e), appears as the first of the tragedians (595b), we can perceive the importance of this problem. Is the *Republic* perhaps an esoteric response to tragedy?

Therefore it is rather consequential, that Plato in the *Republic* explains very detailed, what has barely left a trace in the chorus-songs of Sophocles' *Antigone* and Euripides' *Hippolytos*. Plato knows the soul and the desire within the soul (*epithymía*). The tyrannical in the human being is evident in the emergence of desire during sleep, which is to say, when the rational part of the soul is absent. There, while sleeping, it is the animalistic or the wild that asserts itself (571c), balking not even at incest or at lying with a god or an animal. Eros is now desire, but a special one, because it is the leader of all other desires (573e). A man ruled by this desire will finally become a drunkard, a lecher, and a melancholic (573c). He will violate the natural order of the family. If Eros dwells *in* the soul of the tyrant, his life would consist of continuous festivals with comic acts and luxurious meals accompanied by prostitutes. The philosopher lives differently.

Plato has interpreted the tragic Eros as tyrannical and declared the tyrant the adequate image for this Eros. This does not entail, however, that Eros or the erotic is now left to the poets. Rather, Plato gives it a new meaning, presenting in the *Symposium* a discussion of philosophic Eros. The true Eros is not the tragic one – this Eros appears only as one aspect of the soul and, thereby, as a violent expulsion of reason. Sensual or erotic desire defeats every form of temperance or prudence. It is only through the cruel displacement of his sensory vision with a non-sensory vision that Oedipus comes to see truly.

With the story told by Diotima in the *Symposium* and also with the discourse of Alcibiades, Plato inscribes the entire subsequent history of philosophy with his interpretation of a philosophic Eros. After Phaedrus, Pausanias, Eryximachos, Aristophanes, and Agathon have given their discourses on Eros, heretofore conceived as a God, Socrates takes the stage and brings the discussion to a head in the Diotima-*anamnêsis*. Although the five Pre-Socratic discourses on Eros are not presented by Plato merely as strange curiosities and thus should be taken seriously in the context of the dialogue, they do not achieve the intensity and significance of the Eros-stasimon in the "Antigone," not even the discourse of the tragic poet, Agathon. The tragic, anarchic-anomic Eros is not brought to language. Plato has, it seems, already domesticated the discussion.

What Socrates perceives in all the previous discourses is the celebration of desire, a desire that relates to a desired being understood otherwise. Eros has been praised as the most beautiful and the best, because it incorporates this desire. This desire is described as an irresistible attraction. But this entails that the lover is more noble than the beloved, especially in that he is exposed to this movement, to this attraction. Socrates then focuses primarily on this motion, this striving. Indeed, it is here that we recognize the strongest echo of tragic Eros, insofar as Eros is characterized by Socrates as the one who placelessly rambles around dislocating the human being in the impersonal contingency of an event that has a specific temporality. The tragic as well as the philosophic Eros move the lover, they let him strive. However, now departing from Sophocles, this striving is understood as a property of the soul. Plato has psychologized the myth not only in relation to the poets, but in his own works. The motion of the horse-team representing the soul in the *Phaedrus* is in the *Republic* the soul (and the city) itself.

Nevertheless with this psychological interpretation Plato did not pursue a mere reduction of Eros. On the contrary, the striving of Eros is now identified with *life as a whole*. Life is motion, it is always heading somewhere. But in which direction? Here begins Socrates' critique of tragic Eros. If Eros himself is already the most beautiful and the best, one could not understand why there is still this motion, this striving desire. For the one who is on his way and desires must desire what he is lacking, what he still does not have or is lacking again. Even if he were already to possess what he desires, he would still desire that this remain. Thus, Eros is the desire and the desired at the same time. Eros unfolds the sphere of desire and constitutes an *in between* as the beginning and end of desire.

This step in the interpretation of the erotic cannot be overestimated. It opens up the way, the ascent of desire, which is finally described by the probably mythological priestess of Mantineia, Diotima. The true and thus philosophical way of Eros consists in those steps by which one can finally touch the idea of beauty itself: starting with one beautiful body coming to all bodies of that kind, i.e. to the provisional knowledge that beauty is a general predicate; transcending this knowledge to that of the beautiful soul and those features that mark the soul as beautiful; striving onward from the beautiful soul to the beautiful activity of knowing itself, i.e. to the knowledge that knowing is beautiful; and finally, suddenly, to a view of the eternal idea of beauty itself.

Plato, it seems, judged this final fulfilment of Eros to be impossible in life. On the one hand, wisdom, as we know, is reserved for the god (Apollo) and, on the other hand, motion is unthinkable once in the eternal presence of the desired. A fulfilled desire could only amount to its own annihilation, or to a last and total transformation of the desiring one. Oedipus extinguishes his sensory vision in order to gain the true one, the supersensory. But for Plato even non-sensory seeing, or thinking, is only able to make an approach toward the idea. It cannot become an idea itself. However, a full discussion of this final step in the erotic ascent to the idea would take us beyond the confines of the present discussion.

In any case, it must be said that philosophic Eros is the desiring of the supersensible. Because Socrates embodies this desire, he himself is desired by the most beautiful participant in the *Symposium*, Alcibiades. The philosopher is the true lover. In the *Symposium* of Xenophanes, Socrates even pretends that the very best thing he could do would be to couple with another. Without a doubt, Alcibiades misunderstands the philosopher in this claim if he then desires him bodily, if he wants to lie with him and seeks to fulfill his lust. Although Alcibiades is aware that the philosopher refuses this sensuality, he does not want to recognize that the reasonable man must leave behind the world of the body. Alcibiades confuses philosophy with the philosopher.

At this point, there arises a mistrust which, after Nietzsche and after Freud, must adhere in principle to philosophical desire. This mistrust addresses itself to the idea that there is an interiority capable of coming into contact with the supersensible. We also see here the impetus for those compulsions that can invoke a "crucification of the flesh": sin, guilt, the bad conscience, and all those canny and uncanny desperations. What emerges here is a "subject" that must be constantly at war with itself. For the tragic Eros there is no supersensible sphere that could attract divine and human desire. This Eros remains in the presence of the body of the other, without identifying it with a "person;" an impossibility which is, by the way, endorsed by Plato. This remaining in the presence of the body has for Sophocles nothing to do with knowledge, but with the mere exteriority of an event, by which gods and human beings are consumed. *Happiness*, which is for Socrates in the *Symposium* the ultimate end of human life, seems to be given in the realm of tragic Eros only together with balefulness. For the philosopher, tragic Eros can not reach happiness. It is this that Plato attempted to show with his image of the tyrant. Only philosophic Eros can lead to happiness. In order to do so, however, this happiness has to overcome the body, the body of the other and of oneself. Nay, happiness thus understood simply is this overcoming.

4. Appendices

1. The Poetic and the Philosophic Life

Setting out from the work of Georges Bataille, one could ask whether poetry and the erotic really realize themselves in the abolishment of all differences. In this sense, the poetic life would entail a willingness to collapse into an ambivalence that would remain unknown to the poet. It is only from the position of philosophical life that we could claim to understand this ambivalence – it would be the ambivalence of a "happiness" that is the violent disintegration of order and that must therefore always transform itself into a bitter balefulness. Philosophical life remains in all drunkenness sober, it conserves order; or if it abolishes an old order, as Socrates did, it concerns itself with a new, better one. Philosophy knows a happiness beyond violence, a happiness, which – as in the image of the cave – leaves violence behind by means of violence. It is ultimately a happiness in the presence of the motionless, of eternal and changeless being, a happiness of encircling silence.

Indeed poetic life does not aim for knowledge, at least not for one that would overcome the sensible presence of life. Nevertheless it does not seem to be interested in abolishing of all differences, in confusion and lack of all order. If it "leads" to such an abolishment, then it does so not by desiring it. But perhaps such statements are in general fruitless. We must begin more originally.

In this sense the Platonic alternative between a poetic and a philosophic life guides us to a *question*, which we can find in both modes of life, namely the question of *truth*, of the truth of life. Could this truth consist in striving for a happiness beyond violence and pain, beyond dolefulness and desperation? Or could it consist of a happiness, where we recklessly search for erotic entanglements with bodies along with all the consequences thereof? The celebration and the lament of poetry are dedicated to a human life, which finally is an impenetrable unity of happiness and unhappiness. Philosophy tries to reach the source, where such celebration and lament become a lie.

2. The Temporality of Eros

It has become significant that the erotic, in its motion, presents itself as a certain temporality. This intra-erotic temporality must necessarily be distinguished from the extra-erotic one. This becomes clear through the consideration of a certain phenomenon: Eros happens as a disruption, an opening of exposure. It is not only Sophocles, but Plato as well, who acknowledges this opening, when the latter declares that a glimpse of the idea of beauty itself must occur "suddenly." Thus, we do not share in the opinion that every kind of life is in and of itself erotic. We must ask, rather, what kind of time is to be found in this peculiar exposure?

Primarily, it can be claimed that the temporality of Eros should be conceived as *ecstasis*. This ecstasis builds a sphere,[5] in which ecstasis is not only the center of the erotic, but the last denudation as mutual penetration. This ecstasis also begins as the periphery of this sphere, which unfolds around this center. Whoever finds him or herself surrounded by this sphere does not necessarily need to reach the center. The erotic has many realities. Nevertheless, it also seems to be true that the periphery of this ecstasis can only be understood in relation to its center. The periphery lives from its center.

For Plato the center of erotic temporality is eternal being, i.e. timelessness. It is wise that the philosopher shows caution when it comes to the question of whether the human being could enter this center. Such a situation, such a pathos, might be characterized as divine, a motionless dwelling in the truth. In the *Phaedo*, Socrates seems to demythologize the possibility of reaching this place in death.

Plato's circumspection here does justice to the following experience: the temporality of the last and highest ecstasis withdraws. But one might say as well that this last ecstasis, this center of the erotic, attracts, contracts, and intensifies the usual extension of time. It is obvious that, at the very end of this intensification, metaphors will present

---

5. Obviously it is always questionable to use spatial concepts in speaking about time. Already "ecstasis," as is well-known a term used by Heidegger, is a spatial concept. However, using spatial terms to speak about time and vice versa depends on the fact that what we experience is always a unity of time and space.

themselves as what transform the experience of "orgasm" into concepts of space and time.

More accessible might be that temporality of the periphery. At the periphery of this temporality a kind of soft rapture begins. We have already departed here from the usual progression of day and night. Indeed, this is the reason that we very often connect the erotic with happiness (e.g. in Freud). This peripheral situation or pathos could be characterized as an "already" or a "still." The "already" seems to be the beginning, the "still" the ending of this temporality. But – and this is essential – strictly speaking it is one and the same phenomenon, which is already or still happening.

The erotic presence of the other is an "already" and a "still." Even if we could say that this "already" and this "still" are one and the same phenomenon, a shift in the meaning occurs if we remember that the phenomenon is an event. In this sense the erotic presence of the other is always finite. Therefore it may be more adequate to emphasize the "still," for the "already" is itself a "still," right from the very beginning. He or she is appearing – still. This also seems to refer to the unforeseeable contingency of this other. Outside of erotic temporality we actually cannot relate to the other – this is a claim I do not wish to defend. Only if he or she has shown him- or herself can we desire him or her, can we invoke him or her to stay. Therefore it seems to be possible to conceive the temporality of Eros as a "still." It is so beautiful that you are *still* here with me.

3. Poetry and Eros

Obviously Bataille had his own very personal access to poetry. He refers to it in terms of "eternity," "death," and "continuity." These concepts certainly discussed as forms of "transgression" are inscribed into a collapsing metaphysic of framework. Poetry and eroticism as the "blending" or "fusion" (in French: "confusion") of distinctions are transgressions. But it is evident that eternity builds a contrast or even a contradiction to transgression, and we have to think a different possibility to speak about the relation between poetry and eroticism.

Sure, tragic Eros as he is described here is a blending and a fusion. The world loses its shapes, definitions are only relevant as the representations of anti-erotic institutions (most of all the pólis itself). Tragic Eros transgresses the usual permanence of reason and economy. But in this movement of transgression an experience opens up, which can not be thought any more as mere transgression. This experience can be called *intensity*.

Intensity and transgression can at the first sight be distinguished by the difference between the "in" and the "trans." The "trans" is not only a movement, but a movement of dispersion. The "in" emerges from such rupturing movement, but it is also a gathering. This gathering is not eternity, it can never be eternal, because it will become a loss. Even if transgression is a dispersion – and in this respect also a loss – eternity remains a positive being. "Dissipation" would transgress even eternity.

The gathering of intensity in poetry is the trembling presence of nakedness as well as the softer wind of serene nearness as a moment of life. In this intensity of poetry transgression stops and the abyssal clearness of the world appears. Here poetry is not a bending and fusion and one could ask, whether poetry ever could be this kind of decomposition. Even tragic Eros as intensity can never be only disintegration. Poetry and Eros are the gathering intensity before a loss, which can not be kept.

Dionysian *Dankbarkeit*
Friedrich Hölderlin's Poetics of Sacrifice

ELIZABETH B. SIKES

But, my friend, we have come too late. Though the gods are living,
  Over our heads they live, up in a different world.
Endlessly there they act and seem to pay little mind
  Whether we live, just that much the celestial ones safeguard us.
For not always can a frail, a delicate vessel hold them,
  Only at times can humans bear the full bounty of the gods.
Dream of them is life ever after.[1]

During his last productive years, from 1800–1805, with the descent
into madness immanent, Friedrich Hölderlin's thoughts were fastened
upon that god of mad revelry, Dionysus, and the art form dedicated in
his honor, tragic poetry. In general the late work marks a preoccupation with celebration – hymns and elegies, like *Bread and Wine* (1802,
1804), that ask: Why are the theatres empty? Where is the song?
Where is the dance? Where is the celebration? Enlightened reason,

---

1. "Aber Freund! wir kommen zu spät. Zwar leben die Götter,
   Aber über dem Haupt droben in anderer Welt.
Endlos wirken sie da und scheinens wenig zu achten,
   Ob wir leben, so sehr schonen die Himmlischen uns.
Denn nicht immer vermag ein schwaches Gefäß sie zu fassen,
   Nur zu Zeiten erträgt göttliche Fülle der Mensch.
Traum von ihnen ist drauf das Leben." Brot und Wein, Friedrich Hölderlin,
Sämtliche Werke und Briefe, 3 volumes, ed. Jochen Schmidt (Frankfurt am Main:
Deutscher Klassiker Verlag, 1992), II: 289, v. 109–115. Henceforth DKV. Though
translations are mostly my own, I have also consulted Friedrich Hölderlin: *Poems
and fragments*, trans. Michael Hamburger (London: Anvil Press Poetry Ltd., 1994).
Henceforth, PF.

drunk on the possibility of its power to replace the world with its own mental products, had utterly forgotten the sacrifice at the source of its vitality and nourishment. Such hubris seems to be central to Hölderlin's concerns, especially in works like the *Death of Empedocles*. It stands as the main obstacle of the age in becoming Hesperian, and thus also in becoming *historical*. Could the Hesperians, those occidental moderns, overcome a paucity of heart and mind to bear the challenge of joy, love, and gratitude? Dare they be thankful? The question reverberates today for the post-Hesperians too. Dare *we* be thankful? And if so, how? For we have become so unused to love, and poetic dwelling seems beyond us. Friedrich Hölderlin's *Bread and Wine* entreats us to love more daringly, exhorting us to give thanks beyond the limits reason can bear. His elegy invites us to sing with Dionysian gratitude the destiny of the gods and the earth, one in which everything, including the gods, takes on a mortal, earthly hue.

To love and celebrate more intensely meant for Hölderlin, perhaps somewhat surprisingly, that a new religion was in order. Indeed the new religion would be just this celebration of gratitude in tragic-poetic song. Taking tragedy as a religious text, its song as liturgy, the new religion does not seek, with neurotic intransigence, to recover and fix all that is lost and dissolved in time. Rather, it celebrates the downfall and flight of the gods as the *origin of time and earth*. Tragedy sings the earth while abandoning itself to the dance of its vernal and autumnal rhythms. The elegy *Bread and Wine* insists that the poetic word be the bread and wine of Dionysus (or Jesus, as another "half-god"). In partaking of the god, he is, once again, called back to earth and consumed in word and world. I call this the poetics of sacrifice.

Interwoven in the discourse of celebration are the thematic threads of time, the turning of the ages, and remembrance. In a more daring show of love and gratitude, the new tragic-poetic religion performatively takes up the task of historical remembrance. This speaks to the calling of the poet, as "priest of the wine-god" and singer of the movements of the earth. The turn toward the performative or liturgical role of poetic language belongs to Hölderlin's conception of a new Hesperian word and song that will usher in the age. Thus my analysis of *Bread and Wine* will weave on two levels, the first bringing out the theoretical problems associated with what we might generally call becoming Hesperian, and the second showing how they are resolved in the structure of the song, a poetics of sacrifice. It seems that to become historical, to become Hesperian, one must become Dionysian in one's gratitude and love. In this way the Dionysian *Dankbarkeit* of Hölderlin's *Bread and Wine* contributes to a philosophy of love.

1. *The God of Hesperia*

The destiny of an age is characterized for Hölderlin by the way that the god appears in the element, or *Lebenssphäre*, that is, the sphere of life, in which a people find themselves. When god and mortal are joined in the element, the era of that people will have a destiny. The destinies of the great bygone eras of aether are thought in the elegy in terms of the three half-gods, the fraternal trinity: Dionysus; Heracles and Christ.[2] In the first era, aether rolls from tongue to tongue, the "ancient sign" from heaven, catching fire in temples filled with song and dance (DKV: 288, v. 65–70). In the second era – that of the republican Heracles – aether forms not only words, but deeds, and is reflected in the "gloriously ordered" nations and cities. The advent and death of Christ is told in stanza eight. Upon their leaving, "the heavenly choir" offers a few gifts, traces of their having been there and of their return: bread and wine, the elements of the Eucharist. However, not only is Christ thought in these lines; it is the heavenly choir, not Christ, that has left traces, and Hölderlin often uses this term syncretically to implicate both the religion of the ancients and of the

---

2. The identification and progression of the eras can be grounded looking carefully at the following clues. At the end of stanza three, an allusion to Dionysus is made by naming his haunts and homeland, Thebes (v. 51–53). Stanza four then begins, "Blessed land of the Greeks!" announcing to the reader that this first age, the Greek, which we identify as ruled by the ancient laws of the gods in Homeric myth, has begun. The second era, that of a republican Heracles (the one who pulled down Zeus and his pantheon) is signified by the self-rule of the city-state that creates nations: "Nations rise up and soon [. . .]" (v. 95). In the eighth stanza, Christ is addressed in the lines, "Lastly a Genius had come, dispensing heavenly comfort,/He who proclaimed the Day's end, then himself went away" (v. 130–131). Hölderlin also constellates these three, Dionysus, Heracles and Christ, as brothers in *The Only One*, DKV I: 345, v. 50–55.

Christians.[3] Thus we find evidence of Demeter and Dionysus leave their in these traces, radiating in the light of father Aether, who brings forth the "fruits of the earth." Dionysus and Christ find themselves both implicated in vineyards and fields, in the sphere of collective work and the celebration of its yield. This links beginning with end, showing how Dionysus can be called, in the beginning of the poem, "the god to come," and explaining the movement in the eighth stanza, from the age of Christ toward that of Dionysus.[4] He is not only Christ's predecessor, but his successor as well: the herald and sign of the last era in the land of evening. Dionysus is the god of the future, of Hesperia. He is found at the beginning of the poem and is the god we are left with at the end – an ending that overshadows the entire elegy. For even though Dionysus' presence, both at the beginning and end, clarifies to some extent why the poet writes, "Yes rightly they say he reconciles day with the night [...]" (v. 143), it is this daylight, father

---

3. Cf. Michael Knaupp's commentary to the elegy in Friedrich Hölderlin, *Sämtliche Werke und Briefe,* 3 volumes, ed. Michael Knaupp (München: Carl Hanser Verlag, 1992), III: 215. Henceforth K.

4. According to the myth, Dionysus traveled from East to West, from India and Asia Minor to Greece. Hence he was the named the 'god to come.' Schelling, in his *Philosophy of Revelation,* tells us that Dionysus was called to Eleusis from the East by solemn celebrations and invocations. By virtue of this trait, this coming to Eleusis, he was designated as the 'one to come.' Schelling then postulates that the Eleusis itself means only this coming, the future or advent, of the god. Through a mere change of the accent, he says, the word eleusis, the coming, is transformed into the name Eleusis. Thus the highest object of the Eleusian mysteries was none other than this coming of God, and this coming belongs to his essence. In Jochen Schmidt's commentary to the elegy, he discusses Schelling's interpretation and sees this coming as the state of historical completion that will be fulfilled in the Hesperian age, in his view ultimately in Germany, when the god is called from Hellas to Hesperia. This corresponds with a certain chiliastic interpretation of Hölderlin's philosophy of history. As I hope to make clearer in the course of this essay, if Dionysus represents the future for Hölderlin, it is one that arrives incomplete, breaking up before arrival, and creating a gap at the origin. Then the challenge presents itself to understand how these gaps, breaks, and interruptions can constitute historical continuity – this is the paradox Hölderlin himself puts forth in the *Notes on Oedipus,* and it comes to the fore in the figure of the caesura. Cf. DKV I: 731.

Aether's radiance, that never dawns in the poem. Dionysus is god of the night.[5] It is already evening when the elegy begins:

Around us the town rests; the lamplit street settles into silence [. . .][6]

It is evening when the elegy comes to an end:

More gently dreams and sleeps in the bosom of the earth, the Titan,
Even that envious one, Cerberus, drinks and sleeps.[7]

2. The Dreamers

Dionysus reigns over that lunar realm of sacred sleep, dream, and trance. The lines quoted above are reminiscent of the hymn *Mnemosyne*, which sings of that soporific rocking of the skiff upon the waves; such rocking is connected not so much with the future or the past but with the moment in between. The future of Hesperia lies in its devotion to the god Dionysus, in the moment of being taken in by his wine-induced divine sleep. The aether distilled in wine creates the dream that divinizes the sleep. For after the gods have flown, seeking out heartier spaces than those fragile human vessels can provide, Dionysus remains on earth ministering aether through the fruits of his vine. Henceforth, we consort with the heavenly ones through his oneiric medium:

Only at times can humans bear the full bounty of the gods.
Dream of them is life ever after. But madness,
Wandering, helps, like sleep [. . .][8]

---

5. In Ancient literature we have confirmation of Dionysus' nocturnal affiliation; in Plutarch he is called *Dionysos nukterinos* (*Quaest. conn.* 4, 6.10), and similarly in Virgil, *nocturnus Bacchus*. Cf. DKV, I: 727.
6. "Rings um ruhet die Stadt; still wird die erleuchtete Gasse [. . .]" DKV I: 285, v. 1.
7. "Sanfter träumet und schläft in Armen der Erde der Titan,
Selbst der neidische, selbst Cerberus trinket und schläft" DKV I: 291, v. 159–160.
8. "Nur zu Zeiten erträgt göttliche Fülle der Mensch.
Traum von ihnen ist drauf das Leben. Aber das Irrsaal
Hilft, wie Schlummer [. . .]" DKV I: 289, v. 114–6.

Those who live in the land of evening, the Hesperians, are those who dream – who must dream – and this becomes the task of the poet grown from Hesperian soil in "penurious times."

> Meanwhile often I think it's
> > Better to sleep than to be friendless as we are, alone,
> Always waiting, and what to do or say in the meantime
> > I don't know, and what are poets for anyway in penurious times?
> But they are, you say, like those holy ones, priests of the wine-god
> > Who in holy Night roamed from one place to the next.[9]

At the end, the poet performatively takes up the calling he has announced for himself. Having just called his readers in the preceding lines "the godless," he exhorts them in a kerygmatic and priestly or apostolic style:

> What the song of the ancients presages of the children of God,
> > Look! we are it, ourselves; fruit of Hesperia it is![10]

Das Abendland, land in the west or land of evening, translates *Hesperia* from the Greek, which refers generally to *the Western land*. Hesperia in ancient Greece is also connected with the *Hesperides*, which names both the daughters of Night or Hades and the garden placed under their protection where the golden apple of immortality grew. Thus, as

---

9. "Indessen dünket mir öfters
Besser zu schlafen, wie so ohne Genossen zu seyn,
So zu harren und was zu thun indeß und zu sagen,
Weiß ich nicht und wozu Dichter in dürftiger Zeit?
Aber sie sind, sagst du, wie des Weingotts heilige Priester,
Welche von Lande zu Land zogen in heiliger Nacht." DKV I: 290, v. 119–124. The apostrophe here addresses Wilhelm Heinse, to whom the elegy is also dedicated. Wilhelm Heinse (1746-1803), author of *Ardinghello und die glückseligen Inseln* (1787) was one of the models of *Hyperion*. The reference to the "blessed Isles" also refers to Hesperia. Friends with Hölderlin, they were in Bad Driburg, near Kassel, together, along with Susette Gontard and family. Surely this time spent together with Heinse and Gontard, Hölderlin's beloved Diotima, represented a kind of lost golden age, or time spent on the blessed isles for Hölderlin.
10. "Was der Alten Gesang von Kindern Gottes geweissagt,
Siehe, wir sind es, wir; Frucht von Hesperien ists!" DKV: 291, v. 149–150.

the "fruit of Hesperia," we might be the ones endowed with immortality of the soul, redeemed through the coming of the "Son of the Highest," "the Syrian." Yet such a strictly Christological interpretation is problematic in that these attributes could be predicated of both Dionysus and Christ. Furthermore, the elegy speaks not of man's ascension into heaven, but rather of the descent of the god down "into our gloom," that is, earth. This speaks to one of the great ideas in Hölderlin's work, which I would characterize generally as *love for the earth*. It takes poetic form as the tendency of all the gods to move toward the earth, with Zeus as "Father of the Earth" or "Father of Time," and Dionysus, as we see in this poem, Gaia's greatest lover. This love for the earth is born of and for its mortal nature, and marks the finitude of the gods. The songs that Hölderlin constructs about the death of the gods in the modern Hesperian age, which we hear of not only in *Bread and Wine* but in so many other places in his work, also sing a mythological history of consciousness, one profoundly changed by the caesura signified by Kant's critical project and its ban on intellectual intuition. In these myths, *thanatos* and *eros* are never far from each other. First, *thanatos*.

The history of *Hesperia* and the *Hesperides* is intimately tied to that which is *hesperos*, of the evening or the dark. Sophocles in *Oedipus Rex* connects it with the penumbral realm of Hades, the god of darkness, and the moment of death: "You can see life after life speed away, like a bird on the wing, swifter than irresistible fire, to the shore of the western god" (*aktan pros hesperou theou*, v. 177). Hölderlin's translation reads: "*zum Ufer des abendlichen/Gottes*" (K II: 257, v. 184)[11]. Placed in the context of that infamous realm of evening, Hades, the Hesperian gods go underground, leaving the age without any ground. We might then liken Hölderlin's Hesperian gods with Plato's sky gods, or *the ideas* with which we once flew prior to birth in a kind of eternal intellectual intuition. Translating the *Phaedrus* myth into the Hesperian idiom, the gods' falling below the earth would mean the Idea or Spirit becoming unconscious. In one version of the intellectual intuition

---

11. DKV I: 1048. Cf. Henry George Liddel, Robert Scott, *A Greek-English Dictionary*, The Perseus Project, http://perseus.mpiwg-berlin.mpg.de, entry for *hesperos*.

operative in Kant's thinking according to Moltke Gram, this ever-desirable *visio Dei* is the Archetype of mind.[12] As a form of knowing prohibited to the faculties of human consciousness, the hesperianized intellectual intuition becomes an *archetype of the unconscious*. Once thought to be the highest noetic act, if one is to encounter it at all, intellectual intuition can only be accessed through the unconscious, and all that is associated with this realm: sleep, dreaming, death. Only in Dionysian dream – and tragic poetry in his name – can the Hesperians remember those flights with the gods once again.

Hesperia is riddled with paradox. It is the land rich in resource, *poros*, the home of the golden apple. Yet it is a land nonetheless bankrupt, *penia*, its inhabitants searching for a way into the very garden that is ostensibly its inheritance. As the lines from *Hyperion* lament: "A god is the human being when he dreams, a beggar when he reflects, and when enthusiasm is long gone he stands there, the failed son father drove from home, regarding the meager pennies sympathy threw to him along the way" (KI: 615).

3. Eros

Love is the only consolation in this mythological history of consciousness. As we know from Plato surrounding the birth of Eros, *Poros* and *Penia* mated. "Do you ask when that was?" Hölderlin writes. "Plato says: on the day Aphrodite was born. So then, as the beautiful world commenced for us, when we came to consciousness, at that moment we became finite" (DKV II: 208). We also know from Plato's myth how on that particular evening Resource found himself unusually without, whereas Poverty showed herself to possess hidden resources, in more ways than one. And the clouds gathering to encircle this primordial scene sound the distant thunder of the god to come, Dionysus, when Resource, drunk on the nectar of the gods at the celebration of Aphrodite's birth, falls into a divine torpor beneath the trees, and Poverty conspires to have a child by him. Thus Eros is born. Perhaps it is better said that Resource was most plentiful in the moment when

---

12. Moltke Gram, "Intellectual Intuition: The Continuity Thesis" (in *Journal of the History of Ideas*, 42 1981: 287–304).

he dreamt, for his dream prophesied Aphrodite and Dionysus, the Beautiful and Love.

In Plato's story, retold by Hölderlin's Stranger in *Hyperion*, Hölderlin constructs a mythopoeic description of Kant's critical project, at the center of which stands the ban on intellectual intuition.[13] The delineation of intellectual intuition as Archetype, as we saw before, relegates it to the oneiric sphere of the unconscious; the prescription of the limits of consciousness and knowledge simultaneously proscribes intellectual intuition. This ban shows human beings their limits, while at the same time "discovers the infinite striving within the human heart" (KII: 726). Hölderlin writes, "We cannot deny the drive to liberate ourselves, to ennoble ourselves, to press on toward the infinite; that would be bestial. Neither can we deny the drive to be determined, to receive; that would not be human" (ibid). In Eros these two contradictory drives – one skybound, one earthbound – are united, and Eros becomes the symbol of our ambiguous mortal nature. Common mortality binds us to one another; consciousness of mortality makes us human. This consciousness also enables human beings to love, for it is knowledge of mortality that makes us love life with the fierceness of Antigone, irrecusably, with a depth and intensity, *Innigkeit*, that makes us love others who may or may not survive us. And when the capacity to love reveals mortality, as is the case with Antigone, the suffering this entails, inherent in all *pathē*, has the countenance of Aphrodite. The Beautiful traces the infinite strivings of love toward the unique other, whose existence is fleeting beneath the life-giving sun.

Beauty in art is inextricably entwined with this uniqueness or *originality*. Hölderlin writes, "For me, originality is intensity [*Innigkeit*], depth of heart and spirit" (DKV II: 255). Thus we see why Hyperion has to irritate us, scandalize us, with his contradictions, aberrations, his strength and weakness, his love and wrath, his mourning. Herein lies his intensity, his originality, the sign of all his striving and *his mortality* – herein shines his beauty. For the Beautiful shines only in

---

13. Gerhard Kurz, *Mittelbarkeit und Vereinigung: Zum Verhältnis von Poesie, Reflexion und Revolution bei Hölderlin* (Stuttgart: J. B. Metzlersche Verlagsbuchhandlung, 1975), 11.

the glory of its transience. So it appears in the strivings of the hero like Achilles: "[T]he most transient bloom in the world of heroes, 'thus born to live only a short time' according to Homer, precisely because he is so beautiful" (DKV II:510). In this way, Hölderlin transforms all heroes into tragic heroes.

Thus the age of Philia cannot be a static, Edenic state of perfection. Such perfection has nothing to gain or lose, no fetters to struggle against, nothing that would move it. Rather, it is a perfection that, at the brink of its boundary and form, sounds its own demise. This idea can also be connected with the death and earthbound tendencies of the gods. Mortality, then, is the very condition for love. In being-moved and moving simultaneously, love marks and tells us of time. Both love and time are known in passing, in the movement of the moment: in downfall and becoming. And yes, even the gods must reckon with this when, like Zeus, they fall for a mortal. Hölderlin will say this much later, when, in the context of his translation of *Antigone,* he speaks of Niobe's relation to Zeus:

> She counted for the Father of Time
> The sounding of the hours, the golden.[14]

Dionysus is the 'Guest Yet to Come' at the celebration of Aphrodite's birth. He is anticipated in the crucial element, the nectar bringing about the *mixis*, the "mingling" between the unlikely pair, *Poros* and *Penia*, from which love and the world of beauty arise for mortals. Without faithful observance of the god, *Poros* and *Penia* perpetually encircle each other, never crossing paths under the arbor resplendent with the promise of that golden fruit. Rather, Penury goads Resource to use its cunning to possess the fruit in any which way it can, and Resources' repeated attempts create an illusion of wealth that serves merely to disguise an ever growing abyss of poverty.

With only cunning and penury in our hearts, any love or gratitude shrivels up altogether in that garden. And yet, as Hölderlin himself points out, even in reflecting upon the beloved, it seems we always

---

14. "Sie zählete dem Vater der Zeit
Die Stundenschläge, die goldnen." K II: 372.

come up short on love. We are beggars when we reflect. Love must love even more if it is ever going to approximate the beauty and transience of the beloved – or the infinite debt of gratitude owed the beloved for giving the lover life. Thus the need for a more daring love and gratitude, like the kind of tribute only possible when intoxicated by the dream of the beloved. In the dream we become gods. Such a Dionysian dream suspends the human being's impoverished resourcefulness so that from the divine fusion and confusion he inspires, Resource and Poverty may be fruitful and create an erotic bind that ushers in an authentic relation to time and the age.

Thus to go toward the future, we must go toward Dionysus. To be precise, the time, or time itself, characterized by Dionysus, is neither a state to which one can return nor one to be anticipated; it is rather that perpetual flux and fusion arising between states, between synchrony and diachrony, day and night, heaven and hell. Let us go toward Dionysus, and toward the Hesperian, by way of the beginning of the elegy, where his age is first described. There we will see that sacrifice plays a principal role in defining the moment in which Dionysus dwells, one for which the poet must prepare. Only a poetics of sacrifice rooted in the prodigality of celebration can properly remember the god.

4. *The Gift of Sacrifice*

Though wine's associative character emphasizes Dionysus' tendency to bring people together from out of their isolation, forming the bonds and unions at the heart of family and civilization, Bacchus has his shadow side as well. He teeters perpetually upon the alpine ridge between disorganization and organization, mass confusion and articulated unity. The wine in his chalice is always on the brink of overflowing. Roberto Calasso emphasizes Dionysus' more destructive side:

> Dionysus is not a useful god who helps weave or knot things together, but a god who loosens or unties. The weavers are his enemies. Yet there comes a moment when the weavers will abandon their looms to dash off after him into the mountains. Dionysus is the river we hear flowing by in the distance, an incessant booming far away; then one day it rises and floods everything, as if the normal above-water state of things, the

sober delimitation of our existence, were but a brief parenthesis overwhelmed in an instant.[15]

Indeed, whether it be the river that breaks free of the icy fetters of winter or the wine that streams over the rim, the overflow in both cases is the god's sacrifice. As Heidegger remarks, "The consecrated [*geweihte*] drink is what the word *Guss* truly names: donation, sacrifice. *Guss*, 'to pour' in Greek is: χέειν, in Indo-Germanic: ghu. This means: sacrifice. Where fundamentally completed, sufficiently thought, and truly said, pouring is: to donate, sacrifice, thus give [*schenken*]."[16] Pouring and giving are both meant in the German word *schenken*, whose full essence, Heidegger writes, lies in its gathering together as *Geschenk*, gift. What is dedicated and offered to the god is something sacred, consecrated, and as such, it embodies the god's essence. The god courses and streams, pours and spills down, giving himself as the fullness of life: this is the god's gift. He lives as the ultimately unbound and unbindable essence of everything fluid – in the rivers Hölderlin loved and in the oceans of ambiguous portent. Dionysus, taking after his father Zeus, is there in the thunderous wrath of the storm and in the clear aethereal skies that follow. Thus the storm of the poetic word and the storm poured into every wine glass "more full," more sacred, embody the god's essence as an offering and a sacrifice of life's bounty. Calasso writes:

> The sacred is something that impregnates, it pours into the young girl, the animal, the statue, and fills them. Hence the sacred comes to partake of fullness, and fullness with perfection, since as Aristotle puts it, "we offer to the gods only that which is perfect and whole." The *Iliad* speaks of "youths who filled [or crowned: *epestépsanto*] the bowls with wine." The crown was the rim of the goblet, the point at which fullness becomes excess. The perfect brings death upon itself, since one can't have fullness without spillage, and what spills out is the excess that sacrifice claims for itself.[17]

---

15. Roberto Calasso, *The Marriage of Cadmus and Harmony*, trans. Tim Parks (New York: Vintage International, 1994), 45. Henceforth MC.

16. Martin Heidegger, "Das Ding," in *Vorträge und Aufsätzte* (Stuttgart: Verlag Günther Neske, 1954), 165.

17. MC, 111."Uns die Vergessenheit und das Heiligtrunkene gönnen,

The wine that the poet himself drinks and shares with others is the poetic word. Thus Hölderlin's appeal to the Night and the wine-god whose hand she holds:

> O grant us oblivion and holy drunkenness ,
> Grant the on-rushing word, like lovers,
> Sleepless and a wine cup more full a life more daring,
> Holy remembrance, too, keeping us wakeful at night.[18]

Hölderlin dares us to celebrate this much, that our celebration be truly sacrificial. In a wine cup more full, the god is sacrificed; this is his desire, the *Todeslust* of the god. The divine excess of "holy drunkenness," as the overflow of the current, galvanizes *das heilige Gedächtnis*, the holy remembrance of "frenzied oblivion," *die Vergessenheit*. Here, the dissolution of knots also heralds the parturition of a new social fabric. Upon the excesses of sacrifice, civilizations and ages are born. Next let us turn to how this transition is constituted through remembrance.

5. Forgetting Ideational Recollection

The call for Dionysian oblivion and gratitude, as the proper mode of "holy remembrance" stands in contrast to the theory of historical transition and memory worked out in Hölderlin's essay "The Fatherland in Decline." This essay, along with those grouped under the title "On the Tragic," belong to his work on the mourning play, *The Death of Empedocles*. This period marks Hölderlin's attempt to think seriously the turning of ages on the model of tragedy's movement. Yet Hölderlin is arguably never able to bring his tragic vision fully to fruition in these works. The mourning play remained unfinished in three drafts,

---

Gönnen das strömende Wort, das, wie die Liebenden, sei
Schlummerlos und vollern Pokal und kühneres Leben,
Heilig Gedächtniß auch, wachend zu bleiben bei Nacht."
18. "Uns die Vergessenheit und das Heiligtrunkene gönnen,
Gönnen das strömende Wort, das, wie die Liebenden, sei
Schlummerlos und vollern Pokal und kühneres Leben,
Heilig Gedächtniß auch, wachend zu bleiben bei Nacht."DKVI: 286, v. 33–36.

with his tragic hero Empedocles unable to complete the "ideal suicide" that would reconcile the problem of the age, the scission between sky and earth, god and mortal. In contrasting the notion of ideational recollection (*idealische Erinnerung*) espoused in the Fatherland essay, which would have theoretically sealed the circle of historical return in Empedocles' figurative and figural leap, with the Dionysian dissolution embodied in the liturgy of the song, we come to appreciate the full impact of the truly tragic turn of Hölderlin's elegy.

David Farrell Krell's meditation on "The Fatherland in Decline" and the *Empedocles* drafts centers on the tension between dramatic threads spun, tales that weave history and time together, and the knotty points that with every reversal, hiatus, and caesura, ignite in fire and dissolve all that had been woven hitherto. A memory of what was is reclaimed from these ashes, upon which the new will be founded, as Hölderlin's essay explains. Krell poses the question: "When and where and how in Hölderlin's text does the *point* of every *thread* of all narrative *stuff* catch *fire* and burn itself out?" Further on he continues, "Every bit as early in his life as a thinker, Hölderlin tried to meet the necessity of separation and loss with the force of remembrance. Human beings would elevate themselves above mere need and necessity only if they remembered with gratitude their destiny or proper 'skill,' 'calling,' or 'sending' [*Geschick*]."[19] This gratitude, a Dionysian *Dankbarkeit*, should be the celebration of the fatherland's decline, consecrated as a sacrifice to the transition of ages, to the god and fatherland of the future. If this sacrifice is made, civilizations of the past and future will find their destiny. The fatherland goes into decline at the peak of its perfection, unity, fullness, at which juncture it must be offered as a sacrifice to Dionysus. The moment of sacrifice is what Krell calls the point of diremption, which comes to bear when the whole of life swells with too much intimacy, or is too infinitely connected. Krell writes:

> Tragedy rises as a flame from what seems to be a 'primally unified life,' an Edenic state or an Empedoclean sphere in which everything encounters everything else and each thing receives its 'entire measure

---

19. David Farrell Krell, *Lunar voices: Of tragedy, poetry, fiction, and thought* (Chicago: The University of Chicago Press, 1995), 37. Henceforth LV.

of life.' At a certain point in primally unified life [...] separation invariably supervenes and disrupts the unity. Diremption occurs with, in, and through a feeling of *excess*. The parts that constitute the whole of life come to 'feel too unified [*zu einig*].' The hyperbolic, ironic, excessive 'too' [*zu*] [...] marks the moment of scission and separation at the very point of most intense unity.[20]

The moment of decline signals the demise of perfection, repeating again the theme – which we have by no means seen the last of – that perfection calls death upon itself, perhaps even unconsciously seeking it. This fuels the death drive of the gods, which can also strike a people at the golden hour of their age, as Hölderlin sings in *Voice of the People*.[21] Ideational recollection, as Hölderlin says in his essay, presents this moment of decline in order to bridge the gap between old and new:

> After the memory [*die Erinnerung*] of the dissolved, the individual unites with the infinite feeling of life through the memory of dissolution, and after the gap between them is filled, there proceeds from this unification and comparison of the past singularity and the infinitely present the new situation proper, the next step that is to succeed upon the past (DKV II: 448).[22]

Yet such remembrance vexes. The first possible hazard is that dissolution becomes fixed or stamped in the memory, thus belying the nature of its object, the infinite feeling of life that arises in decline. Every attempt at memorializing risks reducing life and lived experience to a dead figure, a monument or "stele," in Lacoue-Labarthe's words.[23]

---

20. Ibid, 38.

21. *The Voice of the People* should also remind us of just how important the symbol of water is; there is no more powerful image than the one found here of the great rivers rushing gloriously unimpeded toward their death, dissolving and mixing indistinguishably with the ocean of the unbound All. This entropic tendency represents one of the great tragic themes in Hölderlin's poetry. It runs through all of his great river poems, and others dedicated to the civilizations they made possible, like the river Neckar in *Heidelberg* (DKV I: 311–312, v 9–20).

22. LV 29. Translation slightly altered.

23. Phillipe Lacoue-Labarthe, "Typography" in *Typography: Mimesis, philosophy, politics*, ed. Christopher Fynsk (Stanford: Stanford University Press, 1989), 63–95.

The second problem, raised by Krell, is whether dissolution can be captured by memory at all. He writes:

> For even if nature and humanity affect one another reciprocally and harmoniously, as Hölderlin notes in '*Das untergehende Vaterland*...,' so that a new world and a new life germinate in the ashes of the old, and even if tragic dissolution can be felt only on the grounds of a nascent and as yet undiscovered unification, it remains the case, as every hermit knows, that the modality of possibility remains fixed, in mournful remembrance of what has dissolved, and is lost forever to possibility. The access and the excess of *pain* [...] rise in the course of dissolution, blotting out any possible apprehension of the new life [...].[24]

And indeed, 'obliviating,' so to speak, any apprehension whatsoever. The very nature of dissolution and of infinite affect, which Krell sees as the excess of pain in diremption, seems to incorporate something recalcitrant to the ideational act of memory: that act falls into the abyss of what one might call an absolute, irretrievable past. The moment of separation marks the vanishing point into which everything dissolves. If excess itself and its attendant diremption – separation pure and simple – are the true objects of ideational recollection, this poses a grave challenge to a memorializing and singing that must offer itself in a form most genuinely mirroring and representing divine excess. It points back to the problem that the infinite properly speaking cannot be presented.

The third difficulty faced by ideational recollection and its memorializing is the entirely momentary, *augenblicklich*, character of this transition of age and world. Or, in Heidegger's terms, its character as *Ereignis* – a momentous event in which the fermentation of time is finally distilled. Past and future, sky and earth, god and mortal converge, gather together, finding themselves intimately entwined in such a way that the gathering constitutes an event in the history of being. In Hölderlin's terms, this collective gathering marks the "possibility of all relations" which predominates in the transition between epochs (KI: 72). If the mode of existence – the relations governing among human beings and in their intimacy (or lack thereof) with nature or the divine

---

24. LV 39.

– determines an epoch, the moment in which the "possibility of all relations" or "infinity" is felt would be the highest mode of existence, as well as the highest point in an epoch of being; it would be a *divine* or sacred mode of being, or a being-with the divine. The divine can present itself, that is, be experienced as a mode of existence and song, only at that liminal point between the downfall and parturition of the moment. Hölderlin writes, "For the world of all worlds, the All in everything, which always *is* and from whose being everything must be regarded, presents itself only in all time – or in downfall or in the moment, or more genetically in the becoming of the moment and the advent of time and world [...]" (ibid). Such dissolution holds its peculiar character between being and nonbeing (KII: 73). Thus it comes as no surprise when I say, the mode of existence of the sacred is *ecstatic*, or *ex-centric*, in Hölderlinian terms. As momentary, ephemeral, and ecstatic, divine presentation as well as divine existence in the song is incalculable and unpredictable – it happens in due course, and we can neither anticipate nor accelerate its due.

Thus memorializing must not only remember and reflect what escapes all rational apprehension and reflection, regardless of how ideal, but it also has to embody a mode of being which itself is only fleeting, ecstatic, and distills in due time only after its fermentation. How the poet accomplishes this is the mystery revealed in and through *Bread and Wine*. Drawing a parallel between Hölderlin's description of transition in "The Fatherland in Decline" with the movement of stanza eight, we see how to rectify the fault of ideational recollection with Dionysian gratitude.

6. Dionysian Gratitude

In the eighth stanza Hölderlin writes of the coming and disappearance of "a genius," Christ, after which the "heavenly choir" leaves behind a few gifts, in which, as before, we may take pleasure in our human way. The 1802 and 1804 versions of the stanza remain the same, except for the next lines, 134–136, which, although differing, explain why Christ had to disappear. In the first version the poem reads:

Since for spiritual joy the Greater had grown too great
Here, among human beings, and still, even now we lack those strong
enough for
Joy's extremity, but silent some thanks do live on.[25]

Already in building a substantive from the comparative form of
"great," *das Größre*, what is grand intensifies, becomes greater. This
intensification of the comparative is redoubled, becoming too great,
grandiose. The entire line takes on entirely too much intensity and an
excessiveness upon which, as Krell points out, diremption is bound to
supervene. This excess is the joy of the wine-god himself, *der Freu-
dengeist*, whose intensity becomes too great for human beings to bear,
thus signaling his departure.

The 1804 version was written after the Sophocles translations and
stands under the influence of that project's intention to "hesperianize"
or modernize certain aspects of Greek myths and the Greek text in
order to bring it into line with current modes of representation. To
hesperianize the language means to spiritualize it, make it more conceptual, abstract, and in this sense also more numinous – and less
graspable.[26] Thus the event of Christ's advent is described as the
revelation of *destiny*, in the face of which human thought doubles over.
Hölderlin writes, replacing the 1802 lines on the "too great,"

Yet, as the scales well-nigh shatter before it may befall, destiny
In shards almost, so that it buckles,
the mind,
In the face of knowledge, it still lives, but thanks prevail.[27]

---

25. "Denn zur Freude mit Geist, wurde das Größre zu groß
Unter den Menschen und noch, noch fehlen die Starken zu höchsten
Freuden, aber es lebt stille noch einiger Dank." DKV I: 290, v. 134–136.
26. Cf. Gerhard Kurz, "Aus linkischem Gesichtspunkt: Zu Hölderlins Ansicht der
Antike" in *Antiquitates Renatae: Deutsche und französische Beiträge zur Wirkung der
Antike in der europäischen Literatur. Festschrift für Renate Böschenstein zum 65.
Geburtstage*, ed. Verena Ehrich-Haefeli, Hans-Jürgen Schrader, Martin Stern
(Würzburg: Königshausen & Neumann, 1998), 182 ff.
27. "Aber, wie Waagen bricht, fast, eh es kommet, das Schiksaal
Auseinander beinah, daß sich krümmt der
Verstand
Vor Erkentniß, auch lebt, aber sieget der Dank." KI: 381, v. 134–136.

Understanding shatters in the face of destiny, even pictorially from the line, representing a caesura in the continuity of the linear historical narrative. Only "thanks prevail" in both versions. What prevail are the very earthly and modest forms of bread and wine, the very gratitude extolled in the last lines of the stanza. What prevails is poetic song *as* bread and wine:

> Bread is the fruit of the Earth, indeed the blessing of sunlight,
>   And from the thundering god comes the joy of wine.
> Therefore in tasting them we think of the Heavenly who once were
>   Here and shall return when the time is right;
> Therefore sing in seriousness the poets to the wine-god,
>   Never idly devised sound the praises of that most ancient one.[28]

Ludwig von Pigenot, quoted at length in Heidegger's Hölderlin-inspired meditation "Jointure of Grace. Thanks"[29] (1945) writes, "If we attempt to forget everything particular in Hölderlin's poetry and intentionally make it vanish, at the end what remains is perhaps merely *one* word, albeit one of such seriousness that it will survive the times: *thanks*" (GSA 75, 311). This word, he continues, is rooted etymologically in others of neighboring rank, namely thinking (*Denken*) and memory (*Gedächtnis*). Von Pigenot highlights these very lines just quoted from *Bread and Wine* in order to bring into relief the quiet intensity and intimacy of these words. The prevailing thanks are secured in bread and wine. *Therefore* (*Darum*), from this secured ground, in tasting them we *think* of the heavenly ones. *Therefore* (*Darum*), the songs devised, or to say it more vividly, thought-up, *erdacht*, in remembrance of the wine god are serious, sung *mit Ernst*. This is the same seriousness, or gravity, which the action in tragedy, according to Aris-

---

28. "Brod ist der Erde Frucht, doch ists vom Lichte geseegnet,
Und vom donnernden Gott kommet die Freude des Weins.
Darum denken wir auch dabei der Himmlischen, die sonst
Da gewesen und die kehren in richtiger Zeit,
Darum singen sie auch mit Ernst die Sänger den Weingott
Und nicht eitel erdacht tönet dem Alten das Lob." DKVI: 290, v. 137–142.
29. Martin Heidegger, *Gesamtausgabe*, 75 (Frankfurt am Main: Vittorio Klostermann, 2000), 301–312. Hereafter GSA 75.

totle, should have; the song is *spoudaios*. As both determined by and determining the relationship between the gods and mortals, poetic song bears the impact of destiny, which brings in its train ethical as well as political consequences for an era and its people. After singling out those lines, von Pigenot comments:

> The passage just quoted also permits us to fill out the word *thanks* with conceptual language in a particularly Hölderlinian manner. Thanks is for Hölderlin nothing other than our being obliged to remembrance [*Andenken*] and memory [*Gedächtnis*]. Thought in this way, his life and poetic work want to be nothing other than *thanks*; thanks to the gods and the genii of the cosmos; Greece itself counts among them. This he has repeated in his work in decisive places (the most moving one perhaps at the end of the poem "Remembrance": "Yet it takes/And gives memory [*Gedächtnis*], the sea,/And love as well keeps its eyes steadily fastened./Yet what remains, the poets provide.") The gratitude owed the gods is none other than that owed of the child its mother. "In the bosom of the gods, the mortals" are "satiated." The gods are the power encompassing us all, the motherly element bearing all, the sources and powers of the cosmos and likewise of our soul. From time immemorial, they have been at work in the development of world substance. It is incorrect to want to conceive Hölderlin's gods solely as physical, external powers; they act as the *genius* in us as well as outside us.[30]

Significantly, von Pigenot mentions *genius* twice as the source of thanks and remembrance in Hölderlin. The "quiet genius" in *Bread and Wine* who came "dispensing heavenly comfort,/He who proclaimed the Day's end, then himself went away" (v. 129–130) belongs to Hölderlin's genii as well. And we might include here as well the genius, mentioned earlier, of the "on-rushing word" (v. 34) (*das strömende Wort*) that the poet hopes will be granted to him. He names the word along with the "oblivion" (v. 33) of holy drunkenness, which nevertheless counts as "holy remembrance" (v. 35) (*heilig Gedächtnis*). As von Pigenot's example from *Remembrance* points out, the element of water haunted by the genius – the sea, the river, wine – Hölderlin always connects with the source of remembrance and forgetting, or a

---

30. GSA 75, 311–312.

forgetfulness that paradoxically retains and remains loyal to a memory, one to which the poetic word is infinitely grateful. The simple flow of gratitude keeps the poet safe, for a while, as she stands exposed to the storm of the divine – until the "god's absence" (*Gottes Fehl*), his dissolution into the song, comes to the poet's aid. In *The Poet's Vocation* Hölderlin writes:

> Our thanks
> Know God. Yet he doesn't hold it easily to himself
> And likes to join with others
> Who help him to understand it.
>
> Fearless, however, he remains, if he must, the man
> Alone before God, ingenuousness protects him,
> And he needs no weapon and no wile till
> The default of God helps.[31]

What then could be simpler than *thanking*? Simpler than a thinking, thinking-on (*Andenken*), and a thinking-up (*Erdenken*) that takes its ground as *thanks* to the genius? As Heidegger writes, thinking and poetizing arise from thanking (GSA 75: 307). Likewise, thinking-on, *das Andenken* or remembrance, rests in and upon thanks (GSA 75: 309). What is said in remembrance of this thanks is the poetic-creative word, which in its reception of and dwelling in the divine, in turn provides a ground for the genius to take root, spring forth – or pour forth, since it is in the god's nature to appear in this manner. Thanks is the true starting point of all tale-telling, *Erzählen* and *Erdenken*, that remembers. As Heidegger writes in "'Andenken' und 'Mnemosyne'"

---

31. "Ihn kennt
Der Dank. Doch nicht behält er es leicht allein,
Und gern gesellt, damit verstehn sie
Helfen, zu anderen sich ein Dichter.

Furchtlos bleibt aber, so er es muß, der Mann
Einsam vor Gott, es schützet die Einfalt ihn,
Und keener Waffen brauchts und keener
Listen, so lange, bis Gottes Fehl hilft." DKV I: 307, v. 57–64.

> To say from remembrance is to think-up [*Erdenken*]; to abide most intimately with what is, that is the most daring spring into beying. The long time necessary for the preparation of what is true, has found its moment [*Augenblick*] through this poetry itself and through the brief being-there [*Da-sein*] of the poet, a moment in which, in the deepest depths of the unbound [*im Tiefsten des Ungestalten*], there 'the god also dwells too' – and everything turns into an originary spring [*Ursprung*] out of beyng[32]

Memory must be in the service of *gratitude*, not an imperialistic consciousness seeking to stabilize and establish or worse, usurp the place of the genius – all of which are impossible in any case. "Thanks prevail" when understanding buckles, doubles over in the face of destiny. Only gratitude remains standing at this crossing; only gratitude can guarantee the possibility of such a kairotic moment ever supervening again. Thanks both receives the genius and prepares and institutes (*stiftet*) the ground for its reception.

7. The Song as Bread and Wine

Now the question arises: how does poetry remember the genius with enough gratitude? This question leads us back to the beginning of the essay, where I spoke of the nature of eros. It seems that the destitution of reflection and indeed, representational thinking in general, cripples our ability to love. It seems we can never love the other enough. If gratitude expresses this love, it must celebrate it, not reflect upon it. Ideational recollection, which we saw seeks to capture the genius within the representation of a figure, must give way to gratitude, which knows the genius in allowing it to pass away within the song. Yet how is this accomplished?

The first principle in a poetics of sacrifice is that every description of the god is a prescription for memorializing, for gratitude and song. To be dedicated to the god, poetry must embody the divine, must resemble it mimetically. With this in mind, let us recall the problems with such remembrance. The main difficulty lies in the nature of its

---

32. GSA 75: 310

object, namely, the god, whom I have alternately designated as Diony-sus/Christ, destiny, the genius, intellectual intuition, and even more abstractly as "the All." Heidegger would add *being* to this nomencla-ture. If there is one undeniable quality with which the genius always appears in Hölderlin's work, it is the quality of excess, of excessive *intimacy, Innigkeit.* This excess is sung as overflow – the streaming of rivers and rivers of words, the overflowing of wine glasses "more full," the nexus where all of life is felt too intimately, too intensely. This quality, never quantifiable, is designated simply (and yet always enig-matically) with Hölderlin's hallmark use of the comparative forms (*unendlicher, kühner, das Größre*) and the excessive "too," *zu* (*zu groß, zu innig, zu einig*). Divine surfeit contains within it a second characteris-tic: inevitable *diremption* and *dissolution.* As something both too unified and utterly dirempt, as something at the threshold of being and non-being, the divine appears, thirdly, as *ecstatic* and *momentary.* Finally, owing to its ecstatic temporal nature, the divine advenes at the op-portune moment as the happy happenstance – as *Ereignis*; it is the distilled essence of time's fermentation. The advent of the god cannot be reckoned; one can only provide and prepare for its arrival.

If every description of the god is simultaneously a prescription for poetry and gratitude, poetic gratitude must be a certain praxis that imitates the divine. Such praxis is *religious* in nature, and more spe-cifically, *liturgical* or *ritualistic.* Liturgy accounts for the processual character of Hölderlin's work, not consciousness' unfolding. This is because the element of sacrifice in ritual is the moment of diremption – caesura – in the process, as we have seen in *Bread and Wine.* It is the moment of the god's absconding as *a gift* – or when the absence of god helps. How does the god disappear irrecuperably in the song? The mediacy and facticity of the word – and the world to which the god has descended – kills him. Or rather, he is consumed in the word and world. In the second version of the elegy we hear:

> Father Aether expends and strives, like flames, toward earth,
>> Thousand-fold the god comes. Below lies like roses, the ground
> Ill-suited, transitory for the heavenly, but like flames
>> Working from above and testing life and us, consuming.

Men however point there and here and raise their heads
   United they share the glowing good.
The consuming...[33]

Likewise, the bread and wine of the Eucharist – or of any celebration – disappears in the act of consumption. The song as sacrifice is not the god mediated in word. It is the utter consumption of the god. Calasso notes something of importance to keep in mind here: a sacrifice that goes unnoticed and fails to elevate something to consciousness is a crime; only in this way does the offering made in sacrifice differentiate itself from murder – the primordial crime, "the action that makes something in existence disappear: the act of eating."[34] But this happens to be the crime upon which all living creatures depend; every living thing exists at the expense of another. Thus sacrifice is necessary to purify a people of *miasma*, the pollution rooted in thoughtlessness and profound ingratitude. Such thoughtlessness and ingratitude constitute the Empedoclean age of *Neikos*, raging disorder, and as Hölderlin says, godlessness and a lack of destiny, "*dysmoron*."[35] Sacrifice is an offering or gift only if it remembers what has been given. In remembering, the gift is recognized, and as Heidegger writes, "The recognition of gifts as gifts is thanks." (GSA 75, 52).[36] Thus the song as sacrifice is the practice that remembers this consumption of the god, his diremption, the very kairotic and momentary crossing of mortal and divine in decline. Thus bread and wine appear – and poetic song, to be enjoyed, as before, *in a human way*; human beings must wine and dine upon the poetic word in which the god is sacrificed, celebrated, remembered. As the very superfluity of life, the god offers itself up for this sacrifice.

---

33. "Vater Aether verzehrt und strebt, wie Flammen, zur Erde,
Tausendfach kommet der Gott. Unt liegt wie Rosen, der Grund
Himmlischen ungeschikt, vergänglich, aber wie Flammen
Wirket von oben, und prüft Leben, verzehrend, uns aus.
Die aber deuten dort und da und heben die Häupter.
Menschen aber, gesellt, theilen das blühende Gut.
Das Verzehrende..." K I: 377, v. 65–71.
34. Cf. MC 164–5.
35. On "*das Schiksaallose*," cf. K II: 374.
36. GSA 75:52

Gratitude swells to meet this abundance, exceeding and overflowing the song.

8. *The Vocation of the Poet*

The song itself must be an offering – a sacrifice *of* the god *to* the god in recognition of infinite gratitude. Yet this only happens in so far as the poet, the one touched by genius – the one who becomes a genius – is sacrificed in the song. Ludwig von Pigenot brings to attention the poet's role as sacrifice in the ritual of poetic song:

1. Hölderlin himself never doubted the secret relationship of his being to Hellenism, and it seems that he recognized it primarily in the desire and willingness that distinguished him above other poets to sacrifice himself, in the power of practiced remembrance and ritual, where the new human being, mindlessly and impetuously forgetful, overlooked the divine ("Indeed it is as before, yet cultivated no longer").[37]

Hence poets receive their calling sent by the murmuring of destiny: their hymns and tragedies must be a sacrificial celebration which, in remembering what is given, give thanks. Or as Heidegger says, they must be a celebration of thanks in which thanks itself celebrates (GSA 75, 303). Gratitude celebrates as offering and sacrifice. As "priests" of the wine-god, the poet's role to perform a liturgy in song is underscored, a liturgy connected with sacrifice, as is the Eucharist. As "priest," he does not simply repeat the liturgy of stale tradition, but serves a newly conceived religion, which Hölderlin, Schelling, and Hegel all had seen as the goal of the *Systemprogramm*. This new religion is poetic in nature, and takes the myth of Dionysus' shattered birth as its inspiration, both as a calling and a cause for celebration. In *As on a Holiday,* the song succeeds when it sounds of the fateful crossing between Zeus and Semele.

So that quickly struck, she, known for the longest time
To the infinite, shakes

---

37. GSA 75, 310.

With recollection, and ignited by the holy ray
She conceived the fruit in love, the work of gods and men,
To bear witness to both, the song succeeds.[38]

The new religion *is* poetry; the poet's calling is not to write religious poetry but to uncover poetic religion. This religion, as song of the earth, sings the shattered origin of the god, one for whom birth simultaneously means death. Thus poetic religion is tragic, takes tragedy as a *religious* text, as Karl Reinhardt proposes.[39] This new priest of the wine-god would act more in the vein of the tragic heroine, as the tragic mother of Dionysus, Semele or Sophocles' Antigone. The poet-priest, as the one who stands closest to the god – close enough to share both his love and his death, indeed all his suffering, and is his *semblable*. Indeed, the poet through his poetry stands in for, represents, the god, so that he might appear. Thus inevitably the poet risks being "the false priest." *As on a Holiday* ends with a caesura and the poet's sacrifice:

Yet, fellow poets, us it behooves to stand
Bareheaded beneath God's thunder-storms,
To grasp the Father's ray, no less, with our own two hands
And, wrapping in song the heavenly gift,
To offer it to the people.
For if only we are pure in heart,
Like children, and our hands are guiltless,

The Father's ray, the pure, will not sear our hearts
And, deeply convulsed, and sharing his sufferings

---

38. "Daß schnellbetroffen sie, Unendlichem
Bekannt seit langer Zeit, von Erinnerung
Erbebt, und ihr, von heilgem Stral entzündet,
Die Frucht in Liebe geboren, der Götter und Menschen Werk
Der Gesang, damit er beiden zeuge, glükt." DKV I: 240, v. 45–49/ PF 397.
39. Karl Reinhardt, "Hölderlin und Sophokles," in *Tradition und Geist: Gesammelte Essays zur Dichtung* (Göttingen: Vandenhoeck and Ruprecht, 1960), 381–397. Reinhardt sees Hölderlin's relation to Sophocles' tragedies, using the example of *Antigone*, as essentially *religious* in nature and takes this as the starting point of his analysis of Hölderlin's translations. Cf. esp. 382.

Who is stronger than we are, yet in the far-flung down rushing storms of
The God, when he draws near, will the heart stand fast.
But, oh, my shame! when of

My shame!

And let me say at once

That I approached to see the Heavenly,
And they themselves cast me down, deep down
Below the living, into the dark cast down
The false priest that I am, to sing,
For those who have ears to hear, the warning song.
There[40]

Thus it seems that this memorializing would need to take a lesson

---

40. "Doch uns gebührt es, unter Gottes Gewittern,
Ihr Dichter! mit entbößtem Haupte zu stehen,
Des Vaters Stral, ihn selbst, mit eigner Hand
Zu fassen und dem Volk' ins Lied
Gehüllt die himmlische Gaabe zu reichen.
Denn sind nur reinen Herzens,
Wie Kinder, wir, sind schuldlos unsere Hände

Des Vaters Stral, der reine versengt es nicht
Und tieferschüttert, die Leiden des Stärkeren
Mitleidend, bleibt in den hochherstürzenden Stürmen
Des Gottes, wenn er nahet, das Herz doch fest.
Doch weh mir! wenn von

Weh mir!

Und sag ich gleich,

Ich sei genaht, die Himmlischen zu schauen,
Sie selbst, sie werfen mich tief unter die Lebenden
Den falschen Priester, ins Dunkel, daß ich
Das warnende Lied den Gelehrigen singe.
Dort " DKV I: 240–241, v. 56–73/ PF 397, 399.

from that mysterious stranger in *Hyperion* who relates Plato's story of Eros' birth. Quoting once again from the Stranger's story: "When our originally infinite essence first came to *suffer* something, and when the free and full force encountered its first barriers, when Poverty mated with Superfluity, Love came to be" (DKV II: 207–8). The ideational recollection upon which memorializing would be founded would have to find itself boarding on that point of scission, of dissolution, just as Superfluity encounters his barriers when he is effectively dissolved in more divine superfluity, that of the gods' nectar. For Hölderlin, a limit, when shown, at the same time always points toward the beyond of what is prescribed and proscribed there. Only insofar as excess – of god, of the poet – is sacrificed, that is to say, finds its limits – which it does in suffering, can this excessive divinity ever come to the fore. Love is born of this suffering and prepares the ground of infinite gratitude, a Dionysian *Dankbarkeit*. In this way, Poverty is given her measure of Superfluity. Correct measure and proportionality constitute the Beautiful. Such balance is also the objective of sacrifice, yet is only brought into being if excess is not reabsorbed within this calculus. Something must go absolutely missing. Recalling Calasso's words, "what spills out is the excess that sacrifice claims for itself;" or, that the *god* claims for himself. Thus the infinite can only be shown in the moment of it going absolutely missing, or in the decline of the moment. In this moment, the poet, too, like the tragic hero, meets his downfall – he is cast down. Everything in the poet's sphere moves downward. Only a poetics of sacrifice, as a celebration of Dionysian *Dankbarkeit*, prevails.

Eros and Poiesis

ANNA-LENA RENQVIST

There are many words for love, and eros is one of them. A fierce power and the sweetest thing. A source of calamities and the manifestation of grace. A blind destiny and yet a future promise. Eros is the name of love, which, mythologically speaking, recalls the presence of a God. In one of the oldest sources available to us, Hesiod's *Theogony*, Eros appears together with the earth and the underworld, Gaia and Tartarus, as the first God emerging from a primordial chaos.[1] He stands for the power to liberate the forces by splitting them, and remains the condition *sine qua non* for their reencounter – of a propagating nature. Eros is the love that produces offspring.

Variations of the myth appear throughout antiquity. Within the Orphic tradition we learn that Eros stems from an egg issued by the union of heaven and chaos, from which he burgeons as the power to restore what he himself has torn apart. The same egg appears in Aristophanes' play *The Birds*, classified as a parody of the ancient version of the Orphic theogony; and with an allusion to the Phoenician creation myth, Sappho presents Eros as he "who come from heaven dressed in a purple mantle." A significant sample of these elements were to become institutionalized in the Eleusinian mysteries, where each new initiate would be given a sacred chest containing a phallus,

---

1. "Verily at the first Chaos came to be, but next wide-bosomed Earth, the ever-sure foundations of all (4) the deathless ones who hold the peaks of snowy Olympus, and dim Tartarus in the depth of the wide-pathed Earth, and Eros (Love), fairest among the deathless gods, who unnerves the limbs and overcomes the mind and wise counsels of all gods and all men within them." *Theogony*, ll. 116–13 (Harvard: Loeb Classical Library, 1914).

seeds sacred to Demeter and a golden egg.[2] For over two thousand years, until the imposition of Christianity as the Greek state religion at the end of the 4th century, Eros was being worshiped as the *Protogonos,* the first-born, endowed with the peculiar ability to unite opposites and, like Dionysus, recurrently referred to as *Eleuteherios,* "the liberator."

As the author of the mythological *Big Bang,* Eros was held responsible for difference as such, considered the power underlying the unity of the manifold and the essential doer of reunification.[3] As responsible for the mythological *Big Bang,* Eros stands forth both as the power of difference and the power of reunification. When, in the 6th century B.C, Eros appears along the border between mythology and philosophy, it will be in the form of such a complex thing. The first philosopher to write in prose, Pherecydes of Syros – the uncle of Pythagoras and one of the Seven Sages – grants us a narrative of this virtual back-and-forth movement: "For when Zeus was to compose the world out of opposites, he had to transform himself into the original shape of Eros, lead it to concordance and friendship, and was thus able to enfold in all things the identity and the unity that co-penetrates it all."[4]

What Eros is to the universe as a whole, he also is to each of its minor revelations: the cosmological Alpha and Omega and the where-from and whereto of any natural being – what on a human level is known as the past and the future. Eros is the power that makes us come into being and by which we, again and again or eventually, will break into pieces – as mere moments of an ever-lasting becoming. Thus, Eros is a fertile love responsible for making and procreation or, with a more technical term, for production.

Many are the voices that have praised the divine primacy of Eros, and one of them is Plato. With him we find the first philosophical

---

2. Thomas Taylor, *Eleusinian and Bacchic Mysteries* (Lighting Source Publishers, 1997), 117.

3. From Hesiod onwards, Eros stands for the power capable of unifying opposites. In this respect Eros has its temporal equivalence in the Greek divinity Kairos, the divine name of a time able to keep the universe together and to model the very measure of a time, kronos, that follows motion.

4. Rodolfo Mondolfo, *El pensamiento antiguo. Historia de la filosofía greco-romana* (Buenos Aires: Ed Losada, 1983), 25.

exposition of the essentially *poietic* nature here implied. I am referring to works such as the *Phaedrus*, the *Republic* or the *Laws*, but above all to the dialogue *Symposium*, a compilation of ancient myths of love by way of six speeches. The exposition has its core in the last of the discourses, held by Socrates in memorial of his old teacher, Diotima. Here Eros is referred to as a demiurge responsible for the becoming of life in general and of its spiritual counterpart in particular, such as knowledge and wisdom and "every kind of artistic production."[5] The argument is pronounced as an elaborated reply to what another speaker had stated as a question: Who will deny that it is the ability of Eros that allows beings to be born and begotten?[6]

Well aware of the fact that the traditional reading of Plato's doctrine of Eros holds *theorein*, pure contemplation or mere vision, to be the highest pursuable goal of a mortal being, and well aware of the fact that *theorein* is commonly held to be the opposite of any sort of activity, I would like to argue that *theorein* is less passive than such a contra-position would maintain, offering, as a consequence, the indispensible step towards the real objective of the gradual ascension here professed: immortality by way of succession.

Recalling the principal argument of this abundantly commented upon investigation on the phenomena of love, we find that Diotima diverges from mythology in several respects. Primarily, the complex nature of Eros is due to his mixed background. Issued by the union of a human being and the divine, Eros is not a God but a half-God, or what in Greek is called a *daimon*: a sort of pagan angel operating as a messenger in-between the finite world of appearance and the infinite sphere of the beyond. Like its Christian equivalent, the *daimon* was held to be a messenger of the heavens, but unlike the later Christian figure, it was considered a channel in two directions. Following Plato's indications, it was through the *daimon* that any contact and dialogue between gods and men could possibly be achieved.[7]

According to Diotima, Eros is the result of a casual encounter between divine abundance and human poverty, Poros and Penia, at a

---

5. *Symposium*, 196 e.
6. See *Symposium*, 197a. The summary is mine.
7. See *Symposium*, 202e–203a.

party held in honor of the birth of Aphrodite, the goddess of beauty. This is to say that Eros was born a bastard; and as a bastard he is to be both cursed and blessed. Thanks to his mother, he is submitted to motion and change as well as the normal mess known to a mortal being, such as poverty, scarcity and need. Existentially speaking, Eros is pure want; but this condition is graciously recompensed by a father able to turn shortage into a peculiar kind of plenty. By Poros, Eros is blessed with abundance, such that it grants him whatever he needs to be ready at hand. This double heritage has made him a lover of what he does not have, and a skilled hunter with the means to achieve whatever he aims at. Eros will capture his prey but due to his mother, he will not be able to keep it. His object will promptly escape him, the loss will present him with poverty, but then again, out of poverty, his hunting-spirit will be kept alive. As Goethe would later remind us, Love is eternal, only the objects are changing.

From Socrtates analysis of Diotimas tale we learn that Eros is love but not – as had been commonly thought – as the love-worthy. Being the child of Penia, Eros is *he who loves*. A lover of something, who desires his object and who wants to possess the object desired. This very something recalls the attributes of the time and place of Eros' conception: the aphrodisian beauty and the things related, such as goodness, justice and wisdom. Eros is the travel companion of Aphrodite, and hers are the attributes that may appear in the eyes of a lover – either it would be in body and flesh, in a beautiful soul, through the order of things or by an expression of knowledge. The divine attributes are of equal value and worth, yet the objects in which they appear are diverse. Although the sensitivity of beauty offers an indispensable initial condition, there is a virtuous path to be followed and an end to be reached: "the visual beholding of the being foreign to generation and corruption, which is eternally." Hence the *paideia*, or education here involved: a systematic proceeding, starting from early age, able to conduct the loving soul in an ascending movement, from the sensual and individual within the world of appearances, through universal knowledge, in order to end up with the vision of what is naturally so: the idea of beauty itself.

The traditional reading of the platonic Eros ends here. The visual, non-practical but "theoretical" illumination of the lover by the presence of beauty herself, through which the lover partakes of wisdom and comes into possession of the beyond, is held to offer the most noble satisfaction proper to Eros and the *telos* of the platonic erotic.

The interpretation is based on a seemingly solid ground. More than once Plato himself has claimed the crowning of the erotic quest to be contemplation; and more than once has he claimed contemplation to be just the opposite of any kind of activity. While the latter was related to a concern with intraworldy things, submitted to time and corruption, *theoria* was the word given to the experience of the eternal and unspeakable (*arethon*) or, with Aristotles' later precision, with the "without words" (*aneu logou*). The two realms were to be clearly distinguished, since eternity would disclose itself to a mortal eye only when all human activities were at rest.[8]

The distinction is of a philosophical nature; yet it does have both a historical and political context. It is tied up with the fact that for Plato contemplation was an attitude reserved for the few, namely those members of the *polis* considered freed from the time-consuming political activity or *praxis* the city-state required.[9] The understanding of *theoria* as a non-activity thus implies a former division between philosophy and politics which, historically speaking, had its expression with the trial of Socrates. Plato was the spokesman of the latter, and the main purpose of his political philosophy was to secure a life unconstrained by political duties – the philosopher's way of life or the *bios theoretikos*. This was also the origin of the phenomenon *skhole*: a time when activity had ceased and truth, as a result, could be disclosed.

The opposition between contemplation and activity is convincing if we consider activity to translate the word *praxis*, but it is less so if we consider other words for activity within the Greek language such as *archein, energein, dran* or *poiein*. A linguistic detail reflected by Plato himself. Turning to the *Symposium*, not only do we find contemplation treated as a verb, hence understood as an act, but moreover it is held to be the highest form of activity given to a mortal being: the activity

---

8. Hannah Arendt, *The Human Condition* (Chicago: The University of Chicago Press, 1998), 26–27.
9. See Fustel de Coulanges, *The Ancient City* (New York: Anchor Books, 1956), 334–36.

denoted by the word *poiein*, in English creation, fabrication, production. Or as Plato defines it: "the cause that brings something from non-being to being."[10] Diotima's final announcement breaks our habitual line of thought: "What love wants is not beauty, as you think it is Socrates [...], but reproduction and birth in beauty."[11]

Eros is linked to the act of production; hence, as the peak of the platonic erotic, *theoria* is seemingly more of an act than a non-act. The exposition of Plato is remarkably insistent and supplies us with guiding materials. A passage from the important fourth book of the *Republic* may serve as an example. "Then, won't it be reasonable for us to plead, in defense of the real lover, that it is his nature of learning to struggle toward what is, not to remain with any of the many things that are believed to be; that, as he moves on, he neither loses nor lessens his erotic love until he grasps the being of each nature itself with the part of his soul that is fitted to grasp it, because of its kinship with it, and that, once getting near what really is and having intercourse (*migeís*) with it and having begotten understanding and truth, he knows, truly lives, is nourished, and – at that point, but not before – is relieved from the pains of giving birth."[12]

Theoria is an act of intercourse and conception of a visual kind, which is to say that it is a visual kind of *poiesis*; and as such it is the ultimate act of the platonic erotic. Even so, given the nature of *poiesis*, the story is not yet concluded. Posed as a question: if *theoria* is the ultimate act of the lover, is it therefore the ultimate object of Eros? According to Diotima, the answer is no. Strictly speaking, *theoria* may be considered the final aim of Eros only in so far as we mean the ultimate act given to a mortal being, which is to say, the act of dying. *Theoria* is an act, but the ultimate object of Eros – partly in line with traditional understanding – is less of an act and more of an overcoming of a condition, since it is the elimination of death through the perpetuation of life, in other words: immortality. To this end, *theoria* is an intermediate step. Plato's concluding remarks, by way of Diotima,

10. *Symposium*, 205b–c
11. *Symposium*, 206e.
12. Translation G.M.A Grube, rev. C. D. C. Reeve. *Complete Works*, ed. John M. Cooper (Indianapolis / Cambridge: Hackett Publishing Company 1997).

may be summarized thus: "Eros is the mortals desire to always exist and to be as immortal."[13] The affirmation recalls the famous message of Sophocles' *Antigone*: While Death is the Lord against whom man "shall call for aid in vain" love will remain "unconquered in the fight." Love will remain, even in spite of death, and, following Plato, so will somehow the lover, "because procreation is everlasting and immortal, as far as is possible for something mortal."[14]

The object of Eros is not an act but the overcoming of a condition, not a mere love of beauty, but the love of birth and procreation in beauty, not a mere appetite to possess, but a want to progress: by succession to reach immortality. Surely, then, it is not incorrect to say that Eros demands satisfaction, but only as long as we keep in mind that his ultimate claim is named *fruit*. Eros, himself the result of a confusing encounter, is essentially fertile.

Eros is known, above all, as the power to unify, nevertheless – or because of it – the playground of Eros is difference. Only what is apart can desire to meet, and Eros can strike the lover in as far as he is not at one with his object, only to the extent that there is a distance to be overcome and a difference to be obliterated. Moreover – as we have seen – the hidden agenda of Eros is immortality by way of succession, in other words, by way of reproduction of this very difference. It is precisely because the past and the future of the lovers' mingling business is difference, that the moment of unity may be lived as a divine instant of gratification.

Now, what does this actually mean? Let us briefly recapitulate the movements of this vital train of events.

The erotic-poietic process points to a beyond; in more than one way does it imply transcendence. While the lover, from his own point of view, is painfully tied to the world of appearance, the beloved one is not. The essence of the beloved is not of this world, nor is the time and the place of the longed-for encounter. For a meeting to be celebrated there is a limit to be passed and a price to be paid. Like most deities, Eros calls for a sacrifice without which the encounter will be cancelled

---

13. *Symposium*, 207d (my abbreviation).
14. *Symposium*, 206e. Plato's argument echoes a poetic insight running from Sappho to the enigmatic Sonnets of Shakespeare and onwards.

and the process revoked. The close linkage between Eros and Tanatos, recurrent in mythology and later recognized, among others, by Freud, is disturbingly present. The mingling business is virtually incompatible with any set individuality or established identity. As Plato prescribes, being the most highly eroticised person, the philosopher should be prepared: "The one aim for them who practise philosophy in the proper manner, is to practise for dying and death."[15] By way of possession, the loving soul will end up dispossessed; by way of a vision, it will become fused with it all; yet here and now it *becomes* – immortal by way of succession.

The intimacy of the event corresponds to the final act of the lovers as separate beings. At least, for the time being. For a brief yet critical moment the negativity of dialectics, through which difference is borne and confirmed, is replaced by an instant of pure *affirmation*. As Hegel later observed: "We have entered the night in which all cats are grey."[16] Or, following Plato, were facing a kind of insanity: a divine madness (*zeía manía*) triggered by remembrance of things forgotten, a precise reminiscence of a former beauty by way of a present object evoking it. The reference occurs in the dialogue *Phaedro* and it gives us a handsome figure of the danger involved: the loss of self-reference, self-oblivion, self-neglect; fusion by way of confusion.[17] The price for an approximation to beauty is madness, which is to say: an erasing of the individual in the sense of a momentous, episodic cancellation of the *principium individuationis*. Eros claims difference as the sacrifice to be made. The poetic experience that will prosper within romanticism is

---

15. *Phaedo*, 64a

16. *The Phenomoenolgy of the Spirit* (Cambridge: Oxford University Press, 1979), 13. The famous line is pronunced as an argument against intellectual intuition present in the philosophy of Schelling.

17. *Phaedo*, 249c–e. Among several attentive readings of this passage, I quote the one offered by Gadamer in his work *Truth and Method* (New York: Crossroad, 1989), Book II § 4 "To be 'outside of your self' is the positive possibility to assist at something entirely. This assistance has the character of self-oblivion; and the essence of the spectator is to give himself over in contemplation while forgetting about himself. However, this state of self-oblivion has nothing to do with a state of privation, since it has its origin in the return to the thing, which the spectator will realize as his own positive action." (My translation.)

eloquently announced: the power of beauty is devastating, the penalty for an approximation is lethal – yet if the end is vital progression, there is no other way. Physical or spiritual life, poetry or science regardless; only this pre-Cartesian *methodos* may lead us to the pre-conceptual intercourse of the known with the unknown, the familiar with the strange, the present at mind with the partly forgotten, that underlies – as a modification of the Aristotelian notion of substance – the discontinuous continuity of the movement at stake.

The process is of a cyclical nature and recalls the old notion of the eternal recurrence of the same – in its many variations. What has been shaped in a blissful moment may be born in time, and what is born in time may grow to love, and so on and so forth. As difference is cancelled and unity thus restored, the outburst is already apt: the indistinguishable time of conception will be succeeded by the time of painful delivery, of partition of beings and differentiation of the world as we know it.[18] As Plato reminds us, Eros is the strongest of all, stronger even than Ares, the God of war, since he is able to make men into poets, "once love touches him, *anyone* becomes a poet, however uncultured he had been before."[19]

There are many kinds of love; all of them name a relation, some of them coincide, but they point in different directions. Naming four of the major love-themes within the western tradition, the first to be mentioned is the caring love of *agape*. In the Christian tradition *agape* is known as the descending love reaching from a You to an I, and in some protestant readings, figured as the teocentric love opposing the egocentricity attributed to eros.[20] In line with St Paul's teachings, *agape* is considered the most noble love since it "does not seek its own,"[21] as is the case with parental love, which is a love for their creation or, by imitation, as is the case with the love of thy neighbour. In each case we speak of a love that is directed to nourish what needs to mature, to

18. A recent investigation of the seemingly paradoxical caracter of an encounter able to errase difference giving birth to difference is found in Jonna Bornemarks thesis *Kunskapens gräns, gränsens vetande* (Huddinge: Södertörn Philosophical Studies, 2009).
19. *Symposium*, 196e
20. Anders Nygren, *Eros och agape* (Stockholm: AB Tryckmans, 1930).
21. 1Kor. 13;5

restore the strength of the weak, to care and to cure. As a counterpart to this benevolent love, we find the sorrowful circular love between an I and an I, a perverted perception mistaking the I for an Other, in line with the handsome Narcissus who fell in love with his own image. Furthermore, there is the love in-between us, spoken by the word friendship, *philia*; possibly the most sweet, or the least painful love, since it is a love that is mutual. And last but not least, there is the ascending erotic love between an I and a You, whose power is to make us aware of a unification at reach, to make us want to recover what was lost and recalled. Mythologically speaking, Eros is the origin of the becoming of cosmos and the destiny of its minor stars, but humanly speaking, it is the love presenting us with the source of a past and a future. The paradox of the fulfilment of an erotic encounter is the ability to mark a difference between what was and what is to come, to draw a line thereby between a past that might serve us or haunt us, and a future that might appear as a promise or drive us insane – by way of a unifying presence of a becoming. Eros claims offspring, and is therefore the word for love of *poiesis* and love as *poiesis*, a productive love that conquers difference for the sake of difference in memory of it All, by way of the Whole, hence, underlies the continuation of the discontinuous processes known as philosophy, poetry, science or life.

The Nature and Origin of the Eros
of the Human Soul in Plotinus

AGNÈS PIGLER

The Erotic Philosophy of Plato and Plotinus

The originality of Plotinus's teaching concerning the concept of eros lies in the fact that Love is found *at the heart of the One*[1] as the source of the procession and the root of the Real, that is to say, *at the heart* of the Intelligible as well as the sensible: the diffusive love of the Principle is here conceived as an "immense life" which emanates, indeterminately, from the absolute Origin, a life the products of which are all differentiated from each other but whose vital energy permits the Whole to preserve its continuity with itself.

In contrast to this, an examination of the main themes related to platonic love permits the conclusion that, for Plato, the seat of love is in the soul and nowhere else. According to the dialogues, Platonic love takes on different functions: intermediary, auxiliary, method, remembrance. But all of these functions have one and the same goal, to attain the True. In this way, Platonic love is a condition of both psychagogy and gnoseology. But even if all these themes are certainly repeated by Plotinus at different places in the *Enneads*, it is essential to note that whereas human love for Plato is the starting point of philosophy – since "true love is the way to the Beautiful, because it is the love of wisdom, philo-sophy"[2] – *the Plotinian eros is not of the same nature and does not have the same purpose.*

---

1. Cf. Enneads, VI, 8 (39), 15, 1: The Good is "in itself simultaneously the loved object, Love and Love of itself (*kai erasmion kai eros ho autos kai heautou eros.*"
2. Lambros Couloubaritsis, *Aux origines de la philosophie eruopéenne. De la pensée archaïque au néoplatonisme* (Bruxelles: de Boeck, 1992), 248.

It is this Plotinian displacement of the Platonic suppositions concerning love that constitute the true originality of the Plotinian erotic. Despite the recurrence of Platonic themes in the *Enneads*, and sometimes even of a Platonic vocabulary taken over almost word for word by Plotinus,[3] what we find, with regard to eros, is not only a different intuition, but even the emergence of a new metaphysics. The first difference, and the most remarkable, is that *the Plotinian eros does not have its seat in the soul*, as in Plato, *but in the One*.[4] This difference is, I would insist, *crucial* in so far as love, as that which is diffused from the One into its derivatives, is the condition without which the procession of beings could not have come about. The Eros is diffused when the One, "turning towards itself," through this movement, generates – without thereby being changed or diminished – the totality of the Real following upon it. Nowhere in Plato do we find the affirmation of an Eros of the Good generating the Ideas. By contrast, it is from the Plotinian One, from its diffusive Eros, that everything comes, and from the innate desire of the derivatives for their generator comes the fundamental process of conversion permitting the constitution of the Intelligible as well as the sensible. Plotinian love is thus *both* at the source of the procession, as the cause of that which derives from the One loving itself, and the driving force of the conversion of the derivatives towards the latter, in that the diffusive love of the Principle is transformed, in the derivatives, into love of the Good: "Everything tends towards the Good and desires it *through a necessity of nature*, as if sensing that without it nothing can exist."[5]

In this way the One, like the Platonic Good, is the supremely love worthy; but the signification of this supreme love worthiness is not the same for the two philosophers. In the first place, for Plato the attraction of what is the supreme value of love is valid *only* for the human soul in its ascension towards the Good in itself. In the second place, the Platonic erotic method is subordinated to a purpose, namely the attainment of the Good conceived as "the most indispensable of

---

3. This is notably the case in VI, 9 (9), 9, 39-43; VI, 7 (38), 32, 25 and 33, 14.
4. Cf. VI, 8 (39), 15.
5. V, 5 (32), 12, 7-9 (my italics); se also I, 6 (1), 7; IV, 4 (28), 35; VI, 7 (38), 23 and 26; VI, 8 (39), 7.

cognitions,"[6] and on account of which this purpose demands the *abandonment* of the erotic method in favor of an intellectual contemplation of the Truth. On the contrary, for Plotinus it is when the human soul goes beyond the intellect in order to be nothing but love, that there is vision of the Principle and union with it, and this, moreover, is valid also for the intelligible realities. This is because the human soul actually loves the Good *"as driven by it* to love it,"[7] and in opposition to the amorous emotion described by Plato in the *Symposium* and *Phaedrus*, it "does not wait for the announcements of the beautiful things down here."[8] The love of the soul is thus connatural to it, precisely in so far as it is *a certain motion of the Good*, as initiated by the presence of the One in the soul. In the third place, finally, the gnoseological perspective of the Platonic erotic is confirmed by the fact that the philosopher, contemplating the Idea of the Good, does not remain at this height but instead, fecundated by this sublime science from which "justice and the other virtues draw their utility and their advantages,"[9] and having seen that which is true,[10] becomes teacher and/or governor as soon as he returns from heaven to earth.[11] This is why Socrates undertakes, in the *Republic*, the investigation of an educational system designed to lead to the intuition of the Good, and to raise the soul to the vision of the Good.[12]

Nowhere in Plato, then, is love a goal in itself. Nowhere is love that which is diffused from the Good into the realities which follow from it, the Ideas, and nowhere is it the only ideal of the soul, as Plotinus

6. *Republic*, VI, 504e.
7. VI, 7 (38), 31, 17–18 (my italics).
8. Ibid., 19.
9. *Republic*, VI, 505a.
10. Cf. ibid., 484c.
11. Cf. ibid., 473c–e; 484b–c; 498b–c; 500e; 519d–521e.
12. It is thus that gymnastics and music, in the *Republic*, correspond to the love of beautiful bodies and the love of beautiful souls in the *Symposium*. Music has no other purpose than to regulate the soul through harmony; for a detailed analysis of this unification of the soul through the study of music, cf. Evanghelos Moutsopoulos, *La musique dans l'oeuvre de Platon* (Paris: Presses universitaires de France, 1959), in particular in the fourth part, "L'esthétique musicale," the first chapter "Axiologie du Beau musical," 229–259.

will say, to "flee alone to the Alone" (*phugê monou pros monou*).[13] Upon the Platonic erotic ascension, upon the ascending dialectic, there must follow the descending dialectic, which is no longer in any way erotic, but instead pedagogic. Thus Platonic intellectualism surpasses the erotic: the amorous ascension carries us to the Beautiful, and is then effaced in favor of the Intellect's vision of the Good. The dialectic is therefore that which crowns the erotic method, in so far as only the dialectic carries us all the way to the contemplation of the anhypothetic. In Plotinus, *on the contrary*, love is neither a method nor an auxiliary of the dialectic, but it is a *dynamic*, it is power and life. What commands this dynamic is *the overflow of the One*, its abundance, and that which structures the Intelligible as well as the sensible is once again the erotic dynamic as conversion towards the Good.

Our study will show how eros, in relation to *the human soul* – in its purification and its amorous ascension towards the Principle – has a fundamental role in Plotinus. But before entering into the way of the erotic ecstasy of the soul, we must understand where this love inhabiting the human soul comes from and what is its nature. We will show that the eros that moves the human soul is the trace of henological Love, and that, by virtue of its origin, its nature is divine. We will then be able to explain what is the nature of Plotinian ecstasy: rather than a mystical ecstasy, in the ecstatic experience described by Plotinus it is a matter of a truly metaphysical experience.

The Henological Origin of the Eros of the Soul

The uniqueness of the philosophy of Plotinus resides in the fundamental doctrine of the procession. At the source of the latter is the overflow of the One, diffusing an eros and a life inseparable from each other: emanating from the First, life and love communicate themselves to the derivatives through the mediation of a power by which, with the help of the conversion towards their principle, the hypostases are constituted as complete realities. This is why life and love are connatural in the derivatives and express, in their difference from the One, the trace of the latter in them, its *presence*. The trace or *ichnos* of the One in that

---

13. VI, 9 (9), 11, 51.

which follows it may thus be interpreted as *love*. Nevertheless, *eros* does not signify primarily the ontological difference of the hypostasis in relation to its origin, but rather it is *the expression of an identity*, a *continuity* that traverses the intelligible world (*Nous*)[14] and is found, diminished but not exhausted, in the sensible world as well and, *a fortiori*, in the human soul. In its continuity with the origin, eros is thus foundational: it structures the relation of dependence characterizing the totality of derivatives with regard to their principle, and it manifests, through difference, the mark or imprint of the absolute Origin.

This is true for the *Nous* as well as for the Soul, but in different degrees. In fact, Plotinus conceives the Intellect as pure relation to itself, a self-presence that is pure perfection and self-sufficiency, whereas the Soul is conceived as being in a relation of complete dependence with regard to the Intellect. The self-sufficiency of *Nous* expresses itself as primary life and archetypical of all the forms of life following upon it: the Intellect possesses in itself the totality of the *eide*; it is the Whole.[15] On the other hand, although independent and self-sufficient, it also contains a non-intellectual part through which it remains attached to that which is prior and superior to it, the One.

Through this loving part, living the Life of the One, the perfection of the Intellect expresses itself according to a modality different from that of the One: instead of pure self-relation, it becomes the active and dynamic trace of the First; its life is *love of the Good*. Thus love, superior to thought, is the trace of its origin: it manifests the dependence of *Nous* in relation to its generator, that is to say, the continuity which connects the Intellect to the One beyond their radical ontological difference. Love thus signifies *both* the provenance and the dynamic continuity of the procession *and* the conversion.

---

14. "Wherefrom comes the life high above, wherefrom comes the life which is total, and the Intellect which is total? [...]. High up above everything is overflowing and, in a way, seething with life. From these things seething with life, there issues a sort of flow from a unique source" (VI, 7 (38), 12, 20–24).

15. In the Intellect, "Everything is transparent; nothing is obscure or resisting; each one is clear unto everyone else even in their innermost reaches; it is light unto light. Everyone has the whole within himself and sees everything in every other: everything is everywhere, everything is in everything; the splendour is without limit" (V, 8 (31), 4, 4–8).

But eros is also analogous to the Good, because it is itself without form, a trace of the pure erotic-vital power emanating from the absolute Origin. Nevertheless, even though love is the trace of the One in the Intellect, even though it is the presence of it, does it on no account establish a relation of strict identity with the Principle. In fact, eros is simultaneously the sign of the *absence* of the One, since the latter, in its absolute transcendence, its irreducible alterity, is never found *as such* in the hypostasis which immediately derives from it: the desire and the love of the Intellect for the Good are thus equally the traces of its infinite difference from it. In this way, as the trace of the presence of the First, love manifests an infinite dependence, a proximity in the tension of the desire for the supremely love worthy; it permits a living tie to unite that which is originally different. But the absence of the Principle is also visible in the fact that it never manifests itself other than in the guise of an infinite power *derived* from its pure Act, a power in which the diffusive love and life of the Absolute are fused. Thus, the erotic dynamic power emanating from the One manifests *simultaneously* the tie that unites it with its derivatives *and* its absence in that which it has produced: eros as the trace of the Principle is the manifestation of its presence/absence.

But love is also a generative power since, in the act of producing, the origin leaves its trace.[16] This is why Plotinian love, understood as an act of generation, is not metaphoric but *absolutely real*: eros permits the passage, the continuity between that which is absolutely other, the One, and its immediate derivative, *Nous*. In this way, love emphasizes not only the distance from the eminence, but also and above all the

---

16. Cf. III, 8 (30), 11, 14–23: "In attaining the Good, the Intellect takes its form from it; from the Good it receives its completion and the form which it possesses in itself comes from the Good and makes it similar to the Good. Such is the trace of the Good which one sees in the Intellect, and it is in this way that one must conceive the model. In fact, it is from the trace of the Good having imprinted itself on the Intellect that one has the notion of the true Good. *The Good has given to the seeing Intellect a trace of itself and this is why there is a desire in the Intellect (to men oun ep' autou ichnos autou tô nô horônti edôken echein. hôste en men tô nô hê ephesis)*; at every moment the Intellect desires, and at every moment it obtains that which it desires" (my italics).

living presence of the absolute Origin:[17] while the One gives that which it does not have, it nevertheless gives a trace of itself which is unfaltering love and life. Still, in the complete Intellect, the primary life is the totality of forms, it is ontological life; it is thus not in the form that the trace of the Origin resides, but in that which permits the form to bear a resemblance to the Good. The formless life issuing from the pure Act of the Principle, becoming ontological life in *Nous*, retains a similarity with it because love is, as such, *acting*. In fact, only eros, as the trace of the Inexpressible, is able to accomplish the transcendence of the ontological, since it itself is somehow the light of that which is without form: it makes the light of the Good shine over the archetypal life of the Intellect, since it is, at the core of the second hypostasis, the presence of the origin, the mark of an *acting continuity*.

This is why, if love is an acting generative power, *Nous* will also produce through love: it will generate the Soul, and this generation will express the continuity of the *processional erotic dynamic*. The generation of the Soul is thus the effect of an active generosity, because from the founding power of the One emanates an erotic-vital power *which is not exhausted* in the constitution of the hypostasis of the Intellect. In fact, this erotic-vital power always exceeds the process through which a hypostasis is actualized and completed; the overflow of the One is *always exceeding*, and this excess is at the origin of another hypostasis, the Soul. But this time, the mode of generation is different, because whereas *Nous* is constituted from that which the One does not give, *Nous* in its turn makes a gift to the Soul of that which it possesses.

The Soul is thus actualized and completed as hypostasis in amorously turning toward its generator. Thereby it receives the form and the limit possessed by the Intellect, as it contemplates the intelligible realities present in the *Nous*; and the thought of the Soul, which is

---

17. Cf. III, 8 (30), 10, 1–5: "It [the One] is the power of everything; if it does not exist, nothing exists, neither the being, nor the Intellect, neither the primary life, nor any other. It is above life and cause of life; the activity of that life which is all being is not the primary; it flows from it as from a source" (*Ti dê on; dunamis tôn pantôn. hês mê ousês oud' an ta panta, oud'an nous zôê hê prôtê kai pasa. to de hyper tên zôên aition zôês. ou gar hê tês zôês energeia ta panta ousa prôtê, all' hôsper prochutheisa autê hoion ek pêgês.*)

dianoetic thinking, nourishes its desire and love for the higher hypostasis.[18] But this is not the whole story. In fact, in contemplating the intelligible, the Soul simultaneously contemplates the beauty shimmering over the forms, and beauty is an indication of the presence of the Good. Moreover, this beauty is also a strong appeal to the Soul's love for its generator and for that which resides beyond.[19] The Soul, which has also issued from the erotic-vital power emanating from the First, but as mediated through *Nous*, thus receives the trace of the One from the Intellect; but whereas the generation of the second hypostasis is the expression of a primary relation to the origin, and thus the first manifestation of the trace of the One, the gift which the Intellect makes to the Soul is only the trace of that which it has itself received from the Good. While the first trace is nothing other than the form, if "the form is only the trace of that which is without form,"[20] that which is transmitted from *Nous* to the Soul is, by contrast, the intelligible forms. Thus, the Intellect and the Soul in their complete perfection express the Good without form. The form may thus be considered as the trace of the One, in so far as the process of generation is the achievement of love and, in the act of production of one hypostasis by another, constitutes an active relation. In the final analysis, then, that which gives the form the trace of the Good is love, *in that it exceeds all forms*. In fact, even if the presence of the Good cannot be thought outside of the identity of form and life, it is nevertheless in love, as trace and presence of the Good in each of the derivative hypostases, that it comes to be expressed.

---

18. Cf. II, 3 (52), 18, 15–16: "The Intellect gives to the Soul which comes after it the forms, the traces of which are found in the reality of the third degree." In the dynamic process of constituting the hypostases, the hierarchy implies a diffusion of the erotic-vital power. This is why, on the one hand, the Soul is always attached, through love and contemplation, to the Intellect with which it fills itself, thus producing its lower part, and, on the other hand, the intellectual part of the Soul is filled with forms by *Nous*. But without the love, which moves the hypostases towards their generator, without the eros assuring the processional passage in its continuity, there would be neither life nor hypostasis.
19. Cf. VI, 6 (34), 18, 47–49: "Its power and its beauty are so great that everything becomes fascinated with it, attaching itself to it [the Intellect], feeling joy on receiving its trace from it and searching for the Good which lies beyond it."
20. VI, 7 (38), 33, 30.

It is the same process, once again, is at the origin of the creation of the sensible world through the lower Soul, and here as well the erotic-vital power manifests its action. In fact, through the function of an intermediary between the Intelligible and the sensible, which is exercised by the Soul-Nature and the individual souls, the presence of the Good – that is to say its trace in the sensible universe – is not effaced but only weakened and diminished. Eros is active *as well* in the living totality of Nature, in the force and generative power animating the sensible world, because every force is, in Plotinus, a trace of the erotic-vital power having its source in the One.[21] In this sense, the love of the Soul, as a life-propagating power, maintains the sensible world in a coherence with the Whole proceeding from the Principle: it is because there is in the Soul a desire which drives it to act that it organizes the sensible world by outwardly projecting the erotic-vital power which it has received from its higher part.[22] And it is because the eros is active in the Soul that the cosmos is a living cosmos filled with a harmony and a universal sympathy of the Stoic kind:[23] everything here is animated, everything is perfect and manifests the splendor of the Intelligible. The wealth of concrete determinations thus expresses the erotic-vital dynamic in the phenomenal world.[24]

It is the particular souls that are responsible for this world not being deprived of love, harmony and universal sympathy. As concerns matter, it is like the dross of the higher beings, and thereby cannot communicate anything to this world except its bitterness. The descent of the particular souls is thus destined for the completion of the sensible universe; but the love that acts in the particular soul, the eros

---

21. Cf. IV, 4 (28), 27, 3; VI, 7 (38), 11, 17.

22. Cf. III, 7 (45), 11 and 12; IV, 4 (28), 16; IV, 7 (2), 13.

23. Cf. in this regard Agnès Pigler, "La réception plotinienne de la notion stoïcienne de sympathie universelle" (in *Revue de Philosophie Ancienne* 19, 1, 2001, 45–78).

24. Cf. VI, 7 (38), 7, 8–16: "What is there to stop the Soul of the Whole, since is it a universal reason (*logos*), from drawing up a first outline, before the animated powers descend from it, and this outline somehow illuminating matter beforehand? In order to produce, the souls only have to follow the design already traced and organize the parts one by one; and each one directs its attention to the part which it approaches, as in a chorus where the dancer unites with the part given to him."

that is connatural to it and that of itself is directed towards the Good, leads the soul to the conversion and restores it in its ontological dignity. In fact, the love which lives in the soul transforms the bodily ties into an exercise of power in order to arrange that which is ontically inferior, just as it permits the soul, which is mixed up with the body, to purify itself and thus turn its gaze towards its true part.

Above all, it is the analysis of the human soul that shows that the erotic power *in us* attaches us with all its force to an originary love of which we preserve the trace. Since love is a gift of the One,[25] it *is* the presence of the Good in us that gives us the strength to undertake "the journey" which will lead us all the way to the ecstasy and the loving union with the Principle – if, that is, it is true that our soul desires to attain the contemplation of the object of our love.[26] By following the soul along the way it has to travel in order to attain the object of its love, we should thus be able to analyze the intermediate stages – of a theoretical, ethical and aesthetic order – which play a preparatory role for its "erotic journey."

In this way the analysis of eros in Plotinus, even if it preserves from the classical Greek philosophical tradition – and in particular from Plato – the idea of an enlightenment through *logos* and the idea of a beautification through the splendor of the Beautiful, goes beyond the conception of a *demoniacal intermediary* attributed to eros by Plato. Instead, eros in Plotinus becomes *reality in act*, revealing to the amorous soul the propitious road leading from sensible beauty to absolute Beauty, and from the contemplation of the perfect forms in the Intellect to the contemplation of the One.[27] So far, we have shown in what way the origin of the eros of the soul is henological love; we will now apply ourselves to a study of its nature.

---

25. Cf. VI, 7 (38), 32, 21–23.

26. Cf. V, 1 (10), 3, 1–3.

27. It is thus that Plotinus exhorts us: "[…] search God with assurance with the help of such a principle and rise all the way up to him; he is not at all far away and you will arrive there: the intermediaries are not many" (V, 1 (10), 3, 2–4).

The Nature of Psychic Love: the Passions of the Soul

The descent of the soul into the body is often presented by Plotinus as the consequence of an *audacity*: "The origin of evil is audacity (*tolma*) and becoming (*genesis*) and the first difference (*hê prôtê heterotês*) and the will to be master of oneself (*heautou einai*)."[28] The audacity thus consists of the will of the individual souls to be independent. This will has led them into becoming, it has separated them from the principle by adding a first difference, matter – difference being defined, in the Plotinian vocabulary, as the principle of plurality and separation.[29] The descent of souls into bodies thus translates into an increase in multiplicity: each of us is several human beings, which however does not mean that we would thereby be separated, for each of these human beings produces another, and all are in continuity with each other, but still without forming, all together, a substantial unity. The role of the purification will thus be to restore our soul to its original purity and unity, to make it reconnect, through the erotic contemplation, with its true part.

It is here that eros, as the driving force of the conversion, intercedes. In fact, on each level of the erotic anabasis of the soul toward its principle, the soul must traverse the multiplicity of its erotes. These different aspects of the eros of the soul are manifested in the form of the material desire characteristic of the soul completely entangled in matter and perverted by it, as well as in the form of divine eros as the attribute of the noetic and wise soul directing its gaze towards the One. In fact, when our soul rises all the way up to the loving and inchoative *Nous*, it contemplates, in its company and in a state of erotic ecstasy, the Good that dispenses love. We may thus affirm that the nature of the eros of the soul is multiple, due to its sensible condition as incarnated. It is this erotic multiplicity that we must analyze. We

---

28. V, 1 (10), 1, 3–5.

29. Plotinian difference may be analyzed as matter. In fact, Plotinus writes, in the treatise 10 (V, 1): *pôs de kai polla houtôs asômata onta hulês ou chôrizousês* (9, 26–27). Thus, even in the intelligible world, difference produces matter: *hê heterotês hê ekei dei tên hulên moiei* (II, 4 (12), 5, 28–29; III, 6 (26), 15, 5–6), but here it is a question of a matter still belonging to being (cf., for example, VI, 4 (22), 11).

will approach the eros of the soul beginning from its condition as a fallen soul, in order to establish that its eros is, even at this degree of fallenness, the driving force of a movement of purification, of *catharsis*, through which it detaches itself from the bad passions generated by its mixture with matter. We will then arrive at the true nature of its eros when, after having lifted itself through purification to that simplicity which makes us similar to the non-thinking and loving Intellect, our soul is no longer anything but love.

The doctrine of love in Plotinus is tied to the doctrine of the love of the beautiful, which is rooted in the unthought love for the Good which moves all being: "Everything tends toward the Good and desires it (*oregetai kai ephietai*) through a necessity of nature, as if guessing that it cannot exist without it."[30] "Every soul desires the Good, even those which are mixed up with matter,"[31] because the Good is "object of an innate desire (*eis ephesin sumphuton*) existing even in those who are asleep."[32] Still, even if men are oblivious of that which constitutes the object of their desire, this desire nevertheless acts in them and produces a perpetual restlessness, a kind of nostalgia, as an inextinguishable desire driving them to always search for something else and not be satisfied with anything. This is the reason why the soul is attracted to everything which shines with some beauty or other, a beauty through which the soul is seduced by the sensible world. For the soul loves sensible beauty but, at the same time, forgets that the sensible is beautiful only through the grace of its intelligible model. Because of this forgetfulness of the intelligible, the eros of the incarnated soul may become a bad *pathos*, a passion for the sensible appearance of beauty, which always threatens to end up in ugliness and evil. Thus Plotinus warns us: "the desire (*ephesis*) for the Good often leads to a fall (*ekptôsin*) into the bad."[33] The soul is oblivious because it has the will to be by itself, because it loves itself and because it has a narcissistic desire for autonomy that drives it to seek out the opposite of its intelligible origin. But the incarnated soul is ignorant also because

---

30. V, 5 (32), 12, 7–9.
31. III, 5 (50), 3, 36–37.
32. V, 5 (32), 12, 10–12.
33. III, 5 (50), 1, 64–65.

matter constitutes a serious hindrance in the process of conversion. The eros of the soul is not only divine and/or demoniacal, it may also turn into a *pathos*. This is not to say that every *pathos* is necessarily and absolutely bad; even for the passions of the soul, Plotinus proposes a hierarchy separating the bad *pathos*, the purely material desire, from mixed love and pure love. However, it would seem that *pathos* is, for the most part, in Plotinus, a desire whose proper tendency is the ugly. The original movement of desire towards beauty is thus transformed, because of the matter contained in the composite which we are, into an unwholesome desire polluted by vice and intemperance. As Pierre Hadot emphasizes[34] in his commentary of treatise 50, there are several kinds of erotic "irregularities." There is of course homosexual pleasure, but the irregularity may also occur in a heterosexual union, if mere pleasure is its only purpose. Thus, whereas in the general context of the Plotinian treatises homosexuality always constitutes a vice and a fault, mixed love for its part may, when procreation is its aim, constitute a temperate sexual union. On this point Plotinus thus distances himself from Plato, for whom the first step of the ascendant dialectic is constituted by pederastic eros. The Alexandrinian for his part wishes to ignore this possible path of purification completely and, therefore, considers pederastic love as the height of intemperate sexuality.

Temperate mixed love is thus superior to the *pathos* afflicting the soul, in the sense that it is, as Plotinus says, "in accordance with nature" (*kata phusin*).[35] The heterosexual desire for beautiful bodies, provided it is accompanied by temperance (*sôphrosi*), is without blame (*anamartêtos*). The reason why Plotinus, along with Plato, characterizes this eros as "mixed" is because it is both desire of immortality and desire of beauty. "As concerns him for which the desire of beauty is mixed up with another desire, that of being immortal, in so far as this is possible for a mortal, such a man seeks the beautiful in the perpetuity of generations (*aeigenei*) and in the eternal (*aïdiô*), and, following a path in accordance with nature (*kata phusin*), he sows (*speirei*) and generates (*genna*) in the beautiful, sowing partly with a view to

---

34. Cf. Pierre Hadot, *Plotin. Traité 50 (III, 5). Introduction, traduction, commentaire et notes* (Paris: Cerf, 1990), 161.
35. III, 5 (50), 1, 51.

perpetuity, partly in the beautiful, because of the kinship (*sungeneian*) of perpetuity with the beautiful."[36] Even if it is "in accordance with nature," this heterosexual eros nevertheless remains ambivalent, since it is made up of different desires and is tied to ignorance and need. In fact, the love which is awakened by the beauty of bodies does not remain pure and carries with it the instinct of generation: "If one desires to produce beauty, it is because of need, it is because one is not satisfied, and because one thinks one will become so by producing beauty and by generating in the beautiful."[37] Love, which is not mixed up with any desire for the woman, is thus superior to love of the mixed kind.

Pure love is not directed towards bodies, "but to the beauty reflected in them,"[38] and this attraction, far from being blameworthy, is an indication of the worthiness of those who feel it. In fact, when their soul is in the presence of beauty, it is touched by grace, "it receives in itself an influence from above, it is set in motion, it is carried forth by the sting of desire and love is born within it. [...] Even if it is impassioned by that which it presently sees close to itself, it becomes light and raises itself towards a higher object, spontaneously elevated by that which has gifted it with love."[39] As a proof of this pure love, Plotinus analyzes the feelings of those in love: "to the extent that they keep to the visible aspect, they are not yet loving; but of this form they make in themselves, in their indivisible soul, an invisible image: then love is born. If they seek to see the loved one, it is in order to fecundate this image and stop it from withering.[40] At bottom, true love cannot be directed toward a real being. With regard to the love which directs itself toward the other in flesh and blood, we ought not to ridicule it as an illusion, but understand that the illusion which consists in attributing to an incarnated being the perfection of essence in fact reveals this deep truth that in the imperfect being which we love, we see and love the reflection of its intelligible essence. This is why

---

36. Ibid., 40–44.
37. Ibid., 47–50.
38. VI, 7 (38), 22, 4–5.
39. Ibid., 17–19.
40. Ibid., 33, 22–27.

Plotinus can affirm that "love is at the level of essence,"[41] that is to say eros makes the essence of mortal beings shine forth through the matter that obscures and weighs them down.

Pure love does not have any other nature than this intelligible one, nor any other power than to transfigure matter. As for the love contrary to nature, that which is a simple accompaniment of the vice of the soul, it is nothing but a feverish phantasm, completely deprived of psychological value. Incidentally, nowhere in Plotinus is sexual love accorded any cathartic value, even if, as in the case of mixed heterosexual love, he recognizes that it may have a certain nobility of origin that renders it morally tolerable. But sexual love apparently never has any propaedeutic value. Pure love is thus preferable to mixed love, and the lover who prefers not to generate is self-sufficient (*autarkesteron*), since his love does not require anything but the beautiful. Moreover, the *pathos* he experiences does not run any risk of falling into vice and ugliness, something from which mixed love is never exempt. This is why the earthly love most highly valued by Plotinus, and which he considers as the typical example of pure love, is that which a young girl feels for her father, the most adequate metaphor for the love of the Good.[42]

At this point of the analysis we may already draw the following conclusions. First of all, every *pathos*, including that which is pure, is a rapture of the soul toward sensible beauty. But this *pathos*, if it is accompanied by a love for the beauty in itself, revealed in the sensible images, manifests its co-originarity with the desire for the Good, with love as the initial movement toward the Good. Further, every *pathos* is the manifestation *hic et nunc* of a higher eros which gives the multiplicity of loves down here their unity. The eros of the incarnated soul is thus no doubt of the same nature as the higher eros, which is, in the final analysis, the manifestation of the innate and original desire for the Good, and the expression of the overflowing of the One, the expression of its diffusive love.[43]

---

41. III, 5 (50), 7, 42.
42. Cf. ibid., 12, 35–38.
43. Cf. concerning this Agnés Pigler, *Plotin: une métaphysique de l'amour. L'amour comme structure du monde intelligible* (Paris: Vrin, 2002).

Ecstasy: A Metaphysical Experience
Initiated By the Living Eros in the Soul

The simplicity that the purified soul finally attains, after having sur-
mounted all alterity and every relation,[44] allows it to enter the absolute, that is to say, a state of plenitude free from all negation. In this
state, the ecstatic soul fuses with its Principle, signifying a momentary
loss of the personal consciousness that, by limiting the soul, separates
it from the Good.[45] Nevertheless, the ecstatic soul is neither annihilated nor unconscious, since it *sees*, even if it has stopped seeing *itself*.
Thus, in the ecstasy, "the soul is at the same time conscious of itself,
since it is no longer anything but one and the same as the Intellect."[46]
This conservation of the self in the consciousness of the Whole (*Nous*)
is comprehensible in so far as even the desire of the Good necessarily
implies the existence of a being different from the Good and aspiring
toward it. Nevertheless, the soul which is inebriated by the beautiful
cannot see the god who possesses it, it merely feels its presence; and
even if the soul can neither think of the One nor describe it, in no way
does it ever have any doubts about its presence, since it is able to *grasp*
it.[47]

This ecstatic union is nevertheless different from that of Christian
mysticism, which is based on the close relation uniting the creature
and its Creator. In Plotinus, by contrast, the initiative lies with *man*,
not with divine grace, which is the reason why it is better, according
to us, to talk of this ecstasy as a *metaphysical*, rather than as a mystical,
experience. In fact, in the mystical experience the ecstatic feels the
intimate union of his deified humanity as subsumed in the innermost
of the divine being; it manifests, as in the cases of St John of the Cross
or St Theresa of Avila, the violent and dazzling encounter between
divine and human love. But nowhere in the ecstatic experience
described by Plotinus do we find any suggestion of the fact, fundamental
to every mystical experience, of a divine initiative, of a condescension
on the part of God and of his love for his creation and for all men. This

---

44. Cf. VI, 9 (9), 11, 8.
45. Cf., for example, VI, 7 (38), 34, 16–19.
46. IV, 4 (28), 2, 30–32.
47. Cf. V, 3 (49), 14.

is why we judge it preferable to account for the Plotinian ecstasy as a metaphysical experience. In fact, the Plotinian ecstasy is the exact opposite of the Christian mystics, in that the One does not give itself – because if such were the case, it would exercise an activity directed outwards, incompatible with its utterly simple and transcendent unity. The success of the erotic journey, such as Plotinus represents it, lies entirely in the hands of man himself, and the soul cannot count on any obliging grace in order to reach the term of its ascension. Man is thus the sole artisan of his own perfection and salvation. Immobile and self-sufficient, "present to him who is able to touch it,"[48] occupied by an audacious desire and an infinite love, the Good lets things happen (to itself), without itself issuing any hint of appeal, any hint of desire. And if the soul is filled with joy by its possession, this is in no way in virtue of any generous condescension, which the Good would communicate in order to make the souls happy; rather, it is because it is in the nature of things that such will be the case. In fact, once the soul is united to that which it loves with an inexpressible love, there is no longer anything for it to desire. The Good is thus the supremely love worthy, even without itself wanting or calling for it. This is manifest also in the Plotinian analysis of prayer as the soul's concentration in order to comprehend why the One has manifested itself,[49] rather than as an imploration of the divine. The Plotinian prayer has the character of meditation and elevation, by virtue of which the soul is simplified in the extreme, to the point where it is able to merge with a Principle going beyond it; in no way is it an appeal to the divine grace, and even less is it an expression of having recourse to a saving god. In ecstasy the soul is outside itself, "it shuns the act of thinking," it becomes united with the loving intellect by simplifying itself and thus arrives at this state of joyful plenitude and inebriation that illuminates it with love. And if this ecstasy could last, it would consist in pure receptivity and total detachment from everything else. Now, the ecstatic feels this love and desire for the Good because his soul is driven by it, which is to say by the eros that is like a trace of the One, to love it. Love and desire are therefore not absent from the

---

48. VI, 9 (9), 7, 4-5.
49. Cf. V, 1 (10), 6.

absolute Principle, since the Good is Love and Love of itself. Moreover, since it is from the generosity of the first Principle that everything Real flows, from its overflowing which is nothing other than its diffusive love, this love has nothing to do with any kind of love for its creation; the Plotinian One is "a god which is goodness without love,"[50] or as one would rather have to say: without love for its 'creation' and, because of this, without any lowering of the divine towards it.

In the final analysis, we may thus say that at the source as well as at the level of derivative beings, the One is the transcendent model for every love, since it is itself "the object loved, Love and Love of itself."[51] Through the infinite and indeterminate power which emanates from it, it makes a gift of the Love which constitutes it, by diffusing into the beings coming after it the love which is the driving force of the conversion, and the love which is desire for the union, the opening toward the infinite generosity of Love. Not even in the sensible world, in virtue of the mediation of the lower Soul and its eros, is the dynamic erotic current issuing from the One lost or dispersed. Reason (*logos*), in accordance with which the lower Soul orders the sensible world and gives it its beauty, allows the wisest of the individual souls to rise upwards, in an amorous rapture without end, all the way to that which is the giver of beauty and love. This is possible because the Principle, through the diffusion of its Love, is not absent from any being, because it is, on the contrary, present in their innermost reaches:

> For certainly the One is not absent from anything and nevertheless it is absent from everything, so that even though present, it is not present, except for those who are able to receive it and have prepared themselves well for this, in such a way that they will be able to coincide and, somehow, be in contact with it, touch it, in virtue of the similarity, that is to say the power which one has within oneself and which is akin to it: it is only when one is in the state in which one was when leaving it, that one is able to see it, in the way that it can be the object of vision.[52]

---

50. René Arnou, *Le désir de Dieu dans la philosophie plotinienne* (Paris: F Alcan, 1921), 227.

51. VI, 8 (39), 15, 1.

52. VI, 9 (9), 4, 24–30: *ou gar dê apestin oudenos ekeino kai pantôn de, hôste parôn mê*

The sign of this presence of the One in the innermost of all beings, in their most secret intimacy, is love, for only love can manifest itself as that condition "in which one was upon leaving the One." As originary and primary life, carrying in its flow the diffusive Love of the absolute Origin, the primordial power is fused into this love which only life is able to manifest. This is why, at the moment when the Intellect goes beyond itself in order to grasp and receive that which transcends it, it is primitively loving and meta-noetic Intellect, life living of the life of the Good itself, a power derived from the founding power of the One. This is also why, when the higher Soul goes beyond itself in order to unite with the Good, it effaces within itself the contours of the noetic vision so as to no longer be anything but the act of seeing, the originally loving Soul fusing with the pre-noetic love of *Nous*. This is, finally, why individual souls simplify themselves to the point where nothing any longer remains but this desire for union, together with souls essentially illuminated by love for the Good.

Demonstration of the Henological Origin of the Eros of the Soul

The foundation of the metaphysics of Plotinus is thus love. But *life* is also and always that which manifests love, as that which is most similar to the Good: as life multiplies itself without becoming divided – one and nevertheless multiple in its forms – it makes manifest that the First is at the root of all life and of all thought, at the origin of every existence and every fullness. Because Love in the One is a coincidence of Love of oneself and Love in itself, love in that which is derivative *must* express itself in the form of *the infinity of love*, absolute love directing itself towards the absolutely Other, love of the Good infinitely transcending all conceivable modes of love. The infinite power of the Principle, diffusive of love and of life, is the source and origin of every-

---

pareinai all'ê tois dechesthai dunamenois kai pareskeuasmenois, hôste enarmosai kai hoion ephapsasthai kai thigein homoiotêti kai tê en autô dunamei sungenei tô ap'autou. hotan houtôs echê, hôs eichen, hote êlthen ap'autou, êdê dunatai idein hôs pephuken ekeinos theatos einai.

thing that lives and exists; all the way down to the sensible, everything lives only through the motion of the Love of the One.

All the way to the end, then, *love remains the sole dynamic of the procession/conversion* of the creation of the sensible world and the ascension of incarnated souls towards the very source of their love. Such is the signification of that "amorous inebriation" felt by the intelligible realities when they are in the proximity of the object of their love. It is also the signification of the ecstasy for the incarnated souls which end their "erotic journey"[53] by uniting with the Good in a "touching" of this inexpressible, which is their true goal and their only repose, since love is their true nature and the trace in them of the Good. As the unlimited and infinite power of the Principle, *love is thus at work everywhere where there is life*, because life which has received a form carries with it, in its innermost being, this trace of the First *which is love*. This is why *erôs* is coincidence with oneself, as in the One, for in effect, to coincide with oneself is to reach the innermost being of oneself, the presence of the Ineffable. It is to recognize it by shedding all form, abdicating all thought, fused with the mystery of life, in an illumination of love for this presence which still carries the trace of its inaccessible transcendence.

By way of conclusion, we propose to give a brief commentary of the final words pronounced by Plotinus at the hour of his death, which have been reported to us by Porphyrius:

> I strive to make that which is divine in us rise up again towards the divine which is in the whole (*peirasthai to en hêmin theion anagein pros to en tô panti theion*).[54]

Commentators have generally understood these final words by Plotinus in a Platonic sense: death would be for the soul the deliverance from the body in which it has been held 'captive'; it would thus make

---

53. For an analysis of this ascension of the soul towards its Principle, as well as of the conditions required for it, cf. A. Kéléssidou-Galanos, "Le voyage érotique de l'âme dans la mystique plotinienne" (in □□□□□, 24, 1972), 88–100.

54. Porphyrius, *La vie de Plotin* (Paris: Vrin, 1992), II, 25–27. For a deeper study of this passage, grammatically as well as interpretatively, see Jean Pépin, "La dernière parole de Plotin" (in *Porphyre. La vie de Plotin*, vol. II), 355–383.

it possible either to reintegrate the Soul with the Whole from which it comes, or to reascend all the way to the Intellect. Our interpretation is different: that which is played out in the ultimate tension here described by Plotinus is the possibility of a coincidence between the trace of the One within ourselves, a living trace present in the soul, and the trace of the One which acts in the Whole, that is to say, in the sensible as well as in the Intelligible. But this trace is nothing other than the erotic-vital power that emanates from the absolute Origin, the infinite power derived from its pure Act in which the notions of life and love are fused. The text of the *Enneads* is littered with such reminders of our true origin, and the experience of ecstasy is represented as a preparation for the union with the Principle that will take place after our death. But whereas in the course of our existence, the contemplation of the Good cannot be accomplished until the end of an ascension which unites us first with the intelligible Soul, then with the Intellect and finally with this anoetic part of *Nous* whose life is love, death, by contrast, gives us access all at once, without any preliminary stages, to the divine in itself. In effect, death delivers us not only from the entanglement in sensible matter, *but also from form*. For, in dying we return to the Intelligible, which is our true part, *such as we were when leaving the One*. But that which emanates from the One, even before the constitution of the hypostasis of *Nous* and thus of the intelligible forms, is an infinite power, an erotic-vital energy similar to the One in so far as it is itself *one and without form*. Our "ancient nature" is identical to the life that derives from the Principle: it is without form and without love. We are made of this primordial, originary power – which the *form* covers and in a certain way obscures, and which *matter* almost exhausts, but of which there still remains the *trace*. That is why the experience of ecstasy is illuminating: it reveals to our soul that its love carries the imprint of our original and formless unity.

The soul which has understood to prepare itself for dying, through the exercises preparatory to the ecstasy and the amorous union with the Principle, knows that death is nothing but the return to our original state, the return to the infinite power from which we come and of which we preserve within ourselves, intact, a trace. Death delivers us from *the alterity of form* that makes us differ from our origin: the divine within ourselves and the divine in the Whole thus coincide by virtue of their formlessness. Thus, if death is no doubt a passage, as Plato taught, for Plotinus it is a return, certainly not to the One itself, which remains absolutely other in its radical transcendence, but a return to that which manifests its presence with the greatest possible identity: *the erotic-vital power which issues from it and is without form.*

"To make that which is divine within us rise up again towards the divine which is in the Whole" thus means, very precisely, to liberate within ourselves the intact trace of the presence of the One, to once again become this life from which we come and which, through its absence of form, is most similar to the arch-Life of the One. And this ultimately means: to once again become the life which is, through the love moving it, most similar to the ineffable Love of the One for itself.

The Undesirable Object of Desire:
Towards a Phenomenology of Eroticism

JASON WIRTH

For Elizabeth S. Wirth, in memoriam

The untranslatable thought must be the most precise.
Yet words are not the end of thought, they are where it begins.

Jane Hirshfield
"After Long Silence"

Amidst our preoccupation with epistemology, ontology, ethics, and many other familiar endeavors, Eros, as is in ample evidence throughout this volume, has not traditionally been a common theme. As Jean-Luc Marion has recently contended:

> Philosophy today no longer says anything about love, or at best very little. And this silence is for the better, because when philosophy does venture to speak of love it mistreats it or betrays it. One would almost doubt whether philosophers experience love, if one didn't instead guess that they fear saying anything about it. And for good reason, for they know, better than anyone, that we no longer have the words to speak of it, nor the concepts to think about it, nor the strength to celebrate it.[1]

---

1. Jean-Luc Marion, *The Erotic Phenomenon*, trans. Stephen E. Lewis (Chicago: University of Chicago Press, 2007), 1. Henceforth EP. Although this essay attempts to move beyond Marion's containment of the erotic to the realms of the human and the divine, it applauds Marion for moving the erotic decisively from the domain of the *conatus essendi*. The latter protects itself in the fantasy of autonomy (it is enough that I love myself). Marion shows that such self-love is clearly impossible. Who is this lover that assures the beloved that she or he is

Is this because Eros is not an important or even proper subject of philosophy? Or does the erotic expose something that challenges philosophy's capacity to take account of its proper tasks?

That perhaps depends on what we understand about philosophy itself. I will turn to this topic, the philosophy of philosophy itself, shortly.

Before so turning, I would like to orient these reflections by announcing that I will attempt to develop two central theses:

1. The clarity of desire is kitsch. It has nothing to do with self-interest, with the Good insofar as it is understood as something that is obviously *good for me*. As Hermann Broch argued, to know exactly what one wants to do

---

loved? The ego that needs to be reassured that it is loved cannot be the ego capable of reassuring it that it is loved. "A single and compact I cannot become an other that itself, in order to give itself an assurance that responds to the question 'Does anyone out there love me?'" (45). Although conatus-driven philosophical discourses that assume that their own self-preservation and enhancement is what is at stake must ask for an assurance that they are loved, this obscures the domain of the erotic, which begins with the loss of the preeminence of the ego. "Either love is distributed at a loss, or it is lost as love. The more I love at a loss, the less I lose sight of love, because love loves further than the eye can see" (71). The question is not if I am loved, but if I can be taken beyond myself in my capacity to love. The ego, on the other hand, does not venture onto the field of love except in order to escape from the risk of losing itself, thus hoping for an assurance, a return of assurance, the chance to make up the shortfall" (68). Regarding the possibility of extending a discourse beyond the risks particular to the human, see Donna Haraway's new work, *When species meet* (Minneapolis: University of Minnesota Press, 2008). As Haraway argues for a kind of ineluctably complicated erotic becoming after the preeminence of the human: "we are in a knot of species co-shaping one another in layers of reciprocating complexity all the way down" (42). This meeting of species, this vital and vitalizing knot, is an "ontological choreography" (67), a "torque" where "biographies and categories twine in conflicting trajectories" (134), for "becoming is always becoming *with*" (244). The body is its inter-species, kind-complicating becomings, "a vital entanglement of heterogeneous scales, times, and kinds of beings webbed into fleshy presence, always becoming, always constituted in relating" (163).

One must distinguish between annulling death and fleeing death, between shedding light on the irrational and fleeing from the irrational. Kitsch is found in flight, it is constantly fleeing into the rational. The techniques of kitsch, which are based on imitation, are rational and operate according to formulas; they remain rational even when their result has a highly irrational, even crazy, quality.[2]

In Milan Kundera's novels, which eschew the facile world of stereotypes and economies of imitation, kitsch is the "absence of shit" in the sense that it is a rejection of all that does not accord with itself: "Kitsch has its source in the categorical agreement with being."[3] Conventional politics administers what it already knows as true, while the novel for both Broch and Kundera declares such a curatorial and bureaucratic skewering of being to be its enemy. While kitsch may require immense craft, it is ethically repugnant because, in the words of Kundera, it "a folding screen set up to curtain off death" (UB, 253).

Broch was crystal clear that kitsch is an *ethical* problem and that it had nothing to with an absence of taste or any other purely aesthetic category.

> The maker of kitsch does not create inferior art, he is not an incompetent or a bungler, he cannot be evaluated by esthetic standards; rather, he is ethically depraved, a criminal willing radical evil. (EVS, 37)

The question of the erotic is a question that haunts the periphery of philosophy. At the same time it is a demand for a revolution in ethics. Kitsch is the ethical failure of what we shall, following Bataille, call the servile human. Eros, on the other hand, is not a flight to mythic obscurity. It is ever in search of the clear and the undiscovered, and, as such, it wanders (and wonders) on the periphery of the properly ethical, artistic, scientific, and philosophical. It is the force of the life

---

2. Hermann Broch, "Evil in the value-system of art" in *Geist and Zeitgeist: The spiritual in an unspiritual age*, ed. and trans. John Hargraves (New York: Counterpoint, 2002), 35. Henceforth EVS.

3. *The Unbearable Lightness of Being*, trans. Michael Heim (New York: Harper and Row, 1984), 256. Henceforth UB.

of life, the life beyond life and death, not the imitation of a particular formula for living. I do not aim to present any great and inviolable philosophical laws here, either in terms of a phenomenology of eros or philosophy in general.

2. Eroticism is not an activity initiated by a subjective agent, nor is it an activity that renders an otherwise subjective agent passive. "What or who desires?" is not a well-posed question. This is not to deny the political expediency of discourses of agency nor is it a descent into a murky, mystical realm where everything is everything else and desire affirms everything in general and therefore nothing in particular. Rather, it is an attempt to pose the question of erotic desire more precisely in the hopes of revealing some of its more obscure valences.

In pursuit of these two theses, I will directly and indirectly engage in some of the stepping-stones towards a phenomenology of eroticism as such. Following Bataille, I do not wish to offer an apology for eroticism, but rather to delineate a "set of reactions that are incomparably rich." In so doing, in delineating the possibility of a phenomenology of eroticism, indeed, of any kind of philosophy of eroticism, I hope to indicate that Eros brings phenomenology and philosophy, properly construed, construed as something proper, to their boiling point.

In an effort to minimize confusion, I am not exactly proposing an "erotic reduction" in the manner of Marion,[4] although my approach shares his disavowal of the *conatus in suo esse perseverandi* as having anything fundamentally to do with the erotic. My proposed technique is less tidy, more of an *erotic detonation*, or, better, a welcoming invoca-

---

4. The erotic reduction is neither epistemic nor ontological. Rather: "in order for me to be appear as a full-fledged phenomenon, it is not enough that I recognize as a certified object, nor as a certifying ego, nor even as a properly being being; I must discover myself as a given (and gifted) phenomenon, assured as a given that is free from vanity" (EP, 22). Given the impossibility for Marion of self-love, the erotic reduction does not flush out the tacit operation of the *conatus in suo esse perseverandi* as central to the reduction and hence it does not reveal the conatus as in need of reassurance, but rather the conatus is taken elsewhere, utterly away from itself, seeking to be able to love.

tion of the erotic in a kind of philosophical act of ξενία, a welcoming of the stranger as a stranger to the table of philosophy. As such, I will offer to host the stranger with a mélange of discursivity, analysis, and description.

Philosophy as the Preparation for Death

In speaking to the nature of philosophy so that I can estimate the extent to which the erotic can be said to belong to it, I am not claiming to settle at last the identity crisis that has haunted the philosophical enterprise. The wonder that gives birth to philosophy does not do so in such a way that one no longer wonders exactly what wonder asks of one. Wonder remains wonder, and hence it does not settle its own question. If wonder does not wonder about itself, it ceases in some way to be wonder. Wonder, in a manner of speaking, is a question that renders the nature of the question being asked questionable. What should we wonder about when we philosophize? This assumes the more basic question: What do we wonder about when we wonder about the nature of wonder?

In this sense, philosophy's other has haunted philosophy from the beginning. As Deleuze and Guattari have argued, "The plane of philosophy is prephilosophical insofar as we consider it in itself independently of the concepts that come to occupy it, but nonphilosophy is found where the plane confronts chaos. *Philosophy needs a nonphilosophy that comprehends it; it needs a nonphilosophical comprehension just as art needs nonart and science needs nonscience.*"[5] Paradoxically, philosophy is not philosophy so long as it is only philosophy, that is, as it orients itself to its own supposedly proper activity. Philosophy does not reduce to any particular philosophy about itself. A lover of wisdom, being a good friend, is wise enough to love the strangeness of wisdom, rather than to wise up to an alleged content of wisdom itself.

Returning to the morning of the Western philosophical tradition, we can recall one of the oldest claims as to the nature of philosophical activity. Readying himself for death, Socrates in the *Phaedo* claims that

---

5. Gilles Deleuze and Félix Guattari, *What is Philosophy?*, trans. Hugh Tomlinson and Graham Burchell (New York: Columbia University Press, 1994), 218.

philosophy is nothing but a preparation for death: "I am afraid that other people do not realize that the one aim of those who practice philosophy in the proper manner is to practice for dying and death" (64a).[6] Other people, whether or not they claim to philosophize, do not know what Socrates, the one who knows that he does not know, here claims to know. Philosophy is not metaphysics or ethics. It is a particular form of practice, the practice for death. And what does death ask of us, what tasks does it prescribe? One can only wonder.

Right from the get go, I want to be very clear about this: philosophy is in this context a practice, not a body of knowledge, a set of facts of a certain disciplinary kind, a body of information, or, most lamentable of all, intellectual capital. As Michel Foucault and Pierre Hadot, as well as some Buddhists, Daoists, and others, have argued, philosophy is more like a way of living.

As Socrates was gradually absorbed into the self-possessed systems of Neo-Platonism, and as philosophy began to settle into fixed and no longer mysterious tasks (even though the history of philosophy includes fundamental debates about just what those tasks might be), one can still detect vestiges of philosophy as part of some techniques of fundamental practice. For instance, in the *Tusculan Disputations*, written in reclusion late in Cicero's life after the death of his beloved daughter, Tullia, philosophy has de facto a kind of apotropaic force. Cicero, who had mourned Tullia's death powerfully, and who had at times been inconsolable, here rejects death as something bad and practices philosophy to disarm death of its evil. It robs death of the evil of being evil.

> But when God himself has given us a just cause, as formerly he did to Socrates, and lately to Cato, and often to many others – in such a case, certainly every man of sense would gladly exchange this darkness for that light: not that he would forcibly break from the chains that held him, for that would be against the law; but, like a man released from prison by a magistrate or some lawful authority, so he too would walk away, being released and discharged by God. For the whole life

---

6. I have used Grube's translation, revised by John M. Cooper, in *Five dialogues*, second edition (Indianapolis/Cambridge: Hackett, 2002), 101.

of a philosopher is, as the same philosopher says, a meditation on death.[7]

Cicero, despite his own impending mortality and his grief over his daughter's death, practices philosophy in order to meditate on death, which in this case, to some extent, already anticipates a dominant trend in what will later become Christian metaphysics: to answer the question of death. For Cicero, death is the transition from the dark prison of earthly life. To be fair, Cicero does not know the answer to death, but, like the reading of Socrates in the *Phaedo*, which holds that Socrates is investigating the mettle of the prevailing myths on the immortality of the soul in order to establish what he hopes and wants to be true, Cicero would like to believe that there is a place in which he can be reunited with Tullia and many of his now departed friends. Philosophy as the practice of argumentation gives us a likely account of all things, including death, putting our mind at ease. Either there is nothing beyond death, and hence there is nothing to worry about, or there is something beyond death, and this inspires hope. In either case, one makes one's peace with death. One may wonder if this peace held during Cicero's brutal murder and decapitation.

Many centuries later, after this kind of thinking became entrenched in the European philosophical and theological imagination, we come upon the fresh air of that iconoclast Montaigne, who argued that the "advantage of living is not measured by length, but by use." [8] It is not a question of how much life you are granted, but what you do with it, how you live whatever quantity of life you are given. Meditating on the prospect of an immortal afterlife, that is to say, the proposition that a good and desirable life is an infinitely lengthy life, Montaigne found the thought repulsive. "Chiron refused immortality when informed of its conditions by the very god of time and duration, his father Saturn. Imagine honestly how much less bearable and more

---

7. Cicero, *Tusculan meditations*, trans. C. D. Yonge (New York: Harper, 1877), section 30.
8. "That to philosophize is to learn to die," *The complete works of Montaigne*, trans. Donald A. Frame (Stanford, California: Stanford University Press, 1967), 57. Henceforth PLD.

painful to man would be an everlasting life than the life I have given him. If you did not have death, you would curse me incessantly for having deprived you of it" (PLD, 67). One can think of Odysseus, who was not swayed by Calypso's promise of immortality, or of the historical Buddha, Prince Siddhartha, who learned that one cannot solve the problem of sickness, old age, and death.

For Montaigne, death was the ever-present limit that illuminated life itself as a question and as the possibility of a "voluptuous" life. Among the principal benefits of virtue is disdain for death, a means that furnishes our life with a soft tranquility and gives us a pure and pleasant enjoyment of it, without which all other pleasures are extinguished." But most people live in denial or neurotic avoidance of even a hint of the idea of death. "The goal of our career is death" (PLD, 57). There is no escaping it and it comes largely on its own terms and on its own schedule. "How many ways has death to surprise us" (PLD, 58) because "at every moment it is gripping us by the throat" (PLD, 59). Hence, Montaigne vows never to be caught off guard by death, never to live as if death were not already a part of life. "Never did a man prepare to leave the world more utterly and completely, nor detach himself from it more universally, than I propose to do" (PLD, 61).

This does not mean either denying death or imagining that death is a problem that can be solved by religion, the latter understood as the denial of death via the promise of an infinite prolongation of life as the reward for a diminishment of actually living. Montaigne quips, "Our religion has no surer foundation than contempt for life" (PLD, 64). He vows rather to live life virtuously, that is to say, voluptuously, without the illusions of metaphysical comforts, remembering, as Bataille did later, that in Montaigne's words "death is the origin of another life." Indeed, not only does death make room for new life, not only does fatality insure the miracle of natality, but creation is rife with the specter of its origin. "Death is the condition of your creation, it is a part of you" for those who flee death "are fleeing from your own selves. This being of yours that you enjoy is equally divided between life and death. The first day of your birth leads you toward death as towards life" (PLD, 65). In a sense, Montaigne anticipates Heidegger's phenomenological demonstration of the "constant tranquilization of death" (§51) in the self of *das Man*, and Montaigne's words echo Heidegger's famous citation from the Ackermann aus Böhmen, "As soon as a human being is born, he is old enough to die right away" (§48).[9]

Death is a peculiar object with regards to desire (understood here as the hypothesis that desire is a relationship between a subject who desires and an object that is desired). Typically desire recoils before it, and hence, Socrates, Cicero, Montaigne, and even Heidegger, speak of the folly of living in denial of that which one does not want, but which nonetheless shares the ground of one's being. Cicero, as well as the tradition of Platonism in which the *Phaedo* is typically ensconced, approach death by attempting to demonstrate that although prima facie it appears undesirable, upon closer, rational examination, it is actually quite desirable. As Cicero counsels, death is the "exchange" of "this darkness for that light" and the soul's liberation from the prison of the body and mortal human life. This kind of philosophy is predicated on a kind of magic reversal whereby darkness becomes light and death becomes life.

Montaigne and Heidegger, on the other hand, will have nothing of this game of bait and switch. Death is the kind of object of desire that reveals that it is not really fundamentally an object at all, and, in so doing, reveals that the subject, who either would or would not desire this object, shares a peculiar commonality with this object. Death is the kind of non-object that shares the object position in such a way that it reveals that the subject is analogously a non-subject that shares the subject position.[10] One's own death is one's most fundamental property. It cannot be given any more so than fire can give away heat and still be fire. No one can die the death of another. Yet *what* is it that one owns? What cannot be given away is the permanent possibility that everything else will be taken away, rendered accidental by the

9. Martin Heidegger, *Being and time*, trans. Joan Stambaugh (Albany: State University of New York Press, 1996 [1927]), 228.

10. Kitarō Nishida also argued this forcibly: "When I realize my own eternal death, my eternal nothingness, I become truly self-conscious. I become aware that my very existence is an absolute contradiction" *Last writings: Nothingness and the religious worldview*, trans. David Dilworth (Honolulu: University of Hawaii Press, 1987 [1945]), 67.

return of the dark night that was the condition of one's birth. Before the non-object of death, I know that in having death I do not have myself. I never had myself, or anything else objective.[11]

Hermann Broch unleashed this force in his remarkable novel, *The Death of Virgil*.[12] Returning to Brundisium from Greece on the verge of death, Virgil realizes that he has perjured the realm of death, oblivious to its "one duty, earthly duty, the duty of helpfulness, the duty of awakening" (DV, 132). The *Aeneid*, intoxicated by the sweep of its metaphors and symbols, signs which gather peoples into their sway, into the mobs that comprise the empires to which true and powerful metaphors give rise, was on the side of life, and had thereby *perjured* death.

And flight was no longer possible, only its breathless gasping, and there was no going on – whither could it have led now? – and the

---

11. One can also think here of Yukio Mishima's novel, *Confessions of a Mask*, where the narrator tells of the wide array of masks that comprised his life. During the final year of the Second World War he is sent, having just turned twenty, to work "at the N airplane factory," a dusty expanse so large that it "took thirty minutes simply to walk across it from one end to the other." But this was not the typical work in which we busy at bettering ourselves: "This great factory operated upon a mysterious system of production costs: taking no account of the economic dictum that capital investment should produce a return, it was dedicated to a monstrous nothingness. No wonder then that each morning the workers had to recite a mystic oath. I have never seen such a strange factory. In it all the techniques of modern science and management, together with the exact and rational thinking of many superior brains, were dedicated to a single end – Death. Producing the Zero-model combat plane used by the suicide squadrons, this great factory resembled a secret cult that operated thunderously – groaning, shrieking, roaring. I did not see how such a colossal organization could exist without some religious grandiloquence." *Confessions of a Mask*, trans. Meredith Weatherby (New York: New Directions, 1958), 133.

12. Hermann Broch, *The Death of Virgil*, trans. Jean Starr Untermeyer (New York: Pantheon, 1945). Henceforth DV. Since Broch worked with Untermeyer, herself an accomplished poet, for some years on this "translation," it is, in its own right, an independent version of the German version appeared after this one. That being said, the German version of this and other works by Broch have been impactful in the German speaking world, while this novel has largely been ignored in the English speaking world.

gasping was like that of a runner who, having passed his goal, knows
he has not met it and will never meet it, because in the no-man's land
of perjury, this perjured un-space, through which he had been driven,
only to be driven on and on ... That which surrounded him no longer
symbolized anything, it was a non-symbol, the every essence of the
unreflectable and beyond reflection ... divested of all symbol and yet
containing the see of every symbol. (DV, 159)

Virgil resolves to communicate this realm, to redress the perjury that
renders his art so powerful, so mobilizing, so capable of gathering the
living into the sway of its metaphors. He will burn the *Aeneid*. Of
course, Octavian, recognizing the founding power of Virgil's work of
art for the world of the new Roman empire, the new metaphor enabled
Reich, will not allow Virgil to destroy this politically expeditious work.
Born of life, the poem's resplendence must capture life, the power of
Roman life! Yet Virgil argued that "the perception of life, earthily
bound to the earth, never possessed the power to lift itself above the
thing known and to endow it with unity, the unity of an enduring
meaning, a meaning by which life was and is maintained by creation
... only he who is able to perceive death is able to perceive life" (DV,
325). Aeneas' journey to the underworld, to the realm of death, for
example, simply resulted in metaphors of death, death perjured by the
perspective of life. It evaded "the real task" and was neither "perception
nor help – in short, it is not art and cannot endure" (DV, 335).

In this sense, "death vision" moved to Virgil to regard the uncon-
tested natural attitude of "life vision" as a betrayal. The Caesar, on the
other hand, "was greedy for glory ... even if it outlasted death, could
never annul death, that the path of glory was an earthly one, worldly
and without perception, a false path, one of reversion, of intoxication,
a path of evil" (DV, 328). It may be the goal of empire, including even
the empire envy of philosophical systems, but it is not the goal of enlightened poetry, "the strangest of all human occupations, the only
one dedicated to the knowledge of death" (DV, 81). It demands the
"interrealm of the farewell (DV, 81), the vantage point of death *and*
life. The pledge of poetry is born of death perception, not the glory of
true and powerful metaphors. Octavian wanted the *Aeneid* in order to
close the deal on the glory of a new empire, an empire for the ages.
Virgil, on the other hand, want to burn his work because it perjures

death, and thereby perjures its pledge to pursue death enlightenment and work tirelessly to render help to the community of living beings (human and otherwise) that cannot be gathered, only perjured, in metaphors.

Virgil tells Octavian that even "philosophy is no longer capable of finding it" (DV, 344). Philosophy, which too easily succumbs to the intoxication of the daylight, of the metaphors that comprise "life vision," seeks the infinite in the heavens, and "has come to have no base for its perception ... having been obliged to grow upward to touch infinity, philosophy's roots do not reach down far enough ... where the roots fail to grip, there is the shadowless void" (DV, 346). Thinking, bereft of true metaphors, pledged not to perjure death, must seeks deeper roots, roots that go below the earth's surface, that seek to love its elemental humus.

I shall return to this philosophy rooted in humus (the abyssal element of life, which produces the tilth of thinking and love from death and ruin) – or perhaps a non-philosophy that haunts the properly self-possessed activity of philosophy itself – when I turn to the erotic nonphilosophy of Bataille.

What, at this moment in my argument, does the question – death, chaos, humus, nonphilosophy – which haunts and dis-completes philosophy, rendering its glories vainglorious, have to do with Eros, that child of wealth and poverty?

The Poverty of Wealth and the Wealth of Poverty

Famously the figure of Eros is given its philosophical flesh in Socrates' account in the *Symposium*. However, rather than once again directly rehearse this well-known text, I would like to explore it as it appears in its adaptation in the crisis laden, very rich philosophy of Schelling's middle period.

In the third draft of Schelling's *The Ages of the World* (1815), an unfinished text that occupied Schelling for many years, promising an account, a divine comedy as it were, of being in its three-fold potency (the past, present, and future), and which scarcely escapes the past, we find the following passage:

Therefore that force of the beginning posited in the expressible and exterior is the primordial seed of visible nature, out of which nature was unfolded in the succession of ages. Nature is an abyss of the past. This is what is oldest in nature, the deepest of what remains if everything accidental and everything that has become is removed. This is precisely that constant tendency to restrict the being and to place it in darkness. (I/8, 243)[13]

That is to say, in Schelling's account of nature, the very appearance of nature, the very appearance of appearance itself, restricts the plenum of being and hence the emergence of the present is simultaneously the disappearance of the ground of nature into an abyssal past, in the humus of death perception as it were. In a sense, the appearance of nature as presence, as something there, is the simultaneous movement of what Nishida Kitarō was later to call self-predication through self-negation. In order to predicate nature of itself, nature negates itself in order to appear as something, even as "nature."[14] This self-negation is the past, never present, abyssal ground of appearance. Nature is then something like what Nishida called *zettai mujunteki jikodōitsu*, "absolute contradictory self-identity."[15] The primordial seed of visible nature is negated by the fruit of its own germination. This is self predication through self negation.

Schelling continues:

---

13. I am using the standard pagination based on the edition established by Schelling's son, Karl, which lists the volume number followed by the page number. The translation is my own, taken from *The Ages of the World*, 1815 draft (Albany: The State University of New York Press, 2000).

14. To be clear: nature is not here to be thought as a natural kind, a category of things, over against another irreconcilable category of things. This is not "nature" as opposed to "culture," "history," "artifact." It is nature beyond nature and culture, expressing itself variously yet ambiguously as "nature" and "culture." In this respect, see also Donna Haraway, *When Species Meet*, who argues that humans are not uniquely historical beings (66–67); dogs "have not been unchangeable animals confined to the supposedly ahistorical order of nature [...] Relations are constitutive; dogs and people are emergent as historical beings" (62).

15. C.f., Kitarō Nishida "The unity of opposites" in *Intelligibility and the Philosophy of nothingness*, trans. Robert Schinzinger (Honolulu: East-West Center Press, 1966).

The true primordial and fundamental force of all things corporeal is the attracting being that grants a thing form, that delimits it in a place, that incarnates that which in itself is spiritual and incomprehensible. Indeed, the spiritual and the incomprehensible constantly contradicts the thing and announces itself as an evaporating, spiritualizing being, hostile to all limits. Yet it appears everywhere only as something coming to the fore out of an originary negation in respect to which that attractive force comes to the fore as its mooring, as its actual ground.

That tendency (to restrict the being) is even recognizable in customary expressions like: "Nature eludes the eye and conceals her secrets" or "Only when pressed by a higher power does she discharge, from an originary concealment, what will be."[16] In point of fact, everything in nature becomes only through development, i.e., through the constant contradiction of a swathing, contracting force. Left to itself, nature would still lead everything back into that state of utter negation. (I/8, 243–244)

Nature progresses, that is to say, has a future, and hence knows fatality and natality, through the "constant contradiction" of its two potencies: the hidden trace of nature (its primordial but always past seed) and the presence of visible nature. Schelling understands the contradictory progression of nature from its ever receding, abyssal ground, as the erotic self-development of being itself.

Considered in itself, Nature is like Penia showing up at Zeus' feast. From the outside, Penia was the picture of poverty and extreme need. On the inside, she shut away divine plenitude which she could not reveal until she had wed Wealth, Excess himself, that effusively and inexhaustibly garrulous being (A^2). Even then, however, the child wrested from her womb appears under the form and, so to speak, press, of that originary negation. It was the bastard child of Need and Excess. (I/8, 244)

Schelling of course is drawing an analogy for the appearance of nature from one of Diotima's stories that Socrates recounts in the *Symposium*

---

16. The two expressions read in German: "Die Natur entziehe sich dem Anblick und verberge ihre Geheimnisse." "Nur durch eine höhere Macht gedrungen entlasse sie alles, was wird, aus der ursprünglichen Verborgenheit."

(203b–204b). The gods had a feast to honor the birth of Aphrodite, and the guests included Poros [Πόρος], whose name originally meant something like a means to cross a river, like a ferry or a ford, and which more generally means something like "way," "passage," or "resource." An aporia, the lack of *poros*, is the inability to further ford the river of thinking. Schelling, following a long tradition, further translates *poros* as *Reichthum* and *Überfluß*, wealth and excess. Poros is "inexhaustibly garrulous," a discourse without end, a language whose resources are inexhaustible. Poros got drunk on nectar and sleepily headed to Zeus' garden where he fell asleep. Penia [Πενία] ("poverty" or "need"), and here for Schelling the impoverishment of visible nature without the absolute wealth of its past ground, arrived, as was her wont, to beg and when she discovered Poros asleep, she devised a way to free herself from her apparent poverty (the poverty of appearance itself, for she had "shut away divine plenitude"). She seduced Poros and eventually gave birth to the illegitimate child of past plenitude and the restrictions of presence. She bore Eros, who Socrates recounts was "neither mortal nor immortal," "neither ignorant nor wise," neither destitute nor rich for "anything he finds his way to always slips away" (203e).[17]

Penia (the negation that is the possibility of presence, the repression inherent in visible nature) is what Schelling elsewhere designated the A^1. Poros (affirmation, excess, garrulity, and the abyssal past ground of nature) is the A^2 and their illegitimate offspring is the most powerful of all, the birthing fire of progression, Eros (A^3).[18] The birth of visible nature is the repression of that which lacks presence. The repression of Poros, of the inexhaustibly rich ground of nature, is the lack of presence whose displacement first makes possible the secondary and merely apparent lack, need, and poverty of presence itself, the penury of visible nature. The primary lack, which, considered in itself, is an

---

17. Nehamas and Woodruff translation (Indianapolis: Hackett Publishing, 1989).
18. In the 1842 *Philosophie der Mythologie*, Schelling discusses the "effusive Being in the second potency" which "therefore brings the proper Being of the other [the first] to silence so that it remains as *potentia pura*, as a pure Can (*reines Können*), not demanding to go over into the Being of its own. " He remarks on this issue in a footnote by again returning to the *Symposium*: "In the unity 1 and 2 are the eternal sufficiency: together they both represent, so to speak, Poverty and Excess out of whose liaison that famous Platonic poem has Eros come forth" (II/2, 50).

unrestricted and unrestrictable wealth, can be thought of as a deeper lack that makes possible the lack that is presence. In the *Philosophical Introduction to the Philosophy of Mythology* (between 1847–52), for example, Schelling argues, "All commencement lays in lack [*Mangel*], the deepest potency, everything is hinged upon that which does not have being, and this is the hunger for Being" (II/1, 294). The beginning, the humus of death perception, is immemorial – the past as an abyss of thoughts.

All of this talk of lack is easily misleading. It is not that Eros, or his mother Penia for that matter, are abandoned, bereft forces, eternally deprived of their heart's desire. Their initial lack, that is to say, the poverty of merely being something, whatever that something is, is only an apparent lack. This lack appears when they assume *that they are only what they appear to be*. Their wealth is not the accretion of ever-new predicates to satisfy their hunger, as if they were constantly grasping for more in some futile attempt to fill their emptiness.[19] Their wealth is what they *have* paradoxically as what they *lack*. Their wealth is their lack of a present ground. They are fundamentally more than what than what they appear to be, than the penury of appearance itself.

In this sense one could say that Poros is the non-subject in the subject position, the subjectless subject, the "hunger for being," which exceeds any being of its own. Lack is the wealth of the subjectless subject. Lack is not the lack of objects to satisfy an ever-hungry subject who can never have enough. There are plenty of objects, indeed, a plenitude of objects, although what is true of the desiring subject is true of all objects: they are not merely what they appear to be. They are irreducible to their "visible nature" and hence are something like what Melanie Klein, and, eventually Deleuze and Guattari called "partial objects." In fact, death is the kind of object of desire that reveals that objects do not possess their own being, that they lack their own being as the great Buddhist "philosopher" Nāgārjuna insisted, just as the subject cannot posses itself as a subject. The erotic wealth

19. Levinas rightly understood this as the difference between need and metaphysical desire. In need, the conatus "strives to be *me* through living in the *other*." Emmanuel Levinas, *Totality and infinity: An essay on exteriority*, trans. Alphonso Lingis (Pittsburgh: Duquesne University Press, 1969), 117.

of being is nature as the subjectless subject, endlessly verbose with partial objects, revealed to the subjectless human subject amidst the garrulity of her own excessive partial objects.

Erotic desire – the very progression of nature for Schelling – cannot be understood by locating its specific object of desire. It is the richness of the subjectless subject. This strikes me as exactly what Deleuze and Guattari said of desire in *Anti-Oedipus*: "Desire does not lack anything; it does not lack its object. It is, rather, the subject that is missing in desire, or desire that lacks a fixed subject; there is no fixed subject unless there is repression."[20] Eroticism is desire without a fixed subject as it opens up beyond the subjugation of nature. It is *not* the desire for fulfillment in some transcendent object. In fact, it rejects the subjugation of erotic philosophy and its subjectless subject to any master object. There is not some *summum bonum* understood as a transcendent object that organizes all of human desire.

Schelling concludes his meditation on nature's auto-eroticism by noting:

> In accord with its ground, therefore, nature comes out of what is blind, dark, and unspeakable in God. Nature is the first, the beginning in what is necessary of God. The attracting force, the mother and receptacle of all visible things, is eternal force and might itself, which, when set forth, is seen in the works of creation. (I/8, 244)

What is "blind, dark, and unspeakable in God," the verbose silence of the past, the mother, or nurse, what Schelling, following Plato's *Timaeus* calls the χώρα or receptacle, the darkness out of which light appears, exerts an attracting force. If appearance is the expulsion of light from darkness, and if Penia before the birth of Eros is the penury of mere appearance, the illusion that a being has its own being, then darkness, while displaced into the past by presence, nonetheless exerts a gravitational force on presence. In a sense, gravity is the counter pull, a counteracting attraction, to a thing's propensity, found within the

---

20. Gilles Deleuze and Félix Guattari, *Anti-Oedipus: Capitalism and schizophrenia*, trans. Robert Hurley, Mark Seem, and Helen R. Lane (Minneapolis: University of Minnesota Press, 1983 [1972]), 26.

inert force of thingliness itself, towards itself and away from a center that does not lie within itself. As such, gravity permanently threatens a thing's integrity, nay, exposes its integrity as a lie born of inertia and contested by the counterforce of gravity. The latter is the attracting force, the force that magnetically pulls things away from themselves and into the general economy of nature. Gravity is a general center that attracts away from the inertia by which a thing strives to maintain its center of gravity within itself. Yet the individual center of gravity, the fallenness of light, resists the general gravity that contests it. The more the individual contests contestation itself, the more it swells within itself on the periphery. As Schelling describes this double contestation in *The Ages of the World*:

> But even now, intensified into selfhood (into Being-in-itself), these wholes are still retained by the attracting force. Yet, precisely because they are now selfish and because they have their own point of foundation (center of gravity) within themselves, they strive, precisely by dint of this selfhood, to evade the pressure of the attracting power. Hence they strive to distance themselves on all sides from the center of force and to become themselves away from it. Hence, the highest turgor of the whole emerges here, since each particular thing seeks to withdraw itself from the universal center and eccentrically seeks its own center of gravity or foundational point. (I/8, 323–324)

The more an individual insists on its own individuality, the more it seeks gravity within itself, the sicker it becomes. For humans, the celebration of the self in the flight from gravity, from what Schelling once called the "silent celebration of nature" (I/7, 230)[21] is the experience of evil and the possibility of such uniquely human perversity marks the very *humanity of humanity*. Resistance to gravity is the light of humanity's attempt to center itself within itself, to imagine itself as a *subject* for which *freedom* is a predicate. If I imagine that freedom is something for me, an object for a desiring subject, then I fight for my slavery as I were fighting for my liberation.

Freedom is repressed in light's obliviousness to its original darkness, in its attempt to locate its center of gravity within itself, in its delusion

---

21. From the *Aphorismen über die Naturphilosophie* (1806).

that it is most fundamentally attracted to itself and that desire is consequently self-interest. It is humanity's sense of itself as a subject, as fundamentally centered within itself and thereby on some kind of adventure in which it seeks to appreciate both its essential and accidental predicates. The human, in its flight from nature itself, seeks itself as the fundamental point of reference for all predicates. Sin is the flight from the general economy to which general gravity pulls the creaturely. "The beginning of sin is when the human steps out of authentic being into non-being, out of truth into the lie, out of light into darkness in order to become a self-creating ground and to dominate all things with the power of the center that they have within themselves" (I/7, 391).[22] The desire to be oneself, to be a discrete being, is the flight away from the cision between being and what does not have being, and towards the lie that is the fallenness of nature that cannot yet know itself as such.

Yet the oblivion of gravity in the flight to the integrity of humanity does not vitiate the attracting force. Rather gravity in the ethical dimension erupts as a monstrous secret within, pulling one away from oneself in a vortex of heretofore-concealed madness. Freedom returns as the screaming, to lift a phrase from Büchner, that ordinary humans call silence. Perhaps one is "seized by dizziness on a high and precipitous summit" and "a mysterious (*geheim*) voice seems to cry out that one plunge from it." Or perhaps it is like that "old fable" (*The Odyssey*) in which "the irresistible song of the Sirens rings out from the depths in order to attract the passing sailors down into the whirlpool" (I/7, 382). In any case, within the cool, silent evil that is the narcissism nascent in every self-understanding, the monstrosity of freedom can suddenly erupt, as if from nowhere, deducible from no conception of the comprehensible self. This is the explosion of integrity into the orgiastic abandon of the Maenads, the frenzied reassertion of the A^2, by which Pentheus is not recognizable as a mother's son. This is the rage that Homer laments in the *Iliad*, in which the dogs of war rule

---

22. So ist denn der Anfang der Sünde, daß der Mensch aus dem eigentlichen Sein in das Nichtsein, aus der Wahrheit in die Lüge, aus dem Licht in die Finsternis übertritt, um selbst schaffender Grund zu werden, und mit der Macht des Centri, das er in sich hat, über alle Dinge zu herrschen.

and one is blinded by one's own rage, thinking oneself invincible and killing without limit. This is the "murky and wild enthusiasm that breaks out in self-mutilation or, as with the priests of the Phrygian goddess, auto-castration" (I/7, 357).

Eros and Laughter at Oneself

After he had begun his *History of Eroticism* as the proposed second book of *La parte maudite*,[23] and before some of these reflections appeared in a slightly different form in 1957 in the text *L'érotisme*, Bataille was fascinated by the art in the caves of Lascaux.[24] There was something about these paintings, from the dawn of the human condition, with their powerful, almost divine animals, which encapsulated the erotic. "A sense of magnificence and beauty seizes him when he faces bulls, horses, bison, not when he faces himself." The Caves were a Holy of Holies in which some lost power was invoked. Before the artistic "presence" of animals, the human animal felt awe. Before themselves, however, the human animals felt no such thing. "Facing himself, he most likely had to laugh."[25] Such laughter at oneself is far from the "sudden eminence" that Hobbes described as the fruit of *Schadenfreude*. The animal gods did not know laughter, which, for Bataille, was "unique to the human." It was not merely that human beings could laugh, but that laughter for the human animals has a unique form, at least in its most sovereign moments: human laughter is the laughter "of which the human is the unique object" (CH, 80).

Laughter for Bataille is not some kind of halcyon and miraculous return to the lost paradise of nature. In the *History of Eroticism*, he claims "these impulses cannot be mistaken for those of animals" for "there is nothing more contrary to animality than laughter" (AS, 90).

---

23. Georges Bataille, *The Accursed Share, volumes II and III*, trans. Robert Hurley (New York: Zone Books, 1993). Henceforth AS.

24. For further discussion of this and related issues, see my "Animal desiring: Nietzsche, Bataille and a world without image" (in *Research in Phenomenology* 31, 2001), 96–112

25. Georges Bataille, "The passage from animal to man" in *The Cradle of Humanity: Prehistoric art and culture*, ed. Stuart Kendall, trans. Michelle Kendall and Stuart Kendall (New York: Zone Books, 2005), 79. Henceforth CH.

Laughter is one of the sites where humanity invokes its lost animality, but we should be clear that, for Bataille, this meeting place is the meeting place between opposites. For Bataille, only human beings laugh.

At first glance this seems to be yet another chapter in the long and tedious history in which the esteem of humanity is maintained at the expense of all other non-human animals. Human beings have long insisted on the singularity of their species and have done so not simply as a judgment of fact, but as a judgment of value. In what way is the human animal different than all other animals and thereby (tacitly or explicitly) better than all of them? In *On the Parts of Animals*, while discussing tickling, Aristotle claimed that it was exclusive to human beings and this was because of the delicacy of human skin and, more importantly, because humans "are the only animal that laughs" (De anim. membr. III. 673a8). This has been hugely influential. Does Bataille belong to that long history of those who commit what Peter Singer in *Animal Liberation* dubbed speciesism (the unfounded preference for one's own species over those of others[26])? Would we not also be able to extend the charge of speciesism to Schelling, who in the 1809 *Freedom* essay announced "Animals can never remove themselves from unity, whereas the human can voluntarily rend the eternal bond of the forces. Hence Franz Baader correctly states that it would be desirable that the corruption in humans only extend as far as animalization; but unfortunately the human can only stand above or beneath animals" (I/7, 373).

The scientific discipline of gelotology, that is, the scientific study of the physiology and psychology of γέλως (laughter), indicates that the capacity for laughter may not be unique to the human animal. Rats, for instance, are also ticklish, and furthermore apparently prone to slapstick. Something like laughter is also found in monkeys (chimpanzees, gorillas, orangutans, and bonobos) and dogs.[27] Gelotological

26. Peter Singer, *Animal liberation: A New Ethics for our Treatment of Animals* (New York: New York Review Books, 1975), chapter one.
27. See for example, Jaak Pankseep and Jeff Burgdorf, "'Laughing' rats and the evolutionary antecedents of human joy?" (in *Physiology & Behavior* 79, 2003, 533–547).

research is still in its infancy, but preliminary indications are that Aristotle was wrong on both accounts. Neither laughter nor ticklishness seems to be exclusive to the human animal.

Furthermore, laughter belongs to a primordial part of the brain and perhaps even precedes the capacity for language. Human babies, for instance, are able to laugh before they are able to speak. In this sense, laughter probably belongs to the atavistic evolutionary survival mechanisms and there is furthermore plenty of evidence that laughter is good for one's physical well-being. There is evidence suggesting that humans may have laughed before they knew that they were humans, that is, before the advent of self-consciousness.

The issue, however, is not reducible to the capacity for mirth or ticklishness and its physiological ramifications. In Nietzsche's *Nachlaß* we are told, "The animal that suffers the most invented for himself – *laughter*." [28] And of what does this profoundly afflicted animal suffer? It suffers from itself. Animals laugh like gods because they do not have any need to laugh at themselves. The very sickness of humanity is evident in humanity's need to know itself, to fix its kind, to comprehend its essence, in contradistinction to all other animals. Nietzsche on the other hand is a human becoming animal when he prefaces the second (1887) edition of *The Gay Science* with a motto that concludes, "He will laugh at any master who does not laugh at himself."

What is at stake here, therefore, is not a comprehensive philosophical gelotology. There is rather a particular form of laughter, a human all too human form of laughter, if you will, that emerges paradoxically in our most sovereign moments, that is to say, in our least human moments. In a sense, sovereign laughter, that is to say, human laughter on the brink of its non-humanity, relieves the stress of self-consciousness. Only humans laugh because gods and animals do not need to laugh at the egos that they do not have.

The problem of self-consciousness is not, however, merely a gelotological issue. It is for Bataille listed to a host of related issues, including

---

28. Friedrich Nietzsche, *Werke in drei Bänden*, ed. Karl Schlechta (Munich: Carl Hanser Verlag, 1956), volume III, 467. On the topic of Nietzsche and laughter, see my "Nietzsche's joy: On laughter's truth" (in *Epochē: A Journal for the history of philosophy*, 10 (1), 117–139, 2005).

religiosity, artistic creation, the transgression of the very taboos that mark and insure the limits of our humanity, and a sense of obscenity. Perhaps other animals can learn to feel aversion to their bodies, but only the human being can experience their nudity or the nudity of others as obscene. "It is nudity that, because of a misstep, Genesis speaks of, expressing the transition, through the consciousness of obscenity, from animal to man" (AS, 55). It is not that humans find any particular object obscene, for the abjection of an object is not found in the nature of the object itself. The obscene object, like taboos themselves, can vary and shift because what is at stake is more a "relation between an object and the mind of a person" (AS, 54). Obscenity emerges in the rift between the meaning of something and the contestation of that meaning. My genitals are obscene because they do not belong to what it *means* to have a proper body.

What then is this mythic fall by virtue of which one gains the experience of obscenity? The Genesis account links the loss of paradise to the temptation of knowledge, including self-knowledge and therefore shame before certain categorical elements of one's being. The tree that precipitated the fall of humanity into "humanity" was, after all, the tree of the *knowledge* of good and evil, a theme that Kierkegaard explored to great effect in *The Concept of Angst*.

The account in the *Qur'ān* even more explicitly draws our attention to the Fall as the birth of self-consciousness and selfhood. The prophet Mohammed claimed that "humankind were once but one community" (2:213),[29] but that was before the Fall. Allah had commanded the angels to prostrate themselves before Adam. All of the angels complied except for Satan, complaining that he would not bow to a human, who had been made from clay, when he himself had been created from the eternal fires. Satan's *ressentiment*, as it were, was born of the pride enabled by self-consciousness. Allah humbled Satan, although Allah granted Satan a reprieve until the Day of the Resurrection. Blaming Allah for his prideful nature, Satan vowed to sabotage the human's capacity to walk the "straight path." Meanwhile, Allah forbade Adam and Eve to approach a certain tree, but Satan tempted them, claiming

---

29. I am using N. J. Dawood's (numerously) revised translation (New York and London: Penguin Books, 1999).

"Your Lord has forbidden you to approach this tree only to prevent you from becoming angels or immortals." This was the original temptation: the chance to really be somebody, to be somebody powerful and immortal, to be the privileged child of the eternal fires, to be somebody who really counted, who was better than the rest, to be a contender, to be one who knew that they were something special.

The trap was set, and Adam, in wanting really to be "Adam," fell into the snare of selfhood. And hence, when Adam and Eve ate from the tree, "their shame became visible to them" and they came to see that they had sexual parts, which "they had never seen before" (7:11–24). It would make little sense to say that Adam had never noticed his penis or that Eve had never remarked that she had breasts. So how did the Fall into themselves deliver themselves to themselves as shameful and guilty creatures? From whence the guilt that reveals me to myself as having failed myself, as shamefully obscene? For Adam and Eve, guilt emerges from a kind of Lacanian mirror stage in which, in wanting really to be oneself, to affirm and promote oneself, and thereby also disaffirm all that is not oneself, one fails the original community of humankind. It would not make sense, however, to think of this original community as a collection of individuals gathered together by their membership in the natural kind of humanity.

This community emerges in my guilt for having perjured it and this perjury emerges from my desire to think of myself primarily as something discontinuous and discrete, as a denizen of the empire of the clear and distinct. My genitals emerge as obscene as soon as they emerge as *mine*. Human laughter, in which genitals in their obscenity become comic, is possible because of an antecedent Fall into self-consciousness and the consequent loss of the innocence of animal laughter, the loss of animality's capacity to laugh like the gods. The paradox of human laughter is the return of a vestige of the prelapsarian; it speaks from a Paradise always lost, an abyssal realm of humus discovered in the shame of perjury. In this sense, however, human laughter reflects its bifurcated origin, holding together the lost animal community and the human whose self-possessed presence is coming into crisis. Sovereign laughter therefore has an angelic element, in which one laughs at the wonder of being, and a satanic element, in which that same being is relieved of seriousness, of its proper understanding, of its constant contamination by kitsch. The two-fold of sovereign human laughter is on the one hand joyous, grateful, blessed, and celebratory and on the other hand impish, naughty, impious, and tantalized by the obscene.[30]

This lost community that is magically echoed in sovereign laughter cannot be thought of as something that I would retrieve, since this *I* marks the condition of its loss. The retrieval of original community begins when I shatter the mirror of myself, when I become nothing, when, as Frantz Fanon once argued, the dialectic of superiority and inferiority, master and slave, gives way to the other. "Why not the quite simple attempt to touch the other, to feel the other, to explain the other to myself?"[31]

Sovereign laughter, that is, the procreation of wealth and poverty in one's very flesh, contests the otherwise rarely contested rule of the servile human, the one who "averts his eyes from that which is not useful, which serves no purpose" (AS, 15). Erotic laughter is not very practical. It does not give rise to new bureaucratic institutions. It does not found new states, but it is revolutionary, for it calls radically into question the tacit and overarching regime of the servile humans, who "hold the power nowadays in all quarters" (AS, 15). This problem echoes Heidegger's concern about the tyranny of *das Man* and the iron grip of the *Gestell* or Ortega y Gasset's conviction that philosophy had been held captive to science and science in its turn was hostage to practicality. Ortega, making this argument before he could anticipate the rise of Franco, was optimistic that the "tyranny of the laboratory" was at last giving way to the adventure of thinking and its unflinching

---

30. The great exploration of this bifurcation of sovereign human laughter into the angelic and the satanic is Milan Kundera's *The Book of Laughter and Forgetting*, trans. Aaron Asher (New York: HarperCollins, 1996 [1978]). "Dominion of the world, as we know, is divided between angels and devils. The good of the world, however, implies not that the angels have the advantage over the devils (as I believed when I was a child) but that the powers of the two sides are nearly in equilibrium. If there were too much incontestable meaning in the world (the angel's power), man would succumb under its weight. If the world were to lose all of its meaning (the devil's reign), we could not live either" (86).
31. *Black Skin, White Masks*, trans. Charles Lam Markmann (New York: Grove Press, 1967), 231.

pursuit of the unknown.[32] Bataille was not so optimistic: "Humanity is letting itself be led the way a child submits to a professor; a feeling of poverty paralyzes it" (AS, 105). We do not live and think in the time of the poverty of wealth and the wealth of poverty. Our erotic lives are either functional or they are inconsequential distractions, hobbies, and entertainments.[33] In such a so-called Information Age, the question of nature does not present itself, because Eros wears the chains of practicality and self-interest. As Schelling already lamented, "The moralist desires to see nature not living, but dead, so that he may be able to tread upon it with his feet" (I/7, 17).

Erotic Solitude as the Solidarity of Agape

Erotic desire is not servile. It is not the humiliation of desire in its relegation to self-interest. It is sovereign, that is, no longer subjugated by utility, and as such, it is the experience of solitude. Indeed, Bataille's "starting point is the principle that eroticism rests in solitude."[34] Moreover, "eroticism is silence ... it is solitude. But not to the people

---

32. "In Greece, this utilitarian fruitfulness would not have won a decisive influence over every mind, but in Europe it coincided with the predominance of a type of man – the so-called bourgeois – who felt no vocation for the contemplative or the theoretic, but only for the practical ... Therefore the bourgeois age is honored most of all for the triumph of industrialization, and in general those techniques which are useful to life – medicine, economics, administration ... It was in such an atmosphere that what we might call the 'imperialism of physics' was produced." José Ortega y Gasset, *What is Philosophy?*, trans. Mildred Adams, (New York: Norton, 1960 [1929]), 41. As such, philosophy was robbed of a radical relationship to the future. "Life is what comes next, what has not yet come to pass" (225).

33. "There is within today's man a profound intolerance for the sense of humiliation which is demanded every day of our human nature and to which we submit everywhere: we submit in the office and in the street; we submit in the country. Everywhere men feel that human nature has been profoundly humiliated, and what is left of religion finally humiliates him the face of God who, after all, is merely a hypostasis of work" (AM, 82).

34. Georges Bataille, *L'érotisme* (Paris: Les Éditions de Minuit, 1957), 278. *Erotism: Death and sensuality*, trans. Mary Dalwood (San Francisco: City Lights Books, 1986), 252. Henceforth E with the French citation followed by the English citation, which I have emended.

whose very presence in the world is a pure negation of silence, idle chatter, a forgetfulness of the possibility of solitude" (E, 292/264).

In writing about Nietzsche's tonic of solitude, Bataille once asked, "Is there a silence more stifling, more sound-proof, further beneath the earth?"[35] Yet clearly in asking such a question, Bataille, like Nietzsche, was not keeping silent about silence. At the end of *L'érotisme*, Bataille admits that Jean Wahl has rightly heard the contradiction at the heart of Bataille's mad game of writing. As soon as one is conscious of continuity, it becomes discontinuous. As soon as one thinks infinity, it becomes finite. As soon as one makes the abyssal past present, it has already happened, already relegated itself to the past. As soon as one says silence, silence has become word. "The supreme moment is indeed a silent one, and in the silence our consciousness fails us" (E, 306/276). A phenomenology of eroticism does not in the end accomplish a new set of techniques, even a successful and reliably iterable erotic reduction, for disciples to imitate. "In the end the one who speaks confesses her or his impotence" (E, 306/276).

Yet in *L'érotisme*, Bataille offers a vast range of detailed analyses of social phenomena like taboos, transgressions, sexual plethora, prostitution, murder, the repressed animality at the heart of beauty, cannibalism, incest, nudity, the Kinsey Reports, the works of de Sade, Christianity, the orgy, marriage, violence, feasting, war, hunting, sacrifice, and mysticism. Despite all of these analyses, however, Bataille contends that this is not "any form of verbal apology for eroticism. Eroticism is silence" (E, 292/264). Bataille utterly eschews the typically lurid and sensationalistic temptations of such categories, refusing the petty thrills that gossiping about such things usually affords. Bataille avoids the *vulgarity* of gossip in order to communicate the erotic *summit* of solitude.

Let us be clear: solitude has nothing fundamentally to do with the liberal subject, the self-possessed individual. Solitude can only be perjured by the pernicious anxiety of the conatus. The freedom of the consumer is not only an oxymoron, but also a humiliation of solitude and its many messy becomings. In such a milieu, there is, as Hannah

---

35. Georges Bataille, *Inner Experience*, trans. Leslie Anne Boldt (Albany: State University of New York Press, 1988), 156.

Arendt clearly saw, only the loneliness of the absence of solitude. "What makes loneliness so unbearable is the loss of one's own self which can be realized in solitude, but confirmed in its identity only by the trusting and trustworthy company of my equals."[36] Solitude is the possibility of friendship and solidarity, and hence it is misguided ultimately to contrast endlessly eros and agape (the former being individual and acquisitive and the latter being general and generous). Eros assumes agape and agape fulfills the inner promise of eros. In this sense, one might even say that while many friendships are not sexual, all friendships are erotic. Further, what William Blake once called the "terrors of friendship" have, as the culmination of their promise, the overflowing of their boundaries into agape, into a retrieval of the pledge (to be enlightened and therefore helpful, as Broch puts it) that the deflation of the erotic had obscured and perjured. In a sense, eros, philia, and agape are intensifications of a single, albeit complex, self-differentiating, and never fully calculable, movement. They comprise, loosely speaking, and borrowing a figure from Schelling, a kind of A^3 in which these are valences of the force of desire. That Eros speaks to the longings of an individual perjures agape by relegating it to the humiliating glory of metaphor, and robbing it of solitude and its possibility of *philia* and *agape*.

Philosophy does not in this light ever possess wisdom. It is an erotic relationship to wisdom, and, as such, that which also calls one into friendship and solidarity with wisdom, a relationship that is perjured when wisdom becomes a metaphor by which the lover takes possession of the beloved. Wisdom, as the dying Virgil sees, is "the genuine reality, the reality of the never heard, though never forgotten, ever promised word, the reality of the creation rising anew in the rays of the unbeholdable eye, the reality of the homeland" (DV, 425). As such, this "stillness within stillness" (DV, 446), in the "perception and self-perception of a doubled insight" (DV, 463), calls friendship beyond its boundaries, towards an affirmation of and helpfulness towards all beings.[37]

---

36. Hannah Arendt, *The Origins of Totalitarianism* (New York: Harcourt, 1994 [1951]), 477.
37. Nishida already sees this in his first work: "Love is the deepest knowledge of

Karl Jaspers, in reflecting on the nature of philosophy, once argued that "we may say that wonder, doubt, the experience of ultimate situations, are indeed sources of philosophy, but the ultimate source is the will to communication, which embraces all the rest."[38] Although Jaspers, despite his many subtleties, may have underestimated the difficulty of the problem of communication, he remains sensitive to the problem that animated Bataille, as well as Broch, and many others.

Before the prospect of such difficult communication, attentive readers of Bataille are immediately confronted with the explosive aporia that animates all of Bataille's writing and that quickens his experience of language as such. Writing about silence is contradicted by the very silence of silence, yet such a contradiction births the mad religiosity of writing. Writing is a kind of ontological coquetry, the eroticism of wanting to have what one does not want to have. Bataille once asked, "How to write, except as a usually chaste woman getting undressed for an orgy?"[39] Such writing can only emerge from solitude, from the communion of silence, from a "state of wakefulness pushed to extreme lucidity, the limit of which is necessarily silence" (AM, 82).[40]

---

things. Analytical, inferential knowledge is a superficial knowledge, and it cannot grasp reality. We can reach reality only through love. Love is the culmination of knowledge." *An Inquiry into the Good*, trans. Abe Masao and Christopher Ives (New Haven: Yale University Press, 1990), 175.

38. Karl Jaspers, *Way to Wisdom: An Introduction to Philosophy*, second edition, trans. Ralph Manheim (New Haven, Yale University Press, 2003 [1951]), 26. Authentic communication does not reduce to Habermas' communicative rationality or Rorty's democratic conversation, despite the attractive practicality of such approaches for other activities. Of such communication, Deleuze and Guattari warn that "the idea of a Western democratic conversation between friends has never produced a single concept" (WP, 6) and "discussions are fine for roundtable talks, but philosophy throws is numbered dice on another table. The best one can say about discussions is that they take things no farther, since the participants never talk about the same thing" (WP, 28). Hence, "Philosophy has a horror of discussions. It always has something else to do. Debate is unbearable to it, but not because it is too sure of itself. On the contrary, it is its uncertainties that take it down other, more solitary paths" (WP, 29).

39. Georges Bataille, *The Absence of Myth: Writings on Surrealism*, ed. and trans. Michael Richardson (London and New York: Verso, 1994), 100. Henceforth AM.

40. This is the impossible demand that Deleuze and Guattari locate at the heart of philosophy itself: "Is there a 'best' plane that would not hand over immanence

Yet these are books that seek to communicate, that strive for the intimacy of communion. Even as they sacrifice themselves on the very cold altars of analysis that give them birth, they do not enclose themselves in hermetic fancies and eccentricities. As they move beyond themselves in the gesture of communion that their sacrifice calculates, they do offer themselves to the community of Reason. He does not mistake the mad game of writing in which eroticism itself is invoked for simply going mad, for leading language into the free play of surrealism, in which sentences are bereft of all prepositional content. Despite his early friendship with Breton, Bataille came to realize that surrealism simply decimates the very language that it needs to speak, that it needs to be anything whatsoever. "Surrealism is *mutism*: if it spoke it would cease to be what it wanted to be, but if it failed to speak it could only lend itself to misunderstanding" (AM, 56).[41]

Bataille, on the other hand, deploys meaning and propositional content in order to occasion an eruption, an ebullition, within meaning itself. Such communication is, in a sense, to have your meaning and eat it too. This eruption within analysis is *communication* and, as such, eschews gossip and the debasement of the eroticism of writing into yet more *information* about human erotic life. Speaking in *La parte maudite* about Aztec human sacrifice, Bataille claimed that communication is the expenditure of wealth, not its accumulation. "And if I thus consume immoderately, I reveal to my fellow beings that which I am *intimately*: Consumption is the way in which *separate* beings communicate."[42]

The transaction of information enhances the wealth of one's knowledge in a restricted economy in which one engages in specified ex-

---

to Something = x and that would no longer mimic anything transcendent? We will say that THE plane of immanence is, at the same time, that which must be thought and that which cannot be thought. It is the nonthought within thought" (WP, 59).

41. "I cannot consider someone free if they do not have the desire to sever the bonds of language within themselves. It does not follow, however, that it is enough to escape for a moment the empire of words to have pushed as far as possible the concern not to subordinate what we are to anything" (AM, 49).

42. Georges Bataille, *The Accursed Share*, trans. Robert Hurley (New York: Zone Books, 1991) 58. *La part maudite* (Paris: Les Éditions de Minuit, 1967). Henceforth PM with the English citation.

changes that allow one to accumulate knowledge and grow intellectually. The anxiety and distress, the *angoisse*, of ignorance propel the accretion of knowledge. Learning transpires within a restricted economy, but the solitude of non-knowledge is the eruption of a general economy. It is non-utilitarian expenditure, a waste, of accumulated energy.[43] "My work tended first of all to increase the sum of human resources, but its findings showed me that this accumulation was only a delay, a shrinking back from the inevitable term, where the accumulated wealth has value only in the instant" (PM, 11).

Bataille is not here chiefly marking an epistemological limit, as if there was a line, a Kantian some object = x, beyond which the intellect could not continue to accumulate knowledge. Certainly the expenditure of knowledge, the waste of wisdom, presupposes the cold, patient, scholarly, bibliophilic acquisition of knowledge. But the accumulation of knowledge is not simply inverted and knowledge is not simply discarded, as it was in surrealism. Nor is one disposing of excessive and unneeded knowledge, as if one were pruning the tree of one's learning. Rather, the researcher as such reaches the madness of a writing and a thinking in which the researcher can no longer embrace the humiliation of her or his identity, that is, of identity as such. "Certainly, it is dangerous, in extending the frigid research of the sciences, to come to a point where one's object no longer leaves one unaffected, where, on the contrary, it is what inflames. Indeed, the ebullition I consider, which animates the globe, is also *my* ebullition. Thus, the object of my research cannot be distinguished *from the subject at its boiling point*" (PM, 10).

In the general economy of writing, the study of certain objects occasions a kind of *death* of the discrete thinking subject and, with the thinking subject at its boiling point, all objects likewise lose their self-contained, discrete identities. One studies certain objects that occasion the self-overcoming of the subject who purports to study them. In the sacred wastefulness of such non-knowledge, the subject-object

---

43. As Ortega y Gasset writes: "In the small Oriental patio there arises, sweet and tremulous as the slender thread of the fountain, the voice of Christ, who warns, 'Martha, Martha, only one thing is needful.' And with this, facing the busy and useful Martha, he alludes to Mary, loving and superfluous." *What is Philosophy?*, 91.

dichotomy maintains only a temporal primacy as it comes to stand in relationship to the superiority of a general ground, of a continuity, that exceeds the discontinuity of all identities. In the eruption of the other beginning within the sober pursuit of knowledge, the conditions of knowledge reveal themselves to have been necessary yet false. One can call this practice something like an *erotic-thanotic sociology* or, more daringly, an *erotic natural history*: sociological (that is, natural historical) researches that inflame the researching subject. These are thanotic sociologies, analyses that crave the very death that their impartiality initially denied. They comprise natural history because they evoke the nature, the heretofore perjured humus, beyond the duality of nature and culture. They evoke the sovereign nature of solitude.

In this sense, then, we can hear Bataille's "formula" – he does not call it a definition – for eroticism: "it is the approbation of life up to the point of death" (E, 17/11). The affirmation of life is enacted up to – but without achieving – its breaking point. It is the affirmation of wealth that allows it to cohabitate with poverty, much like the early Nietzsche spoke of the pairing of Dionysus and Apollo. The Apollinian object is mastered to the point that its concealed non-objectivity inflames the non-subjectivity at the heart of my subject position. As Bataille articulated it elsewhere: "The sacred is exactly comparable to the flame that destroys the wood by consuming it."[44]

This inflammation, occasioned by the non-objectivity – the life – of the "object" researched, is addressed in a most curious and profound proposition found in a remarkable essay at the end of the third volume *of La parte maudite* entitled "Nietzsche and Jesus." Here Bataille claimed that sovereignty of solitude can be expressed in the kōan-like proposition: I am a deserted beach. This is not a surrealist terrorism in the realm of meaning, as if the key to unlocking a kōan were merely to decide that it was logically absurd and yet somehow, as such, counter-intuitively meritorious. The erupting subject is indeed a deserted beach and this truth is obviously not true in any conventional sense. It is true in a way in which renders conventional truth untrue. In a sense it is a lie that exposes the truth of the vast lie of truth itself.

---

44. Georges Bataille, *Theory of Religion*, trans. Robert Hurley (New York: Zone Books, 1989), 53.

On the beach I spoke of, nothing separates me from the immensity except for the certainty of being *at issue*: I have recognized my equality with the emptiness and boundlessness, for I know that at bottom I am this subjective and countless existence, but memory ties me to objects, to contents, in the midst of which I situate myself .... I am an object *in question*, an object whose basic content is *subjectivity*, which is a question, and which its differentiated contents bring into play. As a subject I am NOTHING within the immensity that is NOTHING – as an object, in the feeling of being at issue that sets me against the self-sameness of the immensity, I rediscover an equivalence. (AS, 378)

This equivalence, which defies any possible logical equivalence – for classical logic is a restricted economy par excellence, reverses thinking. The primacy of discernment gives way to the re-emergence of the supremacy of ignorance, that is, to the heights of solitude and to communities of those who have nothing in common. This is not the reversion to the innocence of an originary ignorance. It is rather the supreme command of solitude: we were supremely ignorant, we were otherwise than being and that now pertains to our very being. This is not the sudden eruption of skepticism.[45] It is a sacred self-knowledge comprised of non-knowledge.[46] Rather than skepticism, it is the erupting inversion of all moral reasoning into the supreme ethic of self-consciousness that knows nothing about (and the absolute nothingness

---

45. Or one could try to frame this problem within the following parameters, building on distinctions that Frege brought to our attention. 1. These are not mere sentences, which, as such, need only be grammatically correct. They do not have to either make sense or refer to anything. "Black jargon jumps horribly" is only a sentence. It is not a proposition. 2. "Odysseus, the only one to make it back to Ithaca, is a lucky bastard" has sense [*Sinn*] (it communicates an idea), but it does not have reference [*Bedeutung*] (the idea does not refer to anything but a writer's imagination). 3. "This is an essay about eros" has both sense and reference. 4. Surrealism speaks sentences that have no sense, only reference. They speak nonsense to nonsense. 5. Bataille's sovereign propositions have sense that operates to expose the non-meaning of what is proposed in such a way that it more fundamentally exposes the non-meaning of the one who proposes propositions. It does not render sense chaotic, but evokes the secret chaos (nonphilosophy) that dwells within the philosophical.

46. "There can be *nothing* sacred. The sacred cannot be a *thing*. The instant alone is sacred, which is *nothing* (is not a *thing*)" (AM, 99).

of) its self. "Changing from the perspectives of restrictive economy to those of general economy actually accomplishes a Copernican transformation: a reversal of thinking – and of ethics" (PM, 25).

Without such paradoxical self-conscious, without "knowing" that "Night is also a sun," (AM, 48), there is only moral reasoning. This is not to pretend that we can abandon moral reasoning but rather to hold such claims, as necessary and imperative as they are, to the supreme ethic of solitude, to the luxurious and mad love of a general economy. "Woe to those who, to the very end, insist on regulating the movement that exceeds them with the narrow mind of the mechanic who changes a tire" (PM, 26).[47] The servile person does not laugh deeply and does not investigate the richness that eroticism expresses.

By Way of Conclusion

In conclusion, I would like to reflect briefly on the strangeness of the present essay. Although it is dedicated to the problem of the erotic, it quickly turned to the force of death and its embodiment in phenomena like laughter and the practice of solitude. Furthermore, I hoped to suggest that the problem of eroticism is not a problem within philosophy, as if we could already take philosophy itself for granted and simply apply it to the problem of eroticism. Rather, it is the latter that demands that we consider anew what is of value in the practice of philosophy. In this sense, the question of the erotic cannot be detached from the question, What is philosophy?

My point of entry into the erotic dynamic of philosophical practice is death: at once uniquely personal (death admits of no substitution and the death of another is singular); yet it is also that in which all of Nature partakes. As such, Jean-Luc Nancy rightly calls the belonging together of the singularity of death and that all of Nature shares in this singularity the "being-singular-plural" of Nature.[48] Thanatos unleashes

47. For the political implication of this for current US politics, see my, "The dark night is also a sun: Bataille's thanotic mendacity in Red America" (in *International studies in philosophy*, 40.1, 2008, 129–142).
48. Jean-Luc Nancy: "But this circulation goes in all directions at once, in all the directions of all the space-times opened by presence to presence: all things, all beings, all entities, everything past and future, alive, dead, inanimate, stones,

eros, but we do not repeat Freud's tendency to think of the former as *something*, with a specific function or rule, that mechanically repeats itself again and again, reducing experience to the play of its paradigm. Although, as Deleuze argued, "Freud was unable to prevent himself " from "maintaining the model of a brute repetition," he somehow had a sense that thanatos "is above all silent (not given in experience), whereas the pleasure principle is noisy."[49]

This silence demands that philosophy reconsider, reevaluate, and deepen the rigors of its practice. The great thirteenth century founder of the Soto Zen tradition in Japan, Dōgen Zenji is quite clear about this: the most important issue in all of Buddha Dharma practice is "the thorough clarification of birth and death."[50] Living and dying, the noisy joys and tribulations of eros and the silence of thanatos, are the great matter of philosophy and hence the great wealth of its ceaseless pluralism and multiplicity.

If philosophy is to be erotic, if it is the practice for death and dying, than it does not endlessly insist on repeating its accomplishments. It is not therefore a question of merely developing a philosophy or phenomenology of eroticism. Eros as an object of study detonates the philosophy or the phenomenology that would make it an object of analysis or reduction. This does not mean that philosophy should not cultivate ξενία to the erotic stranger. Eros, eschews the perjury of self-possessed philosophy and phenomenology, and illuminates the complex life of philosophy, including philosophy at its boiling point. Good philosophy is also simultaneously the hot and bothered desire for nonphilosophy, for the life beyond life and death that exceeds all the sovereign words to which it has given birth. "Yet words are not the end of thought, they are where it begins."

---

plants, nails, gods – and 'humans,' that is, those who expose sharing and circulation as such by saying 'we,' by saying we to themselves in all possible senses of that expression, and by saying we for the totality of all being." *Being Singular Plural*, trans. Robert D. Richardson and Anne E. O'Byrne (Stanford: Stanford University Press, 2000), 3.

49. Gilles Deleuze, *Difference and Repetition*, trans. Paul Patton (New York: Columbia University Press, 1994 [1968]), 16–17.

50. Dōgen, *Shushōgi*, in *Zen master Dōgen: An Introduction with Selected Writings*, trans. and ed. Yūhō Yokoi with Daizen Victoria (New York: Weatherhill, 1976), 58.

Heideggerian Love

MARCIA SÁ CAVALCANTE SCHUBACK

Das Ereignis hat die Liebe
(The event has the love)
Martin Heidegger[1]

How to develop a phenomenology of love? How to find a thinking-word that might correspond to how love shows itself from itself, that is, to the way loves appears as love? A phenomenology of love is neither a psychological nor a biological description of a set of experiences we might wish to call love. Neither is it for that matter an attempt to describe in concepts what happens with the soul and the living-body when what is called love is experienced. It is rather the search for a thinking-word that corresponds and responds to the multiple ways love gives itself as love. To correspond and respond is, however, already a kind of "love" and it was in this sense that the word *philosophia* was first pronounced by the Greeks. Philosophy already says love, *philia*, in the sense of both a correspondence and a response to the all of being (*to sofón*). A philosophy of love is therefore already entangled with the love of philosophy, and the search for a thinking-word, for a philosophical word about love, is already an act of love.

At the same time that a philosophical discussion about love should not forget that the word philosophy is already saying love, it can, all the same, hardly deny the gap that exists between philosophy and love. Not only the insufficiency of philosophy to grasp with thoughts and words the plural experience of how love appears, but how the un-graspability of love also becomes graspable. Love is more "ponderous

---

1. Martin Heidegger, "Ereignis" in *Gedachtes*, GA 81 (Frankfurt am Main: Klostermann, 2007), 269

than the tongue,"[2] as Cordella is meant to show in Shakespeare's *King Lear*, as the one who loves and keeps silent on love, even when this results in the uttermost suffering, as a banishment from love. To keep silent on the subject of love – respecting here Rilke's poetical lesson of "don't speak about love," which he will prescribe to a young poet – means to correspond and respond to the many faces and names of love. Its many faces and names show how effusive and disseminative love can be. Indeed "love in the singular is itself perhaps nothing but the indefinite abundance of all possible loves," to recall the words of Jean-Luc Nancy.[3] Saying love, one says in the singular the "indefinite abundance" of all possible loves; one says in the singular a multi-various plural that cannot be brought into a general or universal concept. Thus love withdraws and exceeds the thoughts of words and the wording of thoughts. Love is not the general concept of different kinds and manners of loving, but the name of many names, the hymn of many hymns, sounding as several hymns together, as *polymnia*. *Polyminia* was one of the nine muses, sister to *Erató*, the muse of erotic poetry. It is perhaps rather *Polymnia* that shows the proper of *Erató* and thereby of the naming of Eros. As "nursing mother of the dance," as the one who, at the wedding of Kadmos and Harmonia, "waved her arms, and sketched in the air an image of a soundless voice, speaking with hands and moving eyes in a graphic picture of silence full of meaning,"[4] *Polyminia* shows the strange kind of name that love is, the strangeness of the name of many names. This may itself give us a sign as to why, when discussing the love proper to *philosophia*, Plato and the Ancients will talk about Eros, describing *philia* in terms of Eros. Here, what appears is the polymnic rather than the polemic character of love; its indefinite abundance disables the philosophical attempts to grasp it conceptually when, for the sake of finding a common measure of and for love,

---

2. Shakespeare, *King Lear*, act one, v. 24–25.
3. Jean-Luc Nancy, " L'amour en éclats" in *Une pensée finie* (Paris: Galillé, 1991). For the English version, see "Shattered love" in *A Finite Thinking*, ed. By Simon Spraks (Stanford: Cailfornia: Stanford University Press, 2003).
4.Nonnus, *Dionysiaca 5*, trans. William Henry Denham Rouse, Loeb Classical Library 344 (Cambridge: Harvard University Press, 1940), 88 ff. (Greek epic C5th A.D.)

different kinds of love are distinguished from each other. In its own name – *philosophia* – philosophy already experiences its limits and insufficiencies: its love for grasping the all and yet never reaching the all with its thinking words. Precisely in the task of thinking love, philosophy, the love of thinking, is brought to its limits.

A phenomenology of love should therefore depart from its own limit, from the limit of philosophy itself, or at least from a philosophy that has brought philosophy to its own limits. It should depart from the uncanny equation between the generous abundance of forms, names, gifts of love and the poverty of conceptual attempts to grasp the meaning of loving experiences. It should depart from a thought that has acknowledged the coldness and debilitation not only of concepts but even of language to name, showing how seldom thinking words of love are. This is the main reason for "reading" the seldom words of love in Heidegger's thought and for discussing what can be called "Heideggerian love." Because Heidegger thought the end of philosophy, because he brought philosophy to its limits,[5] he offers us the possibility for thinking the relation between philosophy and love when philosophy experiences itself at the edge. Heidegger's seldom words on love are to be understood as words being pronounced from a philosophy that is brought to its own limits, to a placeless place where the seldomness and rarity of every love shows itself from itself.

To philosophize from within the limits of philosophy means, in Heidegger's terms, to philosophize from within the time in which the Gods have abandoned the humans. It is to philosophize from the perspective of the "last man," as Nietzsche would say, of "the one who has to ask: What is love? What is a star? What is creation?"[6] for no longer is one able to ask *from* love, *from* the stars, *from* creation. A time of humans abandoned by the Gods is a time of humans abandoned by Eros. Thus Eros is not only one of the Gods but, according to Parmenides, the first of the Gods, *prôtiston theôn*.[7] Heidegger will translate this fragment in a note as the "highest and mostly first," *höchsten zu-*

---

5. Jean-Luc Nancy, op. cit.

6. Friedrich Nietzsche, *Also sprach Zarathustra. Vorrede. Kritische Studieausgabe* (München, Berlin: de Gruyter, 1988), 2224, 19.

7. Parmenides, *On Nature*, B13.

erst.[8] If we acknowledge Plato's description of Eros as a demi-God, an in-between Gods and humans, connecting abundance and poverty, excess and lack – and this as the very meaning of being "highest and mostly first" – we could say that to philosophize from a philosophy brought to its limits means to philosophize in a time when the tension between Gods and humans is withdrawn. As such, the abandon of Eros reveals however a fundamental trait of Eros, namely of not being in possession by humans. If Eros abandons humans it is because they do not possess Eros. It is rather he Eros who possesses them. The abandon of Eros show that Eros must first overtake and befall humans so that they may fall in love. The humans must first be loved by Eros and only then may they love. Indeed, Eros, love, is overtaking and befalling, reaching existence as an arrow pierces the body of the soul. Eros befalls and shakes the soul, as Sappho sings:

> Now like a mountain wind the oaks o'erwhelming,
> Eros shakes my soul.[9]

In different languages, to "fall in love" is a common way to say "to love." This occurs not primarily because one "loses the head" and falls, as Plato acknowledges, under the tyranny of love[10] but rather because Eros has befallen one, shaking the soul of the body as a catastrophe. In a letter from June 1918, the young Heidegger describes the over-taking action of love, saying that: "The you" of your loving soul over-took me" (*Das "Du" Deiner liebenden Seele traf mich*[11]). In this letter, Heidegger speaks of love as the experience of *being*-struck-by (*Getrof-fensein*), as an immediate and bridgeless "belonging-to-you" (*unmit-telbar, brückenlose "Dir"-Gehören*), affirming in this being joined by hyphen, so to speak, the beginning of the outburst of a belief in one's own self, of a belief in becoming oneself.[12] Eros, the highest and the

---

8. Heidegger, *GA 81*, 258 "als höchsten zuerst freilich Eros unter den Göttern be-dachte (Moira) von allen ...<C Parmenides nach Plato, Symposion 178 b.
9. Sappho, frag 44, *Alcée Sapho* (Paris: ed. Les Belles Lettres, 1966), 228, cited by Maximus Tyrius when comparing Socrates and Sappho on love.
10. Plato, Politeia, 573b
11. Heidegger, GA 81, 16.
12. Ibid.

first among the Gods is the God of the highest first. Eros is the God of an overtaking and befalling in which an overwhelming beginning takes place. Both Eros' incipient overtaking and befalling are so overwhelming that words seem "so cold and bordered, so full of finitude and limitation – (that) the only I wish is to always look into your eyes, profound as mountains and seas, and with trembling lips kiss your pure face,"[13] as Heidegger also wrote. Cold and bordered, full of finitude and limitation are the words when Eros overtakes and befalls, when one "falls in love," discovering the self as belonging-to, as joined by the hyphen, as an immediate and bridgeless towardness in togetherness. The time when the Gods have abandoned the humans, when Eros does not overtake and befall, is a time when humans experience themselves as willing Eros, as willing subjects of the verb to-love, as the ones who can possess love and not who are fallen and shaken by love, and not as the ones who are 'overwhelmed as oaks by mountain's winds.' When humans take Eros for something they possess and want to possess, even assuming that Eros has to be awoken and inflamed through the apparition of the "other," of the "you," they take Eros for what falls under the willing subject. What appears in this time of abandonment by the Gods is a sad and fallen Eros, not an inexistent Eros but an abandoned Eros, that remains, like the dead, as present absence, as distant presence. As band between life *and* death, Eros is a half god, that is, a God that shares mortality and death with the humans. Love begins and gives birth but love also dies. The sadness of Eros is the sadness of a fallen Eros. This is something we can see in old plastic representations around the motif of *Eros funèbre*, the mourning Eros: an Eros lying down as if sleeping, falling down surrendered by beauty, withdrawing itself in its own exuberance.

These ancient images of a fallen Eros remind us that Eros not only overtakes and befalls but is self overtaken and befallen. If the abandonment by the Gods named by Heidegger means the enigmatic uncontrollability of a beginning, of the "highest and the very first," that is, of Eros, than the fallen Eros could be understood as a sign that

---

13. Ibid., 12, "Ach die Worte sind so kalt, so kantig, so voll von Endlichkeit und Begrenzung – ich möchte nur immer in Deine bergseetiefen Augen schauen, mit bebenden Lippen die reine Stirn Dir küssen."

humans do not have the power to "name the bride," "to know and look into love, and how love endures," thus love, Eros, "guards the lightning," as Heidegger writes in one of his poetical drafts.

> With light and sound
> the world is dared in promises.
> Who names the bride?
> Who knows and looks into
> love, how love endures?
> The flash of a full bloom,
> incorporated
> to growth,
> which in blossom
> *remains*
> consecrated,

un-perishing years,
making the court, she guards the lightning[14]

---

14. GA 81, 120. In a free translation of mine
Aus Licht und Laut
ist Welt getraut.
Wer nennt die Braut?
Wer kennt und schaut
die Liebe, wie sie währt?
Der Aufblitz einer höchsten Blüte,
die, ins Gedeihen
einverleibt,
Erblühen *bleibt*
aus Weihen,
unverjährt,
daß freyend sie die Blitze hüte

"Who knows and looks into love, how love endures?" asks Heidegger. This question is about the subjectivity of love. It is not however about how love constitutes, grounds or confers the proper meaning of the subject but how love radically questions the subject, the misunderstanding of the who of love as subject. In asking who knows and looks into "how love endures," Heidegger indicates that it is from the way "love endures" that the "who" of love can be named. Endurance is a precarious translation of the German verb *währen*, related to *"wesan"* an old form of *wesen*, meaning being as continuous form. It serves to highlight endurance as a meanwhile. Endurance means here, therefore, the intimacy of being entirely the finitude of the meanwhile. In this entire intimacy, one loses oneself, becoming this meanwhile as much as the meanwhile becomes one. In love, the certainty that it is the subject that loves and is loved breaks down. What then breaks through is that love loves and this to such an extent that in love it is only love that knows and looks into who loves and is loved, that is, how love endures. The "who" of love appears in love as the way love endures; love's endurance is the "who." Losing oneself, being overtaken, one becomes the "you" that overtakes.

As too intimately and entire presence, love breaks down every "own" existence. Being-in-love means being entirely and intimately in the meanwhile. The entirety and intimacy of this being in "the meanwhile" dissolves the oppositions between inside and outside, interior and exterior, selfhood and otherness into a radical new meaning of difference. Difference can no longer be measured by distances in time and space; being in the meanwhile means being in the timeless time and in the placeless place of a lightening. The whole past and the whole future is here, in this meanwhile. Thus everything that existed before and everything that will or may exist after can only exist through and from the lightning flash of this meanwhile. The meanwhile is not the simple "here and now" of a circumstance. It is the temporality of *being in love* that expands every here and now to the whole past and to the whole future. That is why being in love means being in love with the "whole you," with "your" past and future, where the "you" is the past and the future at one and the same time, the lasting of love. Being in the meanwhile, as is the case when one is in love, means to be in oneself outside and beyond oneself. To be in itself, out of and beyond, itself defines an ecstasy. It defines the temporality that constitutes the way human life is factually, the way it is, its being. It defines what Heidegger called "the ecstatic temporality of *Dasein*." Being in the meanwhile, as one is when being in love, renders clear and transparent the "ecstatic temporality of *Dasein*." *Dasein* is not another name for human existence but the name for the most proper meaning of existence, a meaning that is never given but has to break through when the common meaning of existence as "subjectivity," as "something present at hand," breaks down. When being in love, when being entirely and intensively in the meanwhile – the most proper meaning of existence – existence as *Dasein* breaks through.

In a famous letter to Hannah Arendt from 1925, Heidegger writes an equation of love – "to be in (the) love = to be urged to the most proper existence" (*in der Liebe sein = in die eigenste Existenz gedrängt sein*).[15] To be in love is said here to be in the love, to be in Eros and understood as the same as being urged to experience the most proper meaning of existence. The ek-static meaning of existence *qua Dasein* is, as Heidegger always insisted upon, a "fundamental event" (*Grundgeschehen*), a meaning that has to break through at the point at which the meaning of existence as subjectivity breaks down. Another name for it is *Sorge*, usually translated as "care." Human existence is not given. It has to discover itself continuously as *non-being* in the way things are taken for things, that is as something being *in-itself*, as thinghood. It has to discover itself again and again as being in-itself a non being-in-itself, as being out and beyond itself, as ecstasy of being. *Dasein* means therefore the place of a displacement and the displacement of given places. It means experience, a breaking through while breaking down. Hölderlin described this in terms of "becoming in dissolution" (*Werden im Vergehen*). As such, *Dasein* is no longer a question of identity or of unity. *Dasein* is a question of entire intimacy and intimate entirety. That is the meaning of *Sorge*, a meaning often rendered imperceptible in its translation and understanding as care. *Sorge* indicates the existential meaning of being-whole as intimate and as entire comprehension, a comprehension that means seizing while be-

---

15. Hannah Arendt and Martin Heidegger, *Briefe 1925–1975* (Frankfurt am Main: Vittorio Klostermann, 1998), 31.

ing seized, apprehending while being apprehended. Comprehension translates the meaning given by Heidegger to the German word *Verständnis*, the meaning of standing in the outstanding place of a displacement that Being is.

To be in this most proper meaning of existence would be then "to be in (the) love," to be in Eros. Many years later, this will be Heidegger's response to Ludwig Binswanger's complaint that his philosophy has thoroughly thought care but fully neglected love.[16] In the seminars held at Zollikon, Heidegger will reply saying that "if understood correctly, that is, in the sense of fundamental ontology, *Sorge* can never be differentiated from "love" insofar as it names "comprehension of Being" as the fundamental determination of the ek-static temporal constitution of Dasein."[17] "Correctly understood," love means ecstasy of being, intensive and entire comprehension. Love means the co-apprehension of apprehending while being apprehended, of coming to be while already being and, already being while coming to be; it captures being ahead for and in itself, providing a radical insight into the meaning of existence, which only breaks through when consciousness of subjectivity and the subjectivity of consciousness break down.

During a certain period, Heidegger called "transcendence" this movement of breaking through while breaking down, of "becoming in dissolution." It indicates another kind of temporality, a vertiginous temporality between the falling over (catastrophic) and the about to fall (imminent). Transcendence means here rather the "trance" and perplexity of this being intensively and entirely in the fugacity of a meanwhile that defines the endurance of love. It says that the ecstasy and ex-centricity of existence are in principle distinct from every meta-

---

16. Ludwig Binswanger, *Grundformen und Erkenntnis menschlichen Daseins* (Zürich: Max Niehans, 1942). See also Françoise Dastur's discussions about the relation between love and care in her article in the present volume and her article "Amore, noità e cura. Note a proposito della Grundformen di Lundwig Binswanger" in *Ludwig Binswanger. Esperienza della soggetività e transcendenza dell'altro.* A cura di Stefano Besoli (Quodlibet, Macerata, 2007, 519–534).
17. Heidegger, *Zollikoner Seminare* (Frankfurt am Main: Vittorio Klostermann, 1987), 237. For the eng. version see *Zollikon Seminars*, ed. By Medard Boss (Evanston, Il: Northwestern University Press, 2001).

physical determination of becoming such as willing, wishing, longing, desiring, hankering after, urging to.[18]

In these determinations, transcendence is understood as a moving beyond to a beyond oneself, presupposing both something in itself as a point of departure and as something beyond for the sake of what the movement moves. Here, movement means to move from one toward another, a moving that is seized from where it begins and where it ceases, and not its event. Totally distinct from the teleology of the willing movement and its variations such as wishing, longing, desire, hankering, urging, is transcendence a becoming in dissolution. Tran scendence in this sense is neither transcendent nor immanent. It names the distancing that existence is in "itself." It names a being beyond itself in it-self and not something that strives after a beyond. Love, *Sorge*, Eros can be called "transcendence" when understood "correctly." Thus for Heidegger *Dasein* is transcendence. This would then mean that *Dasein* is *love*, is Eros, and further that only because *Dasein* is Eros, is love, it loves (or not).

Love is for Heidegger *Sorge*, that is, transcendence. But this can only be said when transcendence is "correctly understood" as "becoming in dissolution." Because platonic love also is commonly defined as transcendence, it is decisive to distinguish between these two meanings of transcendence. If platonic love is transcendence, it is in the sense of a movement of intensification. The movement of intensification that characterizes platonic love is the movement of something beyond itself towards the other beyond. Platonic love is intensification of desire that, beginning with bodily love, with you-loving, progresses to spiritual or intellectual love, to all-loving. Platonic love is not really transcendence but a desire for the transcendent. Heideggerian love describes a different kind of movement. It differs from a movement directed towards something else, from intentionality even in the sense given to it by Husserl. It is not a directed movement but a vertiginous one, the vertiginous movement of "becoming in dissolution." This movement cannot be described as a play of intentions and directions. It differs from loving intentionality insofar as in this vertiginous transcendence subjects are overtaken and befallen; in this sense, they

18. See Heidegger's discussions on this in *Being and Time*, § 41.

are dispossessed becoming possessed, taken and befallen by love. What appears here are not the subjects of love, neither the lover nor the beloved, but, as we read in Heidegger's lecture *Was ist Metaphysik?*, the "joy about the present of *Dasein* – not simply of the person – of the beloved," (*die Freude an der Gegenwart des Daseins – nicht der blossen Person – eines geliebten Menschen*).[19] Dispossession of the subject when possessed by love is here understood in terms of a "revelation" (*Offenbarung*) accomplished by the "joy of the present of the *Dasein* of the beloved," of the discovery of the meaning of being in love as being in the meanwhile, and therefore as being in itself out and beyond itself, ecstasy of being. It reveals how the beloved "you" appears as joy of the present of the most extreme meaning of the existence of the beloved.

The reservation that what appears is not "simply the person" is a critique towards Husserl and above all to Scheler's understanding of love intentionality. The "you" of your loving soul that overtakes, for Heidegger, is not the irreducible you in regard to a self as Husserl describes in his studies on the Phenomenology of intersubjectivity. Heidegger and Scheler were both very critical of Husserl's concept of intentionality because it does not really overcome the subject-object dichotomy. In their discussions,[20] Scheler proposes that in love the aporias produced through Husserl's notion of the transcendental subject can be overcome, such that in love what is loved is neither the other nor a "you," but the becoming you in the loving relation. In love, stresses Scheler, self and otherness are not; they become insofar

---

19. Heidegger, "Was ist Metaphysik?" in *Wegmarken* (Frankfurt am Main: Klostermann, 1967), 110, eng. version "What is metaphysics?" in *Basic Writings*, ed. David Farell Krell (Routledge, London, 1993), 99.

20. Heidegger, *Metaphysische Anfangsgründe der Logik*, GA 26 (Frankfurt am Main: Klostermann, 1978). In this course from 1928, Heidegger tells us of the impressive discussions he had with Scheler and about a certain set of discussions connected to a reading of Scheler's text "Idealism and Realism," from which they developed together a kind of phenomenological program, summarized as the "necessity of overcoming the subject-obejct relationship." It is a kind of phenomenological manifesto, in which a controversy with Husserl's concept of transcendental subjectivity can be followed. This particular controversy can be read today as the starting point for a criticism of the ulterior development of Phenomenology in phenomenologies of personal pronouns' perspectives.

as who is loved in love is not the "other" but the becoming one in the other and the becoming other in oneself. It is the being-relation that defines the beings. Scheler defined this becoming oneself as "person," describing it as structure of value, of intensification. Scheler described love as a moving search for *more* than oneself, an intensification of one's own immanence through the power of a transcendent other. Love is here a movement of value, of excess and abundance. Not in the sense that love – and its contrary, hate – discover values, right and wrong, but in the sense that, in love – and hate – everything becomes full of value, disrupting every sphere of indifference and neutrality. In the act of love, the subject disrupts insofar as it becomes full of value; it becomes "person." Here the objectivity of the other as "loving object," as "beloved other" is transformed into the only place where the value of being a "person" can really emerge.[21] Scheler's point is that no one loves the other because this other has a value. Love is not interest, not habit, not self-escaping, not fear of loneliness, not social interest for being considered by others someone with value. No one loves in the expectation that someone becomes a value. Love is never pedagogical. No one can learn from someone else about love or how to love. Love cannot be imitated. The basic structure of pedagogy: the "if...then" finds no place in love. Love, in Scheler's phenomenological account, is love for the other's being and the being of both the lover and the beloved is a movement of intensification, the movement of "becoming who you are," as Scheler used to formulate, quoting a famous verse of Pindar. Love loves the becoming oneself and not the self. That is why, for him, love defines concrete individuality as personality. Therefore Scheler's love is personal and expressive, not intentional. It unfolds not only the "principle of the heart," already sketched by Augustine and Pascal, but also the "works of the heart," something that appears even more clearly in Rilke's poetry.

---

21. Scheler, Max, "Liebe und Person" in *Wesen und Formen der Sympathie* (Bern: Francke, 1974), "Nun gilt aber für die individuelle Person, dass sie uns überhaupt nur *durch* und *im* Akte der Liebe, d.h. also auch ihr Wert als Individuum nur in diesem Aktverlauf zur Gegebenheit kommt. Die Gegenständlichkeit als "Liebes-gegenstand" ist gleichsam der Ort, wo allein die Person existiert und darum auch auftauchen kann," 150.

Heidegger will criticize Scheler's concept of love, because in the attempts to think Being at the basis of a being in relation, he described relation as a being. If the beings partaking in a relation are described by Scheler as becoming and thereby as what cannot be grasped as "something in-itself," as "present at hand," his account on the *being-relation* tends to treat relation as something in-itself and therefore as present at hand. In contrast to Scheler's love, Heidegger proposes the meaning of *Dasein* as *Sorge* and transcendence, as "becoming in dissolution." This explains the reservation "not simply the person" and further why the overtaking "you" in love's meanwhile is the "joy of the present of the *Dasein* of the beloved," the joy of the present of the most proper meaning of existence in the beloved.

In the already quoted letter to Hannah Arendt, Heidegger further adds to his equation of love what could be considered a definition of Heideggerian love. "Amo means volo, ut sis, as Augustine said: I love you – I want you to be, what you are" (*Amo heisst volo, ut sis, sagt einmal Augustinus: ich liebe Dich – ich will, dass Du seiest, was Du bist*).[22] This definition is taken from Augustine and is intimately connected to Hannah Arendt and her readings of Augustine on the concept of love.[23] This definition seems to contradict the interpretation here proposed of being in (the) love as being in the most proper meaning of existence, as being in the meanwhile, beyond the intentional and the personal. This Augustian sentence, which we can read here and there in several texts by Heidegger – even the late ones – seems to contradict above all Heidegger's insistent critique of the subjectivity of the will and the willing subjectivity. Critique of metaphysics is in Heidegger above all a critique of the will and if metaphysics is in itself the problem of overcoming, to overcome metaphysics is to overcome the power of the will and the will to power that defines modern subjectivity. In Heidegger's view, the will always wants itself, it is self-referent; self-reference is the fundamental structure of the subject. Therefore, willing is identified with the "will to power" and the "will to will." Dispossession of the subject, dispossession of self-referentiality means

---

22. Arendt and Heidegger, *Briefe*, 31.
23. Arendt, *Der Liebesbegriff bei Augustinus. Versuch einer philosophischen Interpretation* (Berlin/Wien: Philo-Verlagsgesellschaft, 2005).

therefore dispossession of the will. If this vehement critique defines Heidegger's work as a whole, it is astonishing to discover that precisely and only in relation to love do we find some hints of an experience of the will not coincident with the subjectivity and self-referentiality of the will, not coincident with the "will to power" and the "will to will." Precisely in relation to love – the fundamental experience of being overtaken and befallen by the joy of the present of the Dasein of the beloved – is said in terms of the will. It is said as a quote, in Latin, from Augustine. The Augustinian *volo* says in German – Ich *will*. In other languages, *volo* would be rather translated to I wish or want. In Spanish, it is common to say "*Te quiero*," meaning firstly "I love you" and only then "I want or wish you." Instead of rushing to see in these words, which became the signature of love between Heidegger and Arendt, a formulation of love intentionality and of personal love, it is important to try to figure out what does "will" mean here, what other experience of the will than of power is here pronounced.

In these words of love by Augustine, Heidegger listens to the dimension of coming pronounced in the will. *Volo*, Ich will, I wish, I want is saying as in English I will, not the future but the coming, I am coming to your coming. Heidegger uses the same formulation when discussing Hölderlin's poem *Andenken*. Interpreting who speaks in the poem, Heidegger shows that it is Hölderlin insofar as the being poet of Hölderlin (his essence, *Wesen*) has encountered plenitude in the "will that the northeast wind is what it is."[24] Interpreting in this poem the analogous formulation to Augustine's sentence, "to will that the northeast wind is what it is," Heidegger refers to another verse in the poem, "but it comes what I will," bringing the will to the coming. This enables him to say: "in no way does 'will (*Wille*)' mean the selfish enacted demand of a self-referential and directed desire. Will is the knowing readiness for belonging to a destiny. This will only wants and wishes what comes, because this coming has already interpellated this will to a knowing, "calling" it to stay in the wind of being called by the name."[25] In this passage, to will that you are what you are, to will that

24. Heidegger, *Erläuterungen zu Hölderlin's Dichtung*, GA 4 (Frankfurt am Main: Klostermann, 1981), 81.
25. Ibid., "Wille" meint hier keineswegs die eigensüchtig betriebene Erzwingung

the northeast wind is what it is, is interpreted as the willing of the coming that already has interpellated the will to stay in the wind of its called name. The "you," in several passages written in quotation marks, is not the "you" or the "other" of a person or of an intended subject. It is the named you, the "you" being named and called, the "you" being whispered as wind, an overwhelming wind, "shaking my soul," recalling again the words of Sappho. The named, called, pronounced and whispered "you," the you-wind is a coming rather than a becoming. To will the coming, to welcome the coming is presented here as the source for the words of love in loving, showing them as words pronounced and called as wind, showing the overwhelming fugacity of the words of love.

This rare experience of will as willing the coming that defines love for Heidegger is totally distinct from the metaphysical determination of will. In this determination, will is becoming and becoming the essence of being. In his long critical discussions about the modern metaphysical fundament of the will, Heidegger will bring together two dimensions of this determination: on the one hand, Schelling's "will of love" (*Wille der Liebe*) and, on the other, Nietzsche's "will to power" (*Wille zur Macht*)[26]. "Love and power," as Heidegger sees, are essentially opposing and conflictual, they are bound by "struggle" and "contradiction"[27] but as such they are essentially the same. Heidegger understands Schelling's "will of love" as "serene intimacy" ("gelassene Innigkeit"[28]) accomplished in the entire becoming oneself, an intimacy that is so entire that the will to become oneself does not need any longer to wish or want itself. Non-will in Schelling is for Heidegger the accomplished becoming oneself that only love can enact and in

---

eines selbstisch errechneten Begehrens. Wille ist die wissende Bereitschaft für die Zugehörigkeit in das Geschick. Dieser Willen auf ein Wissen angesprochen hat und ihn "heisst," im Wind der Verheissung zu stehen," 82

26. Heidegger, *Die Metaphysik des deutschen Idealismus: zur erneuten Auslegung von Schelling: philosophische Untersuchungen über das Wesen der menschlichen Freiheit und die damit zusammenhängenden Gegenstände (1809)*, GA 49 (Frankfurt am Main: Klostermann, 1991). Above all, 10–104.

27. Ibid., 102.

28. Ibid., 101

this sense unconditional subjectivity. The other extreme of unconditional subjectivity appears for Heidegger in Nietzsche's will to power. At stake here is a will that wants itself beyond itself, wanting the will, willing the will to such an extent that the will "rather will nothingness than not will," as Nietzsche will formulate. For Heidegger the question of the will is the question about the impossibility for modernity and for contemporaneity to experience the coming beyond the idea of self-becoming.

The gift of Heideggerian love would be then one that indicates a will that wants and is wanted by the coming. In this sense, it could be said that the "event has the love" (*das Ereignis hat die Liebe*). This will is beyond activity and passivity because it is beyond the "domain of the will," following here Hannah Arendt's interpretation of Heidegger's critiques of Nietzsche's notion of the will to power.[29] In contrast to a will of love and a will to power, in contrast to a concept of will grounded upon the active power and empowering of the self and the subject through love, to will the coming – which defines Heideggerian love – asks for an understanding of action beyond the dichotomy between activity and passivity. In the aforementioned interpretation of Hölderlin's *Andenken*, Hölderlin discusses the relation between *Liebe und Taten*,[30] between love and acts. Discussing Hölderlin's verses "listen a lot/to the days of love,/and acts (*Thaten*) that happened," Heidegger stresses the listening, describing the listening that thinks as a reminder (*Andenken*) of the tender endurance of the "days of love," to the meanwhile-temporality of the loving. He describes this listening as having a certain spirit, the "spirit of the will that the beloved would be in the own essence and there remains."[31] The vocabulary of the will that wants the coming is not that of activity or of action. Acts are neither active nor passive. How to conceive then the acts of love? They can be conceived as gestures, to be understood theatrically. Thus a gesture is a gestation, which shows how the condition of being

29. Arendt, *The life of the mind* (New York / London: Harvest Book, 1971), 178–179.
30. Heidegger, *Erläuterungen zur Hölderlin's Dichtung*, 118–119.
31. Ibid., 118.

grasped grasps, how being touched itself touches, how the being called calls, the being wanted itself wants. The vocabulary of this rare will speaks in terms of gestures and gestations insofar as it speaks in terms of how love carries the body of the soul when the soul of the body is shaken by the wind of love.

Neither activity, nor passivity, gestuality is the possible made possible and not the realization of possibilities. Loving gestures do not realize or actualize possibilities because there is no before the being in love. All the gestures are what happened because they bring everything of what has happened to the event of being in love. Love brings to the world another meaning of possibility that only with difficulty can be brought to understanding. To indicate how love makes possible the possible rather than realizing or actualizing possibilities, Heidegger will even use the German verb "*mögen*" (to love), that builds the word *Vermögen*, making possible. In the *Letter on Humanism*, we find some other words of love by Heidegger addressing love's unique capacity of making possible the possible:

> Thinking is – this says: Being has fatefully embraced its essence. To embrace a thing or a person in its essence means to love it, to favor it. Thought in a more original way such favoring (*Mögen*) means to bestow essence as a gift. Such favoring is the proper essence of enabling, which not only can achieve this or that but also can let something essentially unfold in its provenance, that is, let it be. It is on the "strength" of such enabling by favoring that something is properly able to be. This enabling is what is properly "possible," whose essence resides in favoring. From this favoring Being enables thinking. The former makes the latter possible. Being is the enabling favoring, the "may-be." As the element, Being is the "quiet power" of the favoring-enabling, that is of the possible. Of course, our words möglich, possible, and Möglichkeit, possibility, under the dominance of "logic" and "metaphysics," are thought solely in contrast to "actuality," that is, they are thought on the basis of a definite – the metaphysical – interpretation of Being as actus and potentia, a disctinction identified with the one between existentia and essentia. When I speak of the "quiet power of the possible" I do not mean the possible of a merely represented *possibilitas*, not *potentia* as the *essentia* of an *actus* of *existentia*; rather, I mean Being itself, which in its favoring presides over thinking and hence over the essence of humanity, and that means over its rela-

tion to Being. To enable something here means to preserve it in its essence, to maintain it in its element.[32]

Love is not only a possible making possible but also a making possible of the possible. Therefore it cannot be understood as "the passion of *potentia passiva*," of the power of powerlessness in which one becomes able to abandon onself to what cannot be appropriated, as suggested by Agamben.[33] Love does not simply let the other be its own possibilities acknowledging both the powerlessness and the non-appropriation of the other. It favors and makes possible the possible in the being of the beloved.

The loving meaning of the possible proposed by Heidegger is to be distinguished from the dynamics of movement from a potential state to the actuality of another. The "irreality" of the possible, says Heidegger in his interpretation of Hölderlin's *Andenken*, shall be understood as the reality of a "dream" that is the concrete reality of

---

32. Heidegger, *Basic Writings*, 220. "Das denken ist – dies sagt: das Sein hat sich je geschcklich seines Wesens angenommen. Sich einer 'Sache' oder einer "Person' in ihrem Wesen annehmen, das heisst: sie lieben: sie mögen. Dieses Mögen bedeutet, ursprünglicher gedacht: das Wesen schenken. Solches Mögen ist das eigentliche Wesen des Vermögens, das nicht nur dieses oder jenes leisten, sondern etwas in seiner Her-kunft 'wesen,' das heisst sein lassen kann. Das Vermögen des Mögens ist es, 'kraft' dessen etwas eigentlich zu sein vermag. Dieses Vermögen ist das eigentlich 'Mögliche,' jenes, dessen Wesen im Mögen beruht. Aus diesem Mögen vermag das Sein das Denken. Jenes ermöglicht dieses. Das Sein als das Element ist die 'stille Kraft' des mögenden Vermögens, das heist des Möglichen. Unsere Wörter 'möglich' und 'Möglichkeit' werden freilich unter der Herrschaft der 'Logik" und 'Metaphysik' nur gedacht im Unterscheid zu 'Wirklichkeit," das heiss aus einer bestimmten – der metaphysischen – Interpretation des Seins als actus und potentia, welche Unterscheidung identifiziert wird mit der von existentia und essentia. Wenn ich von der 'stillen Kraft des Möglichen' spreche, meine ich nicht das possibile einer nur vorgestellten possibilitas, nicht die potentia als essentia eines actus der existentia, sondern das Sein selbst, das mögend über das Denken und so über das Wesen des Menschen und das heisst über dessen Bezug zum Sein vermag. Etwas vermögen bedeutet hier: es in seinem Wesen wahren, in seinem Element einbehalten.

33. Giorgio Agamben, *L'ombre de l'amour. Le concept d'amour chez Heidegger* (Paris: Payot et Rivages, 2003). The essay was first published in Cahiers du college international de Philosophie, n.6, Paris, 1988.

an in-between. To explain this he quotes the following passage from Hölderlin's essay "Becoming in dissolution":

> in-between being and non-being the possible becomes everywhere real and the real becomes ideal and this, in the free artistic imaging, is a terrible but nevertheless divine dream.[34]

Heidegger elucidates what is terrible about the experience of this possible, of this dreamlike-state in-between the real and the unreal, as the terrible of being thrown into the unreal that is however, at the same time, divine because here reality appears transformed, appears as coming.

Willing the coming, love makes possible and favors the possible, liberating it from the rational and sensible metaphysical distinctions between essence and existence, act and potency, actuality and possibility. Love not only transforms the knowing but the feeling as well. Love is not a feeling but an overwhelming transformation of the feelings. It is not a knowing but a total transformation of what it means to know. Heidegger describes this transformation of love in terms of the non-duality of activity and passivity, of knowing and feeling. This transforming force of love is called favor. Favoring, that is, making possible the possible, is the "nature of love."

With favor and favoring Heidegger also translates *filia* in Heraclitus' fragment "*physis kryptesthai filein*," nature loves (favors) hiding itself.[35] The nature of love is defined as the way nature is nature, that is, loving, favoring, making possible the possible. Discussing the translation of *filein* to favor during his seminars on Heraclitus Heidegger quotes Parmenides' fragment 13, in which Eros is called the one who can be "guessed" as the first among the Gods.[36] Heidegger does not develop the connection between Eros, *filia* and *physis*, between Eros, favor, and

---

34. Friedrich Hölderlin, "(im) Zustand zwischen Seyn und Nichtseyn wird aber überall das Mögliche real, und das wirkliche ideal, und diss ist in der freien Kunstnachahmung ein furchtbar aber göttlicher Traum," from *Werden im Vergehen*, quoted by Heidegger in *Erläuterungen zur Hölderlin's Dichtung*, 107

35. Heidegger, *Heraklit: 1. Der Anfang des abendländischen Denkens; 2. Logik, Heraklits Lehre vom Logos*, GA 55 (Frankfurt am Main: Klostermann, 1979), §6.

36. GA 55, §6.

nature, but admits it as fundamental and as something to be understood as a critique of Plato. *Filia* is in a certain sense assumed as a fundamental way in which Eros eroticizes. Eros eroticizes favoring self-concealment, favoring its own gliding and sliding away.[37] Birthing Eros is also mourning Eros. *Filia*, or this face of Eros eroticizing, brings to conception the experience of the non-duality of life *and* death in everything that lives and dies. Heidegger used to affirm that death is itself non-mortal[38] and that only man is mortal, only man *can* die, facing death as possibility and not as fatality. Saying that, he indicates that in mortals the conjugation of life *and* death not only appears but also become transparent.

The experiential content of this non-dual conjugation of life *and* death becoming transparent in human existence is discussed some years later by Heidegger and Fink in their seminar on Heraclitus. In their discussions, mortals, transparency of life *and* death, are described as being in-between day and night. Human mortal life is a life in-between day and night, a life that takes part both in the clarity of daylight and in nocturnal obscurity, being both comprehension of differences and comprehension of un-differentiation. It is neither only daily nor only nocturnal, but both *at once*. Wakefulness and sleep are concrete experiences of the in-between of human mortal life. During their dialogue, Eugen Fink suggests that this human mortal in-between could be interpreted as the double movement of human self-

---

37. Die Gunst is die Weise, aus der die Rückgründung des Aufgehens in das Sicherschliessen, aber auch die Überholung des Aufgehens durch das Sichverschliessen, aber auch die Vorgründung des Sichverschliessens in das Aufgehen wesen, wie sie wesen. Die Gunst wiederum ist nicht etwas für sich und ausser dem phyein und kryptesthai, sondern das Gönnen hat die Wesensart des Aufgehens und Sichverschliessens. Die Gunst ist die Innigkeit der einfachen Unterscheidung; das Gönnen lässt die reine Klarheit erstehen, in der Aufgehen und Sichverbergen auseinander und aufeinander zugehalten sind und also miteinander straiten um die einfache Gewähr des einfach gegönnten Wesens. Die Gunst ist die Grundzug der eris, des Streits, sofern wir diesen anfänglichen denken und nicht sogleich und nur aus dem Widrigen der Ungunst und der Missgunst als den Hader und den Zwist vorstellen, GA 55, § 6, 133.

38. Heidegger, "Die Aletheia ist nichts Sterbliches, so wenig wie der Tod selbst" in *Das Ende der Philosophie und die Aufgabe des Denkens* (Tübingen: Max Niemeyer Verlag, 1976), 75

comprehension. He connects this understanding to Heidegger's *Being and Time*. Human existence comprehends itself as different from everything else, as not being the other beings, and it is as differentiated from others that human factical life immerses itself in the quotidian. Man says first "I am not this or that, I am not you and you" in order to say "I am." Self-comprehension implies strangely self-alienation, differentiation and opposition to others. It is from out of this self-differentiation that man grounds his knowledge about things and discovers himself as incomprehensible. It is however also within this self-differentiation that human mortal life discovers the whole of beings and the being of the whole, beyond self-differentiation. The Ancients formulated the principle of knowledge regulating this movement as "unlike knows unlike." Experiencing, however, the whole of beings beyond self-differentiation, human mortal life discovers its likeness to nature's abyssal and nocturnal ground, to the life of life, to the non-dual conjugation of life *and* death, to nocturnal and abyssal non-differentiation. At this moment, human mortal life comprehends being through obscurity and not through clarity, following another principle for knowledge, in which "like knows like." This double movement of belonging *at the same time and at once* to a principle of daylight (by which unlike knows unlike) and to a principle of nocturnal darkness (by which like knows like), is discussed, in this dialogue between Heidegger and Fink, in terms of proximity and distance, of seeing/listening in contrast to touching. Human life, the only mortal life, is both distance to things and proximity to the whole of things, it is daily differentiating distance and nocturnal non-differential proximity.[39]

This double principle of knowledge shows how nature loves to conceal itself in human mortal life. Nature favors human existence insofar as human mortal life is nature's own concealment. This is an obscure principle of comprehension where like knows like at the same time that unlike knows unlike. When the difficulty in seizing this principle becomes explicit in the dialogue, Heidegger says: "it can only

---

39. This discussion about awakedness and sleep, daylight clarity and nocturnal obscurity is an interpretation and development of Heidegger's affirmation in *Being and Time* that man is ontically the closest to himself but ontologically the most distant.

be comprehensible through the phenomenon of living-body" (*Das wird erst durch das Leibphänomenon verständlich*).[40] Fink adds immediately after: "somehow in the way of understanding proper to Eros" (*etwa in der Verstehensweise des Eros*),[41] to which Heidegger agrees saying that "Man only incorporates when he lives" (*Der Mensch leibt nur, wenn er lebt*).[42] To "leib," to "incorporate" is here admitted so as to comprehend from the obscure standpoint of Eros the whole of life, and where appearing as such, that is, nature, appears to itself hidden in individual, singular, finite forms of life. To "*leib*," to "incorporate" means then to understand nature's self-hiding from within, from "oneself." In this erotic, incorporated understanding, daylight of differences and self-differentiations appear from the nocturnal obscurity of nature favoring its own concealment. Differences appear from the obscure light of the appearing as such, from the obscure light of the Eros of nature.

The way of understanding proper to Eros sketched out in these seldom and disseminated words of love in Heidegger's work indicates a meaning for the knowing brought to life by and through love, by and through Eros, for philosophy. In one of the texts collected and published under the title *Mindfullness, Besinnung*, Heidegger tries to formulate what happens to the definition of philosophy when it ceases to think being in advance of beings and their beingness. The following passage about the word philosophy can be found there:

> Philosophy means "love of wisdom." Let us think this word out of a foundational mindfulness by relinquishing the representational domains of everyday life, erudition, cultural concerns and doctrines of happiness. Then the word says: "love" is the will that wills the beloved be; the will that wills that the beloved finds its way unto its ownmost and sways therein. Such a will does not wish or demand anything. Through honoring, and not by trying to create the loved one, this will let above all the loved one – what is worthy of loving – "be-come,"[43] be the coming the beloved is.

40. Fink, Heidegger, *Heraklit*, 233.

41. Ibid.

42. Ibid.

43. Heidegger, *Besinnung* GA 66 (Frankfurt am Main: Klostermann, 1997), §14, "Philosophie heißt: "Die Liebe zur Weisheit". Denken wir diesen Namen aus der Wesensbesinnung. Verlassen wir den Vorstellungskreis des Alltags und der Ge-

Philosophizing from within the time in which philosophy is brought
to its limits, the time in which Eros, the highest and the very first of
the Gods, has abandoned the humans can be understood as to begin
to philosophize under the nacre light of Eros, unfolding the way of
understanding proper to Eros. Here it might be perhaps possible to
discover philosophy as the diurnal way of existing in this nocturnal
belonging to life, within which human existence is still enveloped,
with its illusions of power and will.

lehrsamkeit, der Kulturbesorgnis und der Gluckseligkeitslehre. Dann sagt das
Wort: "*Liebe*" ist der Wille, daß das Geliebte *sei,* indem es zu seinem Wesen finde
und in ihm wese. Solcher Wille wunscht und fordert nicht. Wurdigend laBt er erst
das Liebens-wurdige als das Geliebte "werden", ohne es doch zu schaffen," 63. For
the eng. *Mindfullness* (New York: Continuum, 2006), § 14, 52,

The Phenomenological Question of the Relation with the Other: Love, Seduction and Care

FRANÇOISE DASTUR

Love, seduction and care seem at first to be different kinds of relations with others. This implies that our first task should consist in showing in which way they differ from each other. However, because love and seduction are often associated with one another it will be necessary to begin by analyzing them before turning to the problem of the relation of love and care.

From a philosophical standpoint, it seems that love can be opposed to seduction in the same manner that at the very beginning of the philosophical tradition *being* was radically opposed to *appearance*. For seduction can be understood as being related to the mere appearance of the other, to what is immediately visible of him or her, whereas love can be seen as being directed towards the proper being of the other, a proper being which can only be discovered by going beyond what appears at first, and even on occasions in opposition to what is apparent. But the distinction between being and appearance remains nevertheless questionable. For it is indeed quite possible to consider that seduction is nothing else than the anticipation of true love and inversely that love itself, in order for it to arise, has to begin with seduction. There is therefore a very tight relation between them.

They are both two very important ways of relating with the other, but they are nevertheless two quite different forms of relation: there is an asymmetrical relation between the person who seduces and the person who is seduced, whereas, at least ideally, there is a symmetrical relation between two persons who love one another, who are at the same time both loving and loved. Seduction, following its etymology, involves the idea of being separated, of going apart, because the Latin verb *se-ducere* means leading (*ducere*) astray (*se*). The word itself implies that the other is diverted from his own way, driven to a way where he or she loses him or herself, in the sense of the German word *Verführung* – a very important term for Freud, who uses this word to designate traumatic seduction, i. e. the raping of a child by an adult. But the term seduction can also refer to another German word, *Verlockung* – a term also employed by Freud, which means the attraction or fascination emanating from an object or a person to such a point that it is no longer possible to oppose any resistance to it. This is what happens, for example, in the case of hypnosis or diabolic possession when the subject is totally submitted to the will of another person. In both cases, when someone is subjected in a violent manner to the domination of another person or when one is attracted by the irresistible charm of someone else, seduction implies the idea of the omnipotence of the one who seduces over the one who is seduced and is therefore deprived of his or her free will and profoundly divided within him or herself, or separated from her or himself. In this respect, seduction would consequently be reduced to an asymmetrical relation, implying on one side a total passivity – as well as a total self-deprivation – and on the other a total domination, machination and instrumentalisation of the other.

Inversely, love would imply acknowledgement and respect of the otherness of the other person, instead of violent subjection, and it would aim at establishing a symmetrical relation of reciprocity and exchange, in which each partner would find the possibility of fully expanding his or her own being. In this view however, love is not referred to as *eros*, love as desire, but rather as *philia*, love as friendship. For love can adopt two different forms. In *Symposium*, a dialogue which deals with love, Plato brings to light the hybrid character of Eros, this half god who is son of *Poros*, wealth, and of *Penia*, poverty.[1] Consequently, Eros is profoundly defined by the tenseness inherent to desire, which is at the same time plenitude and need, deficiency and abundance, ignorance and science. Eros remains therefore caught in an intermediary state between possession and deprivation, so that all

1. Platon, *Symposium*, 203c sq.

that is acquired can only be lost once again. Eros is in this respect the image of the philosopher, defined by Plato as the one who desires *sophia*, knowledge; he searches for it only because he has the remembrance, the reminiscence of having possessed it in a previous life. In such a conception, *eros* can only be related to the figure of the loving person, whereas the figure of the loved person is here identified with the idea of perfection, which means the realized unity of beauty, truth and goodness. *Philia*, on the other hand, is related to the idea of a love or friendship shared by both partners, which implies a real reciprocity between them, so that they are alternatively active and passive, alternatively giving and receiving. This other kind of love that is *philia* – and that Plato is the first to use for defining the specific love of knowledge that is philo-sophy – is characterised by the idea of harmony and agreement in opposition to the idea of erotic tension. The ambiguity of these two forms of love defines the Platonic figure of the philosopher.

*

From a philo-sophical point of view, love constitutes therefore a fundamental mode of human existence. This is the reason why all philosophical analysis of the human being should give the phenomenon of love a fundamental importance. But, as we know, it was not really the case in modern philosophy, which since Descartes has given more importance to rationality than to the sphere of sensibility in general. But this is no longer the case with phenomenology, in spite of the fact that Husserl, its founder, can be considered as a convinced rationalist. Phenomenology wants, according to its name, to limit itself to the mere analysis of phenomena, to what shows itself from itself, without trying to give it an explanation based on metaphysical or theological postulates. It only wants to go directly to "the things themselves", which is the motto given by Husserl to phenomenology, and this implies a certain mistrust with regard to all kinds of theories. Phenomenology aims at merely *elucidating* the meaning of phenomena, which is something quite different from *explaining* them on the basis of presuppositions which are themselves unfounded. Such a conception of the analysis of phenomena, which leaves aside all kinds of prejudices, immediately had a great repercussion in the domain of psychology and psychopathology. At the beginning of the 20th century, a phenomeno-logical psychopathology and psychiatry began to expand. The key figure was Ludwig Binswanger, a Swiss psychiatrist and philosopher, who was first in contact with Freud and remained his friend until his death – in spite of the fact that he started very early to criticize his naturalistic conception of the human being, which is more or less re-duced in psychoanalysis to a bundle of drives *(Triebe)*. For Binswanger, it is not possible to understand human behavior on the basis of the naturalistic concept of drive, it is on the contrary only on the basis of the fundamental dimension of love, *Liebe*, that what is specific to the human being can be understood. In the big treatise he published in 1942 under the title *Fundamental Forms and Knowledge of Human Exis-tence, Grundformen und Erkenntnis menschlichen Daseins,*[2] Binswanger raises an objection to Heidegger – who was nonetheless his main source of inspiration – namely, that Heidegger has centered his anal-ysis of existence in *Being and Time* on the notion of care without having made room for the notion of love. Binswanger explains that love has to be understood in the perspective of what he calls *Wirheit*, ourness, which in his view is the basis of all possible understanding of human existence as such.

Binswanger's objection to Heidegger is not that he left aside the proper dimension of desire, of *eros*, on behalf of the notion of care (*Sorge*). This is Levinas' objection to Heidegger; Levinas distinguishes in a radical manner *need*, which is always related to some definite thing – and which can be satisfied through the temporary disappearance of this thing – from *desire*, which in his view is what gives access to the absolute alterity of the other, which implies that desire remains in principle unsatiable. As Levinas explains in the first pages of *Totality and Infinity*, a book published in 1960, "desire is desire for the absolute other," it is "a desire without satisfaction which, precisely, *understands* the remoteness, the alterity, and the exteriority of the other". Levinas considers that "we speak lightly of desires satisfied," and "love itself is thus taken to be the satisfaction of a sublime hunger," but "if this

2. Cf. Ludwig Binswanger, *Grundformen und Erkenntnis menschlichen Daseins*, Aus-gewählte Werke, Bd 2 (Heidelberg: Asanger, 1993).

language is possible it is because most of our desires and love too are not pure".[3] It seems therefore that true love is considered by Levinas in its erotic dimension, where the relation remains asymmetrical between the loving person and the loved person, whereas Binswanger understands it on the basis of the relation of exchange that is *philia,* which is the origin of this new kind of being that he names *Wirheit,* "ourness," the existence under the form of the couple formed by two loving and loved persons. We could even go as far as to say that the analysis of the relation to the other in Levinas refers to this kind of relation, that is, seduction, rather than to the image that we commonly have of love as a necessarily reciprocal relation.

It is also the case for Sartre, who has been in this respect a very important source of inspiration for Levinas. Sartre understands the relation to the other as a unilateral relation, as the fact of being looked at by the other without being oneself able to look at him. For Sartre, when the other appears in front of me, I experience the loss of my universe, which means that the experience that I have now of myself is the passive experience of being seen by the other. He declares in *Being and Nothingness*: "Being-seen by the other is the truth of seeing the other," so that "the other is on principle the one who looks at me."[4] The only possible experience of the other is the experience of my being for the other: it is a passive and not an active experience, the "traumatic" experience of becoming an object for the other. For Sartre the other is the possessor of a secret that escapes the ego and which is its very appearance for the other. Sartre explains in a very convincing manner that love necessarily includes seduction: because the beloved is only a look, "he can not will to love. Therefore the lover must seduce the beloved and his love can in no way be distinguished from the enterprise of seduction."[5] For what is seduction? It is, as Sartre shows, "to risk assuming my object-state completely for the other," "to risk

3. Emmanuel Levinas, *Totalité et infini. Essai sur l'extériorité* (Le Livre de Poche, 1990), 21 sq. *Totality and Infinity,* trans. Alphonso Linguis (Duquesne University Press, Pittburgh, 1969), 34.

4. Jean-Paul Sartre, *Being and Nothingness*, english translation Hazel Barnes (Washington Square Press, 1956), 345–346.

5. Ibid., 484.

the danger of being-seen in order to appropriate the other in and by means of my object-ness," because on this level I can "engage in battle by making myself a *fascinating* object."[6] But precisely because the enterprise of conquering love is identified with the enterprise of seduction, the result can only be failure. Fascination cannot by itself succeed in producing love, because being fascinated does not mean being in love: "Seduction will perhaps determine me to risk much to conquer the Other-as-object, but his desire to appropriate an object in the midst of the world should not be confused with love."[7] Love can be possible only between two free subjects. But for Sartre all relation to the other is based on an objectification and alienation that cannot allow any reciprocity. For him, love is a contradictory effort to surmount the separation of consciousnesses: "I demand that the other love me and I do everything possible to realise my project; but if the other loves me, he radically deceives me by his very love. I demanded of him that he should found my being as a privileged object by maintaining itself as a pure subjectivity confronting me; and as soon as he loves me he experiences me as subject and is swallowed up in his objectivity confronting my subjectivity."[8] Sartre's conclusion is the following: "The problem of my being-for-others remains therefore without solution. The lovers remain each one for himself in a total subjectivity."[9] For Sartre, the only possible experience of "ourness" can be found on the level of work or of play, but not on the level of love, because for him the relation to the other is in principle a relation of competition and conflict and not one of harmony and *philia*. This is the same for Levinas, where the very idea of "ourness" cannot be found, because the starting point of his analysis is the solitude of the subject, who can become, as Levinas says in *Otherwise than Being,* the hostage of the other, because he reads an infinite demand in his face.[10] There is here also a kind of fascination or seduction in what Levinas

---

6. Ibid.

7. Ibid., 488.

8. Ibid., 490.

9. Ibid.

10. Emanuel Levinas, *Autrement qu'être ou au-delà de l'essence* (Le Livre de Poche, 1991), 177, *Otherwise than Being or Beyond Essence,* trans. Alphonso Lingis (Pittsburgh: Duquesne, 1998).

calls the "epiphany" of the other as face, the appearance of the other being in itself the seduction of the invisible, of the infinite, of what in the other escapes radically all attempts to possess and dominate him.

To this erotic conception of the relation with others, which can be found in Sartre and Levinas, it is possible to oppose another conception of love as a community of subjects, which can be found not only in Binswanger, but also in Merleau-Ponty, who conceives love on the basis of a true reciprocity and dialogue between two subjects. What is really interesting in this respect in Merleau-Ponty is the fact that there is not for him a definite limit between the subjects who are in relation with each other primarily through their bodies. Instead of giving himself as a basis the solitude of the ego, of the one who is looked at – as it is the case for Sartre – or the one to which the face of the other reveals itself – as is the case for Levinas – Merleau-Ponty considers that there is a real "intercorporeality" between the subjects,[11] which implies that there is a kind of primary familiarity and community with others. Instead of seeing in the struggle of consciousnesses the only possible relation to others, Merleau-Ponty understands on the contrary this relation as originarily based on a common mode of being to the world. This originary familiarity with others comes from the fact that the human being is not completely individualized in the sense that it is not me as a personal subject who sees the world, but a pre-personal and anonymous subject, so that the other can also see the same world and also participate in the pre-personal subjectivity that we both are through our embodiment. It is therefore not possible to conceive of subjectivity as traditional modern philosophy does, that is as a pure immanence or interiority, as a pure identity with oneself, because we are still "natural beings" and because nature is not only outside me, but in me, "discernible at the centre of subjectivity,"[12] as Merleau-Ponty says in the chapter on "Other selves and the human world" in *Phenomenology of Perception*. I am not the author of my own existence, I do not decide upon the passing of time, and this is the reason why I

---

11. Cf. Maurice Merleau-Ponty, *Signs*, English translation Richard C Mc Cleary (Evanston: Northwestern University Press, 1964), 168.
12. Maurice Merleau-Ponty, *Phenomenology of perception*, English translation Colin Smith (Routledge, London, 1962), 346.

cannot really become a full individuality. As Merleau-Ponty says, "my voluntary and rational life knows that it merges into another power which stands in the way of its completion, and gives it a permanently tentative look."[13] This means that "the lived is thus never entirely comprehensible," and that "in short, I am never quite at one with myself. Such is the lot of a being who is born, that is who once and for all has been given to himself as something to be understood."[14] I do not constitute myself, but I am born, which means that I have the foundation of my own being in somebody other than me, and that I am given to myself so that I will never be able to completely coincide with myself, in the sense that an anonymous life will always remain in myself, as something that I cannot completely master. I am already in communication with other living beings through the mere fact that I have sensory functions, a visual, auditory and tactile field, because I experience my own body as the power of adopting certain patterns of behaviour and in this respect I discover the body of the other as "a miraculous prolongation of my own intentions"[15] in the sense that his or her behaviour could have been mine, because it is for me a familiar way of dealing with the world.

This originary being with others is also the basis of this properly human relation that is dialogue. We are already in communication with others through our behaviour, and gestures. The situation is the same on the level of speech, which Merleau-Ponty understands as being "a particular gesture": on this level also, we are not face to face with the other, but insofar as we belong to the same cultural world and to the same language, "we encroach upon one another,"[16] because my acts of expression and the other's have the same basis: the institution of a common language which constitutes already by itself an intersubjective world. There is therefore a similarity between corporeality and language: "The common language which we speak is something like the anonymous corporeality which we share with other organisms."[17]

13. Ibid., 346–347.
14. Ibid., 347.
15. Ibid., 354.
16. Ibid.
17. Ibid.

But this establishes only a "virtual" communication with the other in general, with a species-individual which is not really present. When I really begin to communicate with a real other, when I am no longer on the general level of language and communication, but on the level of *actual* speech, our common situation is no longer only "a community of being, but a community of doing,"[18] which means that here we are on a creative level. As Merleau-Ponty explains in *The Prose of the World,* in a chapter dealing with "Dialogue and the Perception of the Other," on the level of speech, "there is no longer that alternation which makes a rivalry of the relation between minds,"[19] because when I speak, I am at the same time active and passive, as well as when I am listening, so that speaking is not only my own initiative and listening is not only submitting to the initiative of the other.[20] For Merleau-Ponty, dialogue does not consist of the mere face to face of two subjects, who are opposed to each other by way of different views on the real, but it is a common attempt aiming at the manifestation of truth. A dialogue is not a duel between two consciousnesses who want to dominate each other, but a participation of two speaking beings in the becoming of truth. Truth needs to be expressed because, as Merleau-Ponty points out, "the foundation of truth is not outside time."[21] When we express a truth, we have the feeling that it was always true, but in fact there is no truth "before" its expression in actual speech, there is no truth that could "exist" without being expressed, which means that it can and must be shared by others.

Love is therefore nothing else than the creation of a new manner of being with the other, the invention of a dialogue which takes place in a common world, in what Merleau-Ponty calls sometimes an "interworld," which is the world common to several subjectivities that are not enclosed in themselves. Merleau-Ponty, in opposition to Sartre, does not use the word "seduction;" rather, he speaks of "false and illusory love" when describing the illusions that we can have in regard

18. Ibid.
19. *La Prose du monde* (Paris: Gallimard, 1969) trans. John O'Neill, *The Prose of the World* (Evanston: Northwestern University Press, 1973), 143.
20. Ibid., 144.
21. Ibid.

to ourselves.[22] In the case of an "illusory love," what is loved is not "the individual manner of being which is that person itself" but only some of its qualities.[23] In such a love, in opposition to true love, the lover is not himself "wholly captured," for "areas of his past and future life escaped the invasion," and he maintains within himself "corners set aside for other things." Such a love has been described by Stendhal in his essay "On love" where he compares love to the phenomenon of "crystallization:" one can embellish a being by giving him qualities that he otherwise did not possess in the same way that it is possible to convert the small branch of a tree into a jewel of crystal by merely throwing it into the salt mines of Salzbourg.[24] Such an illusory love has a subject which is itself imaginary, because in that case the loving subject is like an actor playing a role, as far as his whole being is not truly engaged in this relation to the other. By his description of "false love" Merleau-Ponty makes us understand that seduction can take a very superficial form, which presupposes, on the side of the one who is seduced as well as on the side of the one who seduces, the playing of a game, the construction of an unreal relation in both of them, which often ends when it reveals itself as unreal without causing too much damage to either partner.

It is therefore possible to show that amongst the philosophers who have participated in the phenomenological movement, some of them, like Sartre and Levinas, have an erotic conception of love, whereas others, like Merleau-Ponty and Binswanger, have a conception of love as *philia*, which alone allows the emergence of a "community of love." The founder of phenomenology, Edmund Husserl, already saw in such a "community of love" the realization of true intersubjectivity, because

22. *Phenomenology of Perception*, 378.
23. Ibid.
24. Cf. Stendhal, *De l'amour* (Paris, Hypérion, 1936), 4 : "Aux mines de Saltzbourg, on jette dans les profondeurs abandonnées de la mine un rameau d'arbre effeuillé par l'hiver; deux ou trois mois après, on le retire couvert de cristallisations brillantes: les plus petites branches, celles qui ne sont pas plus grosses que la patte d'une mésange, sont garnies d'une infinité de diamants mobiles et éblouissants: on ne peut plus reconnaître le rameau primitif. Ce que j'appelle cristallisation, c'est l'opération de l'esprit, qui tire de tout ce qui se présente la découverte que l'objet aimé de nouvelles perfections."

in it the subjects are completely intertwined in one another, because, as he wrote in one of his manuscripts "the lovers do not live side by side, neither the one with the other, but in one another."[25]

*

It is time now to come to the second problem to be solved, the relation between love and care. As was already mentioned, Binswanger raises the objection to Heidegger that he leaves no room for love in his conception of the relation with others, because he understands it on the basis of care, as concern or solicitude (*Fürsorge*). It seems that, in opposition to Medard Boss – another Swiss psychiatrist who belongs also to the phenomenological movement – Binswanger did not show a great interest for section 26 of *Being and Time* in which Heidegger opposes two positive forms of concern to the forms of our relation to others in everydayness, both of which are characterized by a deficient concern or by sheer indifference. In the first positive form of concern, one takes the other's care away from him and puts oneself in his place in taking care. In this concern, the other can become dependant and dominated. In the second form of concern, one does not try to put oneself in the place of the other in order to take care away from him, but one tries first to give it back to him and to let him be free to assume by himself his own existence. Medard Boss was struck by this definition of authentic concern and saw in it the description of the ideal therapeutic relation between the psychiatrist or analyst and his patient. In the seminars that Heidegger gave in Medard Boss' house in Zollikon from 1959 to 1969, he came back to the question of authentic concern, putting it in relation with Socrates' maieutic method,[26] because authentic concern does not allow the domination of the therapist over the patient, but, on the contrary, aims at liberating him so that he can recover his freedom, which implies that therapy has to become super-fluous as soon as possible.

On this basis Medard Boss develops a theory of transference (*Über-*

---

25. Edmund Husserl, *Zur Phänomenologie der Intersubjektivität 1928–1935,* Husserl-iana Band XV (Nijhoff, den Haag, 1973), 174.
26. Martin Heidegger, *Zollikoner Seminare,* ed. Medard Boss (Klostermann, Frankfurt am Main, 1987), 303.

tragung), which is very different from Freud's own conception of transference as projection of an affect on the psychoanalyst and consists of
a temporary interference of the therapist, who has to help the patient
to find by himself an access to freedom and health. The interference
of the therapist in the curing process constitutes only an "occasion"
for the patient to recover the full possession of all his capacities, the
therapist being not at all the efficient "cause" of his recovering. This
authentic concern, which, as Heidegger says, "leaps ahead of the other" is the authentic help which lets the other be as a being which is
constantly and fundamentally caring for itself. It is according to
Heidegger the highest possible form of the relation to the other. This
is the reason why in the *Zollikoner Seminare*, Heidegger's answer to
Binswanger consists in declaring that love as well as its contrary, hate,
is founded upon care.[27]

Binswanger is nevertheless not completely wrong when he points
out that Heidegger does not speak of love. We find indeed in Heidegger
only some hints on this subject. He gives only a brief definition of love
at the beginning of his *Letter on Humanism*, a letter written to Jean
Beaufret just after the war. He explains there that "to embrace a thing
or a person in its essence means to love it, to favor it" so that love can
be understood as "to bestow essence as a gift," such favoring being
"the proper essence of enabling" which "can let something essentially
unfold in his provenance, that is, let it be". And he adds: "It is on the
strength of such enabling by favoring that something is properly able
to be."[28] Love is therefore understood on the basis of authentic concern
as capacity of letting be the other and as "power" to grant to him the
possibility of unfolding himself. Heidegger finds here again the
Augustinian definition of love of which he spoke in his correspondence
with Hannah Arendt, who, in turn, later dedicated her Dissertation to
the concept of love in Augustine.[29] As Heidegger explains in another
letter to a friend of his wife, Elisabeth Blochmann,[30] Augustine defines

27. Ibid., 286.
28. Martin Heidegger, *Basic writings,* English translation David Farrell Krell
(Harper, San Franscico, 1992), 220
29. Hannah Arendt, *Der Liebesbegriff bei Augustin* (Berlin: Springer, 1929).
30. Martin Heidegger – Elisabeth Blochmannn, *Briefwechsel 1928–1969* (Marbach

love by the formula *volo ut sis,* "I want you to be" in the sense of "existing and being such as you are." Such a will is not imposing anything, but on the contrary implies the withdrawal of the willing subject in order to make room for the other. It is a will that wants the alterity of the other, his freedom. In his letters to Hannah Arendt, we also find the idea of a "community of love," which has the form of "ourness." Heidegger wrote to her in May 1925: "All that we can say is that the world is not longer mine or yours, but that it has become ours, that our doings do not belong to me or to you, but to *us.*"[31]

We can therefore find in Heidegger some very interesting sayings about love, especially in his letters to Hannah Arendt, in spite of the fact that this correspondence remains silent on the properly erotic side of their love. Heidegger does not show a lot of interest for seduction, and if we had to clear the space for it in his work, it seems that he could have dealt with this topic only on the level of "inauthentic existence," as an addition to his analyses of these inauthentic behaviours, such as idle talk, curiosity and ambiguity.[32] Idle talk is in fact the meaningless use of language, which aims only at producing an effect in the other. This is precisely, as Plato showed, what constitutes the seducing power of the sophist: the power of giving a being to non being by the sheer magic of the word, in order to dominate the other and place him in a state of dependency. Curiosity is founded on the desire of seeing and has the tendency to give appearances too great an importance, so that the world becomes something like a show or theatre. In this case, it is not the sophist who could be the agent of seduction, but rather the devil himself, the most eminent seducer. In section 36 of *Being and Time*, Heidegger, when analysing curiosity, quotes Augustine again, who pointed out the privilege granted to the eye and to seeing in human existence, but interpreted it in a Christian perspective as concupiscence and lust.[33] The "look" is therefore linked in a fundamental

---

am Neckar, 1990), 23.

31. Hannah Arendt, Martin Heidegger, *Lettres et autres documents 1925–1975* (Paris: Gallimard, 2001), 34.

32. Cf. Martin Heidegger, *Being and Time* (Albany: State University of New York Press, 1996), § 35–38.

33. Ibid., §36 [171].

way to the desire of possession, which reappears again as soon as it has been fulfilled. The curious person can be in this respect identified with the seducer, with for example the character of Valmont in the French novel *Les liaisons dangereuses*, or with Casanova, who constantly needs to seduce another woman and is always searching for something new. Ambiguity, which comes from the fact that the discourse remains undefined and vague, constitutes the very milieu in which seduction can unfold, even if it does not originate out of a an explicit intention to deceive or distort,[34] because seduction requires allusiveness, ambiguity of discourse and behaviour, and involves the possibility of misunderstanding.

Love as the eminent mode of authentic relation to the other could therefore be opposed to seduction as inauthentic relation to oneself and to the other. But this would be a mere repetition of the traditional split between being and appearance, truth and falsity, which dominates the classical way of thinking, but which cannot really explain the power of seduction and the fact that we so often go astray and become the prey of what Merleau-Ponty calls "false love." It is therefore necessary to try to analyse in a more precise manner the phenomenon of seduction, wondering if it is not always more or less at the very origin of true love.

To seduce is in fact always to take the other by surprise, to touch him or her, to force him or her to go out of his or her way, out of his or her habits and out of his or her indifference. If we want to try to rehabilitate seduction, we have to distinguish between two kinds of behavior: on one hand the behavior of the "vile" seducer, who looks for his own pleasure and finds it at the expense of the other and who, like the sophist, plays with non-being and appearance; and on the other hand the behavior of the seductive person who attracts us by his or her natural charm without always being conscious of it and in whom the harmony of being and appearance rather than their discordance is made manifest. The experience of ravishment or rapture – the word indicates in itself the violence of such an experience, but in this case it is an assumed violence – is also the experience of a departure from the normal path. Such an experience can even be

---

34. Ibid., § 77 [175].

deadly, as it is the case in Thomas Mann's novel, *Death in Venice*, which is the story of the involuntary seduction of the old novelist by a beautiful young boy. In both cases, innocent seduction and voluntary seduction, the experience of the seduced person is the same: it is the experience of a de-centering out of his normal sphere of life and of becoming unable to be the master his own existence. Seduction has to do with appearance and its medium is the body. Voluntary seduction consists therefore in embellishing appearances by making use of the multiple tools of seduction which all aim at producing illusion. If the devil is the seducer *par excellence,* it is because he is the master of appearances and illusions, the one who can dissimulate nothingness under the veil of being. The seducer, in opposition to the seductive person, always makes use of violence, because he wants to reduce the seduced person to an instrument in order to use him or her for his own pleasure. But if the seduced person gives way so easily to his or her own bondage, it is because seduction is never sheer violence. Seduction is different from these forms of pure violence which are sadism and masochism; it is a violence that has the appearance of love and which relies upon the victim's approval. This means that the seduced person is never completely passive, he or she remains a self, which implies that there is still a kind of reciprocity in seduction. The seducer relies upon the freedom of the seduced person, upon his or her capacity to be attracted and outwitted. This explains the importance given to the "scene" of seduction, which is very carefully prepared and calculated, especially when the seducer has become something like a "professional" seducer.

"Seduced and abandoned": it was the title of an Italian film from the sixties which gave to understand all the tragedy of seduction.[35] Behind the beautiful appearances, there is nothing, no love, and the unveiling of this nothingness is at the same time the humiliation of the victim, who is at once deprived of her illusions and her virtue. But we have to remember that the victim was never entirely passive, that she responded to the attraction of the seducer, so that she was willing to play the game of seduction and wanted to believe in it. On the side of the seducer, there is also a will to become vulnerable and to remain

---

35. "Seduta et abbandonata", a film of the Italian director Pietro Germi (1964).

open to the signs of love expressed by the seduced person. We cannot therefore oppose in a strict manner activity and passivity, and this implies that there is not on the side of the seducer a sheer decision to seduce, but rather an invitation given to the other to play the game of seduction. Moreover the invitation is not given to anybody but to a definite person who has been chosen and who could be chosen only on the basis of an emotion felt by the seducer. Valmont, who can to some extent be considered as the incarnation of the cold-blooded and machiavellian seducer, is only a literary character and we can wonder if he can ever be found in real life. There is therefore, in spite of all, a co-presence, a being-with of the seducer and the seduced.

Inversely, we have to acknowledge that in order to be loved, it is necessary to begin by seducing the other, by inviting him or her to look in our direction. There is always in the beginning of love a desire to please which can lead to care about one's own appearance in an excessive manner. But this desire to please coexists with the fear of being loved only for some temporary qualities, such as for example beauty or youth.[36] The desire to be loved in an absolute manner can even lead a person to show oneself in a bad light, in order to test the loved person. For what the loving person is looking for is a love deprived of any reason or justification, a love which could be love of the being itself and not only of the appearances.

*

It is quite obvious that love and seduction cannot be understood only in terms of psychology or sociology; they have to do with being itself and are ontological phenomena. In Heidegger's view, their common ontological basis would be care itself, more precisely concern and so-licitude. This makes it impossible for us to continue to oppose seduc-tion and love in a strict manner, following the traditional opposition between being and appearance. If we understand love as being authen-tic concern and seduction as being inauthentic concern, we have to acknowledge that both of them have something in common, which is

36. Cf. Blaise Pascal, *Pensées* (688) : "On n'aime donc jamais personne, mais seule-ment des qualités (...) On n'aime personne que pour des qualités empruntées."

concern itself. The opposition of authenticity and inauthenticity is not similar to the metaphysical opposition of being and appearance, because, as Heidegger emphasizes, we are "at first and most often" inauthentic, authenticity being therefore only a "modification" of inauthenticity which remains our "normal" mode of behaviour in everydayness. Applied to the difference of love and seduction, this means that seduction remains the most common way of relating to others. It therefore has to be acknowledged that wanting to be loved is generally only a desire to be attractive, a want to please, i.e. to dominate the other and to receive pleasure from him. True love would consequently require something like a conversion from inauthenticity into authenticity, which most probably does not happen very often. Seen in this light, true love becomes more improbable than ever.

The Temporality of Sexual Life in Husserl and Freud

NICHOLAS SMITH

Introduction

In this text there are two things I would like to show:[1]

Firstly, that the so-called "timelessness" of the Freudian unconscious, which poses such great interpretative problems, can be elucidated through an interpretation of the concept of *Nachträglichkeit* as it functions in Freud's texts, and showing thereby that there is indeed a temporality specific to the workings of the unconscious. Freud's analysis of early psychic trauma related to sexual phenomena pointed to a serious complication for all believers in the immediate transparency of consciousness. For the "wound" itself was constituted over time, and the possibility of coming to understand the trauma (thereby achieving a certain freedom from its repercussions) was again only possible after the event had passed. The *Nachträglichkeit* involved in the psychoanalytical understanding of sexual trauma thus hinges on a threefold temporal process at work in subjective life.

Secondly, I wish to show (albeit tentatively) that Husserl, in his analyses of time and intersubjectivity, delivered the materials with which a phenomenological clarification of the Freudian idea of *Nachträglich-*

---

1. This text is a reworked version of a paper first presented at the NOSP-conference in Reykjavik in 2006 and then in Stockholm in 2007. I would like to thank the participants there for their comments, in particular Klaus Held and Françoise Dastur. The issues discussed in this text are more fully developed in my book *Towards a Phenomenology of Repression. A Husserlian Reply to the Freudian Challenge* (Stockholm: Acta Universitatis Stockholmiensis, 2010).

keit can be given, at least in its most formal outlines. Since *Nachträgli-chkeit* is essentially tied to the structure of repression (and thus the very constitution of the unconscious), what I am suggesting is a pro-legomenon to a phenomenological clarification of Freudian repression. This clearly suggests the need for further investigations into the phenomenology of sexual life.

It is well known that Freud in virtually all his major works spoke of the unconscious as being timeless (*Zeitlos*). Few attempts have been made – both from phenomenological and analytical philosophers – to clarify what this really means. The same holds *a fortiori* for psychoanalysts. It is also well known that many phenomenological thinkers have argued that the resources of Husserlian transcendental phenomenology are insufficient for a clarification of the Freudian concept of the unconscious. In the general phenomenological debate, Freud's investigations have served as both a welcome and an important contribution, at least from the second wave of phenomenologically inspired thinkers onwards.[2] By incorporating Freud's insights into their own analyses, and thereby also expanding the original sense it had, the phenomenological unconscious has found itself situated at the crossroads of primary sensibility, drives as pre-intentional structures, and

---

2. Disregarding some negative statements pertaining to the unconscious in general by the early Husserl and also by Martin Heidegger, see Husserl: Hua XII, *Philosophie der Arithmetik. Mit ergänzenden Texte (1890–1901)*, ed. Lothar Eley (Den Haag: Nijhoff, 1970), 59; Hua XIX/1, *Logische Untersuchungen*, ed. Ursula Panzer (Den Haag: Nijhoff, 1984), 72, 75, 398f.
Heidegger: *Reden und andere Zeugnisse eines Lebensweges*, GA 16, ed. Hermann Heidegger (Frankfurt am Main: Klostermann, 2000), 23. The more precise first wave critique by Scheler, Geiger (and later on also Heidegger) criticize Freud as being a part of the *Erlebnis*-psychology (Wundt, Lipps etc.) which was guided by the natural-scientific demands of causality: the unconscious, according to the critics, only serves to fill in the gaps in the causal chain of the lived experiences; see Max Scheler, "Die Idole der Selbsterkenntnis" (1911; 2nd revised and extended ed. 1915) in *Vom Umsturz der Werte* (Francke: Bern, 1955), 281f, 249;
Moritz Geiger, "Fragment über den Begriff des Unbewußten und die psychische Realität" in *Jahrbuch für Philosophie und phänomenologische Forschung* IV (1921), 79; and Heidegger *Zollikoner Seminare*, ed. Medard Boss (Frankfurt am Main: Klostermann, 1994), 260.

pathic-emotional proto-experiences in a pre-linguistic surrounding. Arguing that the further investigation of these themes are of some importance in the overall project of articulating the depth-dimensions of subjectivity, many amongst these phenomenologists have accordingly stated that the Freudian unconscious represents not only an unsurpassable limit for transcendental phenomenology in its Husserlian program of an act-intentionality, but also that a step beyond this program must be taken.

For these thinkers, this means that the very project of transcendental phenomenology must, by implication, undergo more or less substantial revision. This, in one way or another, and with internal variations, holds for Merleau-Ponty, Ricœur, Derrida, Levinas and Michel Henry.[3]

---

3. Just to mention some particularly important points of reference, see for instance Maurice Merleau-Ponty, *Le visible et l'invisible, suivi de notes de travail,* ed. Claude Lefort (Paris: Gallimard, 1999), 292f; Jaques Derrida, *La voix et le phénomène* (Paris: PUF, 1967), 70f, *De la grammatologie* (Paris: Minuit, 1967), 97f. Along a less immediate path, Paul Ricœur in *De l'interprétation. Essai sur Freud* (Paris: Seuil, 1965) is positive toward Freud's deconstruction of Cartesian subjectivity, which shows that there is narcissistic desire and drives operative prior to knowledge, while Husserl's analysis of passive genesis according to Ricœur is only helpful in explaining the constitution of objects and cannot be of help in accounting for the constitution of the subject (408ff, 424f). So for the larger project of engaging Freud's "demystifying" hermeneutics and the "restoration of the sacred" (which is lost to modernity) in a "dialectics," by means of an interpretation of equivocal expressions, "symbols," such as the dream (which is given a paradigmatic position), transcendental phenomenology is of little avail. In the cases of Levinas and Henry the substantiation of this claim would call for more general references, but see for instance Levinas, *Autrement qu'être ou au-delà de l'essence* (Paris: Le livre de poche, 2004), 192ff. Henry from early on criticized Husserl for not being able to conceptualize the sphere of immanence in a sufficiently radical way, and developed his version of "material" or "radical" phenomenology to address this lack. In this project Freud is both friend and foe, whereas transcendental phenomenology in its Husserlian form must be fundamentally reinterpreted; see Michel Henry, *Généalogie de la psychanalyse. Le commencement perdu* (Paris: PUF, 1985), 343ff; *Phénoménologie matérielle* (Paris: PUF, 1990), 175.

The Zeitlosigkeit of the Unconscious

Let me begin by giving just one example of this supposed timelessness of the unconscious. In the 1915 essay "The Unconscious," Freud says:

> The processes of the Ucs [unconscious] system are *timeless*; i.e. they are not ordered temporally, are not altered by the passage of time; they have no reference to time at all.[4]

Of course if we take this (and all similar statements) at face value, we would come up against some insurmountable problems in the theoretical foundations of psychoanalysis. But this denial of any relation between time and the unconscious, instead of being construed as a complete separation, should be understood as calling for deeper investigation, i.e. of a *psychoanalytical* investigation into more originary modes of temporality pertaining to conscious life.[5] There are at least two trends of thought in Freud's texts that support such a hypothesis, and these can be connected so as to form an argument validating my first claim. The first step consists in establishing that the links or interfaces between the unconscious and consciousness that Freud presents are precisely of a temporal nature (I will turn to this right away), and the second step will simply be to show that with the concept of *Nachträglichkeit* the unconscious is made to speak, in the language of time.

---

4. "The Unconscious" in PFL 11, *Penguin Freud Library*, 15 volumes, ed. Angela Richards and Albert Dickson (Hammondsworth: Penguin Books, 1973–1986), 191 / SA III, *Studienausgabe*, 11 volumes, ed. Alexander Mitscherlich, Angela Richards and James Strachey (Frankfurt am Main: Fischer, 1969–1975), 145f.

5. Derrida has pointed the way for my interpretation, by saying that Freud's concept of *Nachträglichkeit* "should lead, if not to the solution, at least to a new way of posing the formidable problem of the temporalization and the so-called "timelessness" of the unconscious. The timelessness of the unconscious is no doubt determined only in opposition to a common concept of time, a traditional concept, the metaphysical concept: the time of mechanics or the time of consciousness. We ought perhaps to read Freud the way Heidegger read Kant: like the cogito, the unconscious is no doubt timeless only from the standpoint of a certain vulgar conception of time" ("Freud and the scene of writing" [1966], in *Writing and Difference*, London: Routledge, 1997, 215).

In the brief text called "Zur Einleitung der Behandlung" (1913), Freud seems to argue against his own convictions; there he states that "the 'timelessness' of our unconscious processes" actually *corresponds* to the long duration of the psychoanalytical cure, which implies that there *is* after all a temporal correspondence between conscious processes and the unconscious.[6] This, if we pause and reflect, is indeed what makes the cure possible, for as Freud states elsewhere: "psychoanalytic treatment is based upon an influencing of the Ucs. from the direction of the Cs., and at any rate [it] shows that this, though a laborious task, is not impossible."[7] How then does Freud go about explaining this correspondence or influence of consciousness to the unconscious?

On Freud's view, it falls upon the preconscious to make communication possible between its contents and those of the unconscious, and thereby the unconscious processes are, so he says at one place, given "an order in time" (*zeitliche Anordnung*).[8] The preconscious thus receives the gifts that the unconscious provides, beyond the control of the active and awakened I, so that the unconscious becomes a source of donation of that which cannot be harboured within the I, that which emerges in various well known forms of enigmae in subjective, everyday life. The preconscious thus "co-operates" with the unconscious, primarily through the so-called derivatives (*Abkömmlingen*) of the unconscious, which are described as a continuation (*Fortsetzung*) of the unconscious into the preconscious.

Through these links, the unconscious is, in return, always susceptible to the ongoings and effects of the awakened life, and it therefore

---

6. This text from 1913 (not available in PFL) is to be found in SA *Ergänzungs Band* (Frankfurt am Main: Fischer Verlag, 1975); see 190. Likewise, in *Beyond the Pleasure Principle*, Freud after having enumerated the negative characteristics of the timelessness of unconscious processes – they are *not* ordered temporally, that time does *not* change them in any way and that the idea of time *cannot* be applied to them – states that these characteristics "can only be clearly understood if a comparison is made with conscious mental processes" (PFL 11, 299f). In a similar vein, cf. "The unconscious": "The full significance of the characteristics of the system Ucs. [...] could only be appreciated by us if we were to contrast and compare them with those of the system Pcs." (192).

7. "The Unconscious," PFL 11, 199.

8. Ibid, 193.

stands in a *reciprocal* relation of influence to the preconscious.[9] Amongst these derivatives of the unconscious, which continuously transgress the border, are phantasies, associations, dreams and bodily symptoms. The preconscious is thus not only the passive receiver of the unconscious material, but rather the co-editor or the co-writer, in that it helps in determining which one of these derivatives is chosen in each case. Being open to these often unwanted gifts, that is to say, accepting that kind of otherness within oneself, is at once a necessary condition for the unravelling of these layers of subjective life, *and* an exposure to danger, a putting oneself at risk, since we thereby make the experience in flesh, that our world is made of the same stuff as that of the insane. These phenomena thus represent the primary modes of what Freud calls a "communication" (*Verkehr*) between the unconscious and consciousness, and this communication is essentially *reciprocal*, in that movements in both directions occur. The distinction between the two systems is therefore by Freud shown to be one that is *relative* and not absolute:

> Study of the derivatives of the Ucs. will completely disappoint our expectations of a schematically clear-cut distinction between the two psychical systems.[10]

So far a connection has been established between time and certain phenomena stemming from the unconscious in Freud's texts, indicating thereby that there must be another concept of time operative than the one that was dismissed in relation to the "timelessness" of the unconscious. That is to say, there must besides this "vulgar" or "natural attitude" concept of time, as Heidegger and Husserl would no doubt have called it, also be a concept of time that corresponds more closely to the specific workings of the unconscious. What is this, and in what direction should an interpretation go searching for it?

---

9. "In brief, it must be said that the Ucs. is continued into what are known as derivatives, that it is accessible to the impressions of life, that it constantly influences the Pcs., and is even, for its part, subjected to influences from the Pcs" ("The unconscious," PFL 11, 194).

10. Ibid.

It has been suggested, both by Derrida and Lacan, that the most central idea to be advanced by Freud, directly impacting on the philosophy of time, is that of *Nachträglichkeit*.[11] Not only is it a constant running through Freud's work, but furthermore this concept stands in the most direct relation to the unconscious in its major manifestations, such as repression, sexuality and memory. What then is the structure of this experience according to Freud? In his most lucid accounts of *Nachträglichkeit*, Freud refers to a threefold series of events, related at first to his theory of trauma and seduction in relation to children. First, there is the occurrence of a shocking event, vibrant with both meaning and emotions, and often of a sexual character. This traumatic event is such that the child cannot comprehend; it remains within her as an indigestible core in the form of a passive enigma: it becomes repressed.

Second, there is the revival of this event at a later stage, say puberty, when the sexual implications that were at first withheld from language and understanding in that sense, resurface. This surfacing is motivated by an association from present day life that connects with the repressed event. This is the constitution of the trauma proper: the growing suspicion that something horrible has happened and that it was related to sexuality becomes a wound in the soul that is always open, bleeding. What is most remarkable from our point of view is the fact that it is the second event which is responsible for, so to speak, filling in the first event with a trauma-constitutive force, something that it did not have by itself:

---

11. Jean Laplanche and Jean-Bertrand Pontalis give credit to Lacan for having reopened the issue of *Nachträglichkeit* in Freud's works; see *The Language of Psychoanalysis* (London: Karnac Books, 1988), 111; however, Derrida should also be mentioned in this context. It is no exaggeration to say that Freud's concepts of repression and *Nachträglichkeit* are amongst the most elementary for the whole enterprise of deconstruction and *différance*, in the early phase. This is clearly legible also in the significance that he describes to these concepts: "Let us note in passing that the concepts of *Nachträglichkeit* and *Verspätung*, concepts which govern the whole of Freud's thought and determine all his other concepts, are already present and named in the *Project*. The irreducibility of the "effect of deferral" – such, no doubt, is Freud's discovery" ("Freud and the scene of writing," 203).

... a memory is repressed which has become a trauma only after the event (*nur nachträglich*).[12]

It is the retardation (*Verspätung*) of the sexual development in children that makes this possible in the classical examples that Freud presents. But there is no real *insight* connected with this second event, i.e., no understanding of *why* severe psychic and/or bodily suffering has occurred and why it has taken the particular forms it has: its origin has not been grasped, and therefore its effects on present day living cannot be overcome.

It is only with the third event that we have true insight that qualifies as an experience of what we may call psychoanalytical truth, and whereby the understanding brings about a "dissolution of the symptom," as the early Freud somewhat exaltedly puts it. This usually only takes place – if at all – many years, or even decades after the first event, and this fact has most certainly been a factor for Freud in the determination of the unconscious as *zeitlos*.[13]

So we see that the basis of the whole idea is the fact that certain past events undergo revision when they are brought back to memory, according to which a new meaning comes to be ascribed to the previous event, a meaning that it did not have at the time. This is what lies behind the choice of words of the English translators of Freud's collected works, when they render *Nachträglichkeit* as "deferred action:" the action which is triggered by the trauma, only comes into being *after* the event. Although thus stressing the performative nature of

---

12. *Project for a Scientific Psychology* [1895], *Standard Edition*, vol. I (London: The Hogarth Press and the Institute of Psychoanalysis, 1953–1974), 435

13. When for instance the Wolfman had reached twenty-five, he recounted the trauma-constitutive event which took place when he was four, and which in turn relates back to the supposed *Urszene* (watching his parents make love) when he was one and a half: "We must not forget the actual situation which lies behind the abbreviated description given in the text: the patient under analysis, at an age of over twenty-five years, was putting the impressions and impulses of his fourth year into words which he would never have found at that time [*nach 25 Jahren Eindrücken und Regungen [...] Worte verleiht, die er damals nicht gefunden hätte.*]" From the *History of an Infantile Neurosis* [1918] PFL 9, *Case Histories II*, 278n/SA VIII, *Zwei Kinderneurosen*, 163n.

recollection, its "dynamic" effects (when the trauma-to-be changes its manifestation from *dynamis* to *energeia*), a mechanistic-causal cloud threatens to obscure Freud's intentions: for what is at stake is certainly more than the postponement of an action from time A to time B. What this translation occludes is the ancient light, that black sun that still, through Freud's own words, discloses the fundamental experience which can be said to govern all his undertakings: Œdipus' moment of truth.[14] Thus speaking of the understanding available in the case of the Wolfman as an adult in analysis, Freud says: "This is simply a second instance of *Nachträglichkeit*."[15] What happens here is the becoming flesh, so to speak, of a logos previously hidden (which has always been the central task of psychoanalysis), through the long and arduous task of bringing an experience which was previously wordless to words. This performative or constitutive power of logos reveals itself by bringing into being an event that – perhaps, but how could we ever know? – did not exist prior to its articulation, but which yet, and this is the interesting complication, is not a mere figment of the imagination (whatever that would be): its relationship to truth rules such an option out. The relation between this logos and truth is thus groundless in any empirical sense – at least in the sense that there is no one single event there, in the history of her subjective life, to which

---

14. In his reading of the Sophoclean tragedy, which takes us underneath its Appolinian surface, Nietzsche argues that the "inside and horrors of nature," which manifest themselves there, can only be seen (of course it is the eye that is at stake here) through a kind of inversion or destruction of normal seeing: "When after a forceful attempt to gaze on the sun we turn away blinded, we see dark-colored spots before our eyes, as a cure, as it were [*gleichsam als Heilmittel*]; conversely, the bright image appearances of the Sophoclean hero – in short, the Appolinian aspect of the mask – are the necessary offspring from a glance into the inside and horrors of nature, as it were, luminous spots to cure eyes damaged by gruesome night"; *The Birth of Tragedy*, § 9, tr. W. Kaufmann (New York: Random House, 1967); tr. mod.

15. "*Es ist dies einfach ein zweiter Fall von Nachträglichkeit*" (SA VIII, 163n / PFL 9, 278n; tr. mod.). The English translation has: "This is simply another instance of deferred action"; but that misses the point: it is precisely a *second* instance, one that occurs after the trauma has been constituted (which represents the first instance), and now with the "full" understanding.

a statement could correspond in adequation. Instead it gains another ground by means of recourse to dreams, phantasies and reconstructions of the past. Our experience of truth thus finds itself hovering between an event which at the time of its occurrence was devoid of meaning, and a later reconstruction when its "truth" can no longer be empirically checked with reality. Thus, we are at a loss, hanging over the abyss between on the one hand the craving for solid, empirical truth, and on the other the impulse to give it all up to fancies of the imagination, all the while refraining from accepting either of these alternatives. By way of bringing to a close this first part, it seems as if the "timelessness" of the unconscious is something that can actually be overcome (*Überwindung*), but only by subjecting oneself to the temporality that inheres in the unconscious, as it manifests itself in consciousness for those with eyes that are no longer eyes – eyes that, as Nietzsche has it, are able to see around corners, or as with Oedipus, that are able to see only after they are no longer there. Thus instead of being a question of a mere time-lapse, such as that between stimuli and a postponed response (even in more sophisticated forms), Freud's concept of *Nachträglichkeit* corresponds to Oedipus' moment of truth.

In search for a point of transition to take us from this Freudian topic to phenomenology, and thus to move to my next hypothesis, I will suggest that Husserl's analysis of *conflict* in our engagement with the world, of *Widerstreitsbewusstsein* (which activates concepts such as *Hemmung, Verdrängung, Deckerinnerungen* etc.), played out as it is in the perceptual field, serves as a highly relevant first stop.[16] What primarily characterizes the Freudian unconscious is that it manifests itself precisely in conflicts with our ordinary experience and expectations, i.e. as breaches in experiential life. Without going into details, one must at least state that 1) Husserl did indeed reflect systematically on these issues, and 2) that temporality is undoubtedly at work underneath these phenomena of conflict, so that inner time-consciousness is shown to be the formal framework in which the breaches of experience

---

16. Already in *Logische Untersuchungen* Husserl speaks of the synthesis of knowledge as a consciousness of a certain *Übereinstimmung*, and notes that to this there always corresponds the possibility of *Nicht-Übereinstimmung*, i.e. of *Widerstreit* (XIX/2, §§ 11f, 32–35). This analysis is repeatedly taken up in later texts.

are synthesized, and possibly also therefore the phenomena pertaining to the unconscious.

Phenomenological clarification
of Nachträglichkeit

But in order to reach my last point concerning the possibility of a phenomenological clarification of the formal aspects of the concept of *Nachträglichkeit*, I must proceed to other fields, more directly related to this issue.

In Husserl's analysis of retentional consciousness, it is shown how the relation between the *Längsintentionalität* and the *Querintentionalität* gives an account of both the pre-objective self-manifestation of the flow and of hetero-manifestation (preceding both the constitution of the I and the world).[17] According to this theory, each retention is connected to the whole previous sequence of retentions, thus forming the backbone so to speak of my inner history. This is, formally speaking, what makes possible my return to previous events, memory, recollection etc. Let us see how this takes on a more concrete shape in Husserl's analysis of the intersubjective reduction, first presented in the 1910–11 lecture series, *Grundprobleme der Phänomenologie*.[18]

His analysis proceeds stepwise, first by insisting that the Cartesian reduction to immanence must be extended and complemented by a new reduction: "we discover the noteworthy fact that each lived experience permits of a double reduction," that is to say, one that also reaches into the *horizons* that surround that which is apodictically given in *Gegenwärtigung*, i.e. to include also the sphere of *Vergegenwärtigungen*.[19] This means that we reduce not only the punctual ego

17. Hua X, *Zur Phänomenologie des inneren Zeitbewusstseins (1893–1917)*, ed. Rudolf Boehm (Den Haag: Nijhoff, 1966), § 39; Nr. 54.
18. Hua XIII, *Zur Phänomenologie der Intersubjektivität. Texte aus dem Nachlass. Erster Teil: 1905–1920*, ed. Iso Kern (Den Haag: Nijhoff, 1973), Text Nr. 6 "Aus den Vorlesungen 'Grundprobleme der Phänomenologie' WS 1910/11" (111–194).
19. Ibid., § 34 "Aufhebung einer künstlichen Einschränkung. Die Gewinnung des phänomenologischen Bewusstseinsstromes im Ausgang von der natürlichen Reflexion auf den Bewusstseinsstrom und die doppelte phänomenologische Reduktion," 177.

cogito, but also the sphere of its "retentions, rememberings, expectations."[20] It is only by doing so that the "artificial restriction," which characterizes the previous presentations of the reduction in for instance *Die Idee der Phänomenologie,* can be *aufgehoben.*[21]

Then in a further step, Husserl shows how this also holds in the case of the other, so that we can reduce not only my empathizing with the other, that is to say, my living-myself-into-her-life, but also *her* as empathizing with *me*, i.e. her living-herself-into-my-life.[22] I will briefly return to this intersubjective reduction at the end, or more specifically, to how it is presented in relation to the intentionality of the drives. When for instance the reduction is applied to a memory, a recollection, then we also reduce and thus make available for transcendental inquiry that which was given in the *background* of the thing or event that was then at the center of attention, so that its whole horizon becomes a possible theme. This paying attention to that which at the time one gives scant attention, i.e. to the background, which, Husserl says, can only occur *nachträglich.* So that with this new, double reduction, all that which is in one way or another intentionally connected to the first thing or event, becomes available in the transcendental field for possible retrieval.[23]

But what role is actually ascribed to the concept of *"Nachträglichkeit"* – carefully placed in brackets – here? That is to say, could it be replaced at will, or does its appearance signify something else? It is clear that some concept or other that is able to account for the phenomenon of bringing back to experiential life a whole segment of previously lived experience, must be employed. If *nachträglich* means only this however, then it could indeed be replaced, it seems. But, if we consider the specific context, namely the bringing back of the *horizon* of an object

---

20. Ibid., 178.

21. Ibid., § 34, 177.

22. Ibid., § 39 "Die Gewinnung anderer phänomenologischer Ich durch doppelte phänomenologische Reduktion. Die Natur als Index der Koordination einer Vielheit von Ichmonaden."

23. All this was worked out in greater detail with the notion of intentional implication in *Erste Philosophie II*; see Hua VIII, *Erste Philosophie (1923/4). Zweiter Teil: Theorie der phänomenologischen Reduktion*, ed. R. Boehm (Den Haag: Nijhoff, 1959), 47. Vorlesung: "Intentionale Implikationen und Iterationen."

that was previously perceived, that is to say, the background which was precisely not attended to at the time (and thus not perceived), then, it seems to me, things begin to look different. For what is at stake is the "bringing back" of a background which was never perceived at the time, and which thus has to be constituted *after* the event, for the first time. The hyletic material would be there as a potentiality for constitution, dormant in the sedimented sphere, for it later to be the source of a non-apodictical project of what was there, though one that is always open for confusion and unclarity.

Thus it seems to me that it is clearly not the question of a mere revival of a previously lived experience, but something more along the lines of what Derrida spoke of in relation to the Freudian *Nachträglichkeit*, namely that "it produces the present past."[24] In connection with this, Derrida as an open question asks whether "sexual deferral" really is "the best example or the essence of this movement," and I think that Husserl has been trying to tell him his view on the matter for some time now. This "production" of the past must not be misunderstood; it is not the question of random fabrication, it is of course guided by the object as remembered and other constitutive signals.

The much discussed analogy between the givenness of my own past and the givenness of the other – which is given its paradigmatic presentation in the *Grundprobleme* – for me testify what is at stake: in the deepest respect of the phenomena at hand, i.e. the past and the other, Husserl insists that we must make do with this. The constitution that is at stake occurs in a kind of inevitable greyzone: neither private phantasy nor objective reality, but a reconstruction of a "reality" that was supposed to have occurred. Its evidential validity is of necessity weaker than the object that is at the center of attention, for as far as the latter is concerned, there is always a possibility of comparison with how it is at first remembered, and how it can be presented through an

---

24. "This impression has left behind a laborious trace which has never been perceived, whose meaning has never beeen lived in the present, i.e., has never been lived consciously. The postscript which constitutes the past present as such is not satisfied, as Plato, Hegel, and Proust perhaps thought, with reawakening or revealing the present past in its truth. It produces the present past." "Freud and the scene of writing," 215.

act of recollection, where our searchlight is set upon the recalling of details that we want to fill out. This is why Husserl always insisted how the Cartesian way to the reduction has evidential priority over and above the non-Cartesian ways, which supplement it (such as the psychological way, which is foreshadowed here). The tentative outcome of this is that *Nachträglichkeit* in the more radical Freudian sense is to at least some extent, operative in Husserl's first analysis of the extended reduction to intersubjectivity through an intentional analysis of *Vergegenwärtigung*.

Later on, the development of genetic phenomenology led Husserl to again consider the possibility of unconscious contents becoming conscious at a later point. For as he says in a text from 1926, it is possible that there are affective tendencies arising out of that which is repressed in the "unconscious," whilst our attention is directed to other matters:

> Perseverance. There may therefore exist continuous affections from the unconscious, but such that are suppressed. Intensive attention – this brings about the suppression of affections that stem from an interest, but a different interest than the one that is intensely attended to. In the moving present something new arises, which favours something suppressed and awakens it.[25]

And in a yet later text Husserl also approaches the aspect of *Nachträglichkeit* that Freud calls the "revision" of a former event through a present recollection. "At the time I only had eyes for this and that," Husserl says in this manuscript, "but I could have seen it in a different light, since the recollection shows now that it is different than I thought it was." He goes on:

---

25. Hua XI, *Analysen zur passiven Synthesis. Aus Vorlesungs- und Forschungsmanuskripten (1918–1926)*, ed. M. Fleischer (Den Haag: Nijhoff, 1966); Beilage XXIX "Zur Phänomenologie der Assoziation" [1926], 416. The German text reads: "Perseverance. Es können also aus dem 'Unbewussten' fortlaufend Affektionen da sein, aber unterdrückt. Intensive Aufmerksamkeit – Unterdrückung von Affektionen des Interesses, aber eines andern Interesses. In der beweglichen Gegenwart Neues, das einem Unterdrückten zugute kommt und es aufweckt."

> But precisely this constant possibility to let my present powers of interest play a part in the representified past, and from now onwards not only bring to words how that past concretely was, but also to bring to words *nachträglich* that which "lies" within it, is never the less important also from a constitutive perspective.[26]

Here Husserl indeed seems to discuss something like the general possibility of *Nachträglichkeit*, understood in its Freudian sense, were it not for the lack of references to sexual life. If transcendental phenomenology would have nothing to do with sexuality, then it would be more difficult to pursue the present task.[27]

Now it seems to me that the question can be pushed further, once the intentional analysis advances so that the formal and slightly dry investigation of temporality is disclosed in its concreteness – of course through experiences of the flesh, and notably the flesh of the other. With the reduction to the "living present" (*lebendige Gegenwart*), which is presented in several major later texts, for instance in the C-manuscripts, *Crisis* and Hua XV, Husserl at one place describes what he calls the "originary structure" (*Urstruktur*) of the living present as consisting in originary kinaesthesia, originary feelings and originary drives:

> Now I consider whether not by means of the *Rückfrage* we finally come up with the originary structure in its transformation of primal hyletic

26. D 14/21 [1931–32]. The German text reads: "Aber eben diese beständige Möglichkeit, meine gegenwärtige Interessenkraft in die vergegenwärtigte Vergangenheit hineinspielen zu lassen und vom Jetzt aus nicht nur, sie, wie sie konkret war, sondern was in ihr 'liegt' zu Worte zu bringen, jetzt, nachträglich, ist doch wichtig auch in konstitutiver Hinsicht."

27. It should be now already clear that there is reason for questioning the position reached by Derrida on this issue, both in *De la grammatologie* and *La voix et le phénomène*: "It is the problem of the deferred effect (*Nachträglichkeit*) of which Freud speaks. The temporality to which he refers cannot be that which lends itself to a phenomenology of consciousness or of presence and one may indeed wonder by what right all that is in question here should still be called time, now, anterior present, delay, etc." (*De la grammatologie*, 97f). "Ce n'est pas un hasard si les *Leçons* sur la conscience intime du temps confirment la dominance du présent et rejettent à la fois l'"après-coup' du devenir-conscient d'un 'contenu inconscient,' c'est-à-dire la structure de la temporalité impliquée par tous les textes de Freud," *La voix et le phénomène*, 70f.

matter etc. with its originary kinaesthesia, originary feelings, originary instincts. According to this it resides in the fact that the originary material proceeds precisely in a form of unity that is an essential form prior to the worldliness. Thereby the constitution of the whole world seems to be predelineated for me already "instinctively," such that the functions that make this possible themselves have their essential-ABC, their grammar of essence in advance. That is to say that it lies within the fact that a teleology occurs in advance. A full ontology is teleology, but it presupposes the fact.[28]

The primordiality of this structure is best described as a system of drives, and when we understand this primordiality as an originarily standing streaming (*urtümlich stehendes Strömen*), we see that in this streaming, we also find therein the drives that stem from the other and that are directed to me:

The drive can be in a state of undetermined hunger, which does not yet carry its object within itself as its "where to." Hunger in the ordinary sense is more determined, when it as a drive refers to eating – in the originary mode it is directed in a determinate way [...]. In the case of sexual hunger in its determined direction it is the other that is its affecting, alluring goal. This determined sexual hunger has its figure of fulfilment in copulation. In the drive itself lies the relatedness to the other as other, and to her correlative drive. The one and the other drive can have the mode – mode of transformation – of refraining, or of wanting again. In the originary mode it is however an unmodalized drive "without inhibition," which always reaches into the other and

---

28. Hua XV, *Zur Phänomenologie der Intersubjektivität. Texte aus dem Nachlass. Dritter Teil: 1929–1935*, ed. I. Kern (Den Haag: Nijhoff, 1973); Nr. 22 "Teleologie. <Die Implikation des Eidos transzendentale Intersubjektivität im Eidos transzendentales Ich. Faktum und Eidos>" [1931], 385. The German text reads: "Nun bedenke ich aber dass in der Rückfrage sich schliesslich die Urstruktur ergibt in ihrem Wandel der Urhyle etc. mit den Urkinästhesen, Urgefühlen, Urinstinkten. Danach liegt es im Faktum, dass das Urmaterial gerade so verläuft in einer Einheitsform, die Wesensform ist vor der Weltlichkeit. Damit scheint schon "instinktiv" die Konstitution der ganzen Welt für mich vorgezeichnet, wobei die ermöglichenden Funktionen selbst ihr Wesens-ABC, ihre Wesensgrammatik im voraus haben. Also im Faktum liegt es, dass im voraus eine Teleologie statthat. Eine volle Ontologie ist Teleologie, sie setzt aber das Faktum voraus."

whose intentionality of drives has always reached through to the other through her correlative intentionality of drives. In the simple, originary mode of fulfilment we do not have two separate fulfilments each in the one and the other primordiality, but a unity of both primordialities that is brought about by means of the fulfilment of one-within-the-other.[29]

The transcendental framework should not hinder us from seeing what Husserl is saying: the most basic structure of inner time-consciousness, when reduced in a sufficiently radical way, shows that at the heart of ourselves as temporal beings, that old familiar song is played out once again: "I want you, and you want me;" and we are also promised that this is indeed the very first recording. Behind the sober earnestness of the transcendental façade, we thus find Eros and time united in ecstatic entwinement, as two aspects – one concrete and one formal – of one and the same flow:

> In my old doctrine of inner time-consciousness, I treated the intentionality that has been demonstrated here precisely as intentionality – aimed forwards through the protention and modifying itself through retention, although preserving the unity – but I did not there speak of

---

29. Hua XV, Nr. 34 "Universale Teleologie. Der intersubjektive, alle und jede Subjekte umspannende Trieb transzendental gesehen. Sein der monadischen Totalität" [1933], 593f. The German text reads: "Der Trieb in dem einen Individuum und der Wechseltrieb im anderen. Der Trieb kann im Stadium des unbestimmten Hungers sein, das seinen Gegenstand noch nicht als sein Worauf in sich trägt. Der Hunger im gewöhnlichen Sinn ist bestimmter, wenn er triebhaft auf die Speise geht – bestimmt gerichtet im Urmodus [...]. Im Fall des Geschlechtshungers in betimmter Richtung auf sein affizierendes, reizendes Ziel ist dieses der Andere. Dieser bestimmte Geschlechtshunger hat Erfüllungsgestalt im Modus der Kopulation. Im Trieb selbst liegt die Bezogenheit auf den Anderen als Anderen und auf seinen korrelativen Trieb. Der eine und andere Trieb kann den Modus – Abwandlungsmodus – der Enthaltung, des Wiederwillens haben. Im Urmodus ist er eben 'hemmungslos' unmodalisierter Trieb, der je in den Anderen hineinreicht und seine Triebintentionalität durch die korrelative im Anderen hindurchreichen hat. In der schlichten urmodalen Erfüllung haben wir nicht zwei zu trennende Erfüllungen je in der einen und anderen Primordialität, sondern eine sich durch das Ineinander der Erfüllungen herstellende Einheit der beiden Primordialitäten."

the I, did not characterize it as pertaining to the I (in the widest sense of an intentionality of willing).[30]

The drive is a mode of temporalization, and as such a fundamental aspect of self-manifestation, which at the same time is also a fundamental aspect of hetero-manifestation. That is to say, the drives as originary modes of temporalization, are what makes possible the manifestation of myself and of alterity. This process is also inherently spatializing by means of the proto-kinaesthesia that opens my lived body to myself as flesh, the originary process in passivity that discloses my flesh as always already directed towards the other, prior to a distinct "I" or the objectivated givenness of "my lived body" as "separate" from a "you" and "your lived body." This process can also be analyzed from a worldly perspective:

> "Prior" to the world lies the constitution of the world, lies my self-temporization in the pre-time and lies the intersubjective temporization in the intersubjective pre-time. The intersubjective "act of conception" "motivates" new processes in the other, it changes the self-temporization and in the disclosure of the worldly side, as a human, I experience what shows itself there as worldly and what by means of further inductions can be said about this in relation to the physiology of pregnancy.[31]

---

30. Hua XV, Nr. 34 [1933], 594f. The German text reads: "In meiner alten Lehre vom inneren Zeitbewusstsein habe ich die hierbei aufgewiesene Intentionalität eben als Intentionalität [...] behandelt, aber nicht vom Ich gesprochen, nicht sie als ichliche (im weitesten Sinn Willensintentionalität) charakterisiert. Später habe ich die letztere als in einer ichlosen ('Passivität') fundierte eingeführt." See also the reference to "drive-temporality": "Der Lebenstrieb in seinen modalen Verwandlungen einheitlich in seiner einheitlichen Trieb-Zeitlichkeit in einem ständigen Werden, Sich-Verwandeln in Verwandlung der Sondertriebe, die also einzeln, im Miteinander in einer ständigen Genesis stehen, in einer "intentionalen" Genesis, obschon wir hier zuerst in einer *Vorintentionalität* stehen, die in aller expliziten Intentionalität ihre Rolle spielt." B II 3/16b [1934]

31. Hua XV, Nr. 34 [1933], 597 . The German text reads: "'Vor' der Welt liegt Weltkonstitution, liegt meine Selbstzeitigung in der Vorzeit und liegt die intersubjektive Zeitigung in der intersubjektiven Vorzeit. Der intersubjektive 'Zeugungsakt' 'motiviert' in dem anderen Leben neue Prozesse, abgeänderte der Selbstzeitigung, und in der Enthüllung von seiten der Weltlichkeit, als Mensch,

The radicalized reduction leads to an intersubjective streaming that is the foundation of an "originary empathy," and which manifests itself as reciprocal sexual drives. These drives towards the other are also constitutive of my own, pre-egoic selfhood as flesh (*Urleib*), which at a higher level manifests itself as lived body (*Leib*).[32] This originary spacing by means of my own hyletic-temporizing (*Zeitigung*) becoming proceeds at different levels: first as the originary event of proto-kinaesthetic flesh (*Urleib*), and then as pre-reflective givenness of my own lived body (*Leib*) which, (at least as presented in *Cartesian Meditations*) by means of associative pairing then becomes body as objectivated object in nature (*Körper*). These steps permit the full constitution of my lived body as the *Nullkörper* which is my "absolute center of orientation," which Husserl began to analyze already in the 1907 lectures on *Ding und Raum*. And the constitution of the world necessitates the prior constitution of my lived body as a body in nature by means of reflection (one hand touching the other, my seeing my own hand, etc.).[33] My lived body is thus "non-spatial" or pre-spatial in the sense that it precedes the constitution of objective space as its condition of possibility. In originary experience, my lived body as flesh has no progressive movement (*Fortbewährung*) nor rest, only an inner movement and rest that is unlike that of outer objects; it has "extension" but is not subjected to change or spatial consistency like an external body.[34] The radicalized reduction discloses an important aspect of this at a genetically foundational level, by highlighting the implicit bodily self-awareness, the constant self-affection, which is a touching oneself prior to the touch, that sets this whole process in motion:

---

erfahre ich, was da weltlich sich zeigt und was in weiteren Induktionen in bezug auf die Physiologie der Schwangerschaft zu sagen ist."

32. See Hua XIII, 327f; IX, 107.

33. See Dorion Cairns, *Conversations with Husserl and Fink* (The Hague, 1976), 4, 6. This is also developed in many manuscripts; see for instance D 17 [1934]; published in *Philosophical Essays in Memory of Edmund Husserl*, ed. Marvin Farber (Cambridge MA: Harvard University Press, 1940), 307–325.

34. See D 17, in Farber (1940), 315.

In the streaming primal present we already have a ceaseless perception of the lived body, and so in the temporization of immanent time my bodily perception runs through the totality of this time as it synthetically and identically constitutes this same lived body in an all temporal way.[35]

This analysis of the originary pre-empathic intersubjectivity also enables us to understand better the lacunae or blind spots in the account of the constitution of the other in *Cartesian Meditations*. The whole problematics of how to account for the fact that the other, on the one hand, by necessity exceeds my constitutive powers, and, on the other hand, remains inscribed within my horizontal system of noematical givens, can now be recognized as resting on a ground that is moving from a static egology to a genetic order of being, intersubjective from the outset. When Husserl says that the apperception of my lived body as physical body (or quasi-physical, since I can never wholly transform myself into an object in nature) is a "first presupposition for empathy" to come about, the other and I are already engaged in a reciprocal sexual drive-intentionality in this apperception, by virtue of the most originary temporizing-spatializing pre-egoic life in the living present.[36] Thus in order for my flesh to be able to be perceived as body, it is simply necessary that the body of the other is drawn into the process.[37]

35. Husserliana Materialen 8. *Späte Texte über Zeitkonstitution (1929–1934): Die C-Manuskripte*, ed. Dieter Lohmar (Dordrecht: Springer, 2006); Nr. 23 [C6/Aug. 1930] "Vorstoss zu einer Methode des Abbaus, des radikalen Abbaus der vorgegebenen Welt im Rückgang zur strömenden Gegenwart und systematischer Abbau dieser Gegenwart. <Aufdeckung von Kernstrukturen in der immanenten Zeit und der Konstitution der Natur>" 112. The German text reads: "In der strömenden Urpräsenz haben wir unabänderlich immer schon Leibwahrnehmung, und so in der Zeitigung der immanenten Zeit geht durch diese ganze Zeit kontinuierlich hindurch mein Leibwahrnehmen, synthetisch identisch denselben Leib allzeitlich konstituierend."
36. Hua XV, Beilage LIV, 660: "Die Apperzeption meines Leibes als Körper als erste Voraussetzung der Einfühlung;" cf. CM, § 44, 128.
37. On this point, see the innovative analyses by Dider Franck in *Chair et corps. Sur la phénoménologie de Husserl* (Paris: Minuit, 1981), 153: "La chair n'est objective qu'à condition d'être essentiellement en relation à une autre chair." See also Natalie Depraz, *Transcendance et incarnation. Le statut de l'intersubjectivité comme*

In as much as inner time-consciousness in conjunction with passive synthesis of kinaesthesia is generally said to make up the foundation of subjectivity in Husserl's philosophy, we might now venture the statement that sexuality, as an originary drive, and as a concrete form of this kinaesthetic temporalization, is an integral part of the foundation of subjectivity.

With this final step taken, where the living present is shown to consist of an *Urstruktur* that in part consists in sexuality as a *Trieb-zeit-lichkeit*, I think that at least the major components required for a phenomenological clarification of Freud's concept of *Nachträglichkeit* are in place.

altérité à soi chez Husserl (Paris: Vrin, 1995), 132: "Pour que ma chair puisse s'apercevoir comme corps dans le creusement d'un écart d'abord infime du sein de la primordialité, il est nécessaire que soi supposé dès cet instant un autre corps qui, lui ressemblant point par point, s'intrique dans cet écart."

On Flesh and Eros in Sartre's
Being and Nothingness

HELENA DAHLBERG

> At the still point of the turning world. Neither flesh nor fleshless;
> Neither from nor towards; at the still point, there the dance is,
> But neither arrest nor movement. And do not call it fixity,
> Where past and future are gathered. Neither movement from nor
>   towards,
> Neither ascent nor decline. Except for the point, the still point,
> There would be no dance, and there is only dance.
>
> T.S. Eliot, *Burnt Norton*

In the third part of *L'être et le néant* – *Being and Nothingness* – in the chapter on "Concrete relations with others", Sartre says,

> [...] in desire I make myself flesh in *the presence of the Other in order to appropriate the Other's flesh*. This means that it is not merely a question of my grasping the Other's shoulders or thighs or of my drawing a body over against me: it is necessary as well for me to apprehend them with this particular instrument which is the body as it produces a clogging of consciousness. In this sense when I grasp these shoulders, it can be said not only that my body is a means for touching the shoulders, but that the Other's shoulders are a means for my discovering my body as the fascinating revelation of facticity, that is, as flesh.[1]

---

1. Jean-Paul Sartre, *Being and Nothingness* (Routledge, 1958), 389. (Henceforth BN). "[...] dans le désir, je me fais chair en présence d'autrui pour m'appropier la chair d'autrui. Cela signifie qu'il ne s'agit pas seulement de saisir les épaules ou des flancs ou d'attirer un corps contre moi : il faut encore les saisir avec cet inastrument particulier qu'est le corps en tant qu'il empâte la conscience. En ce sens, lorsque je saisis ces épaules, on pourrait dire non seulement que mon corps est un moyen pour toucher les épaules mais que les épaules d'autrui sont un moyen

In my first meeting with this text, it was the presence of the concept of flesh that made me wonder. The flesh is here equated with facticity. And at the same time, Sartre clearly wants to distinguish the desiring relation that gives birth to the flesh from the handling of a pure thing, or from the seizing of a tool. Sartre, by using the concept of flesh, wishes to make visible a relation with the other that is somehow reciprocal, a relation which requires of me a transformation. When aiming at the other's flesh, I cannot simply grab him; I have to apprehend him with my body. Sartre further emphasizes the uniqueness of the desiring relation to the other by asserting that

> Now at first the Other's body is not flesh for me; it appears as a synthetic form in action. [...] The Other's body is originally a body in situation; flesh on the contrary, appears as *the pure contingency of presence*. Ordinarily it is hidden by cosmetics, clothing, etc.; in particular it is hidden by its *movements*. Nothing is less "in the flesh" than a dancer even though she is nude. Desire is an attempt to strip the body of its movements as of its clothing and to make it exist as pure flesh; it is an attempt to *incarnate* the Other's body.[2]

I would now like to take this concept of flesh in *Being and Nothingness* as my starting point for this article. My aim will be to understand what it means – to make sense of it – In order to explore its possibilities, and maybe try to go beyond them as I use it to understand desire and love.

Let us start with how the flesh comes to be. Sartre makes clear that the flesh is born out of desire. Rather than describing my body's transformation into flesh as something that happens to me, Sartre

---

pour moi de decouvrir mon corps comme révélation fascinante de ma facticité, c'est-à-dire comme chair." Jean-Paul Sartre, *L'être et le néant* (Paris: Gallimard, 2003 [1943]), 429. (Henceforth EN).

2. BN, 389 "Or c'est [chair] qu[e le corps d'autrui] n'est pas d'abord pour moi : le corps d'autrui apparaît comme forme synthétique en acte [...] Le corps d'autrui est originellement corps en situation : la chair au contraire apparaît comme *contingence pure de la présence*. Elle est ordinairement masquée par les fards, les vêtements, etc. ; surtout, elle est masquée par les *mouvements* ; rien n'est moins "en chair" qu'une danseuse, fût-elle nue. Le désir est une tentative pour déshabiller le corps de ses mouvemnets comme de ses vêtements et de le faire exister comme pure chair ; c'est une tentative d'*incarnation* du corps d'autrui." EN, 430.

ON FLESH AND EROS IN SARTRE'S "BEING AND NOTHINGNESS"

states that *I make myself flesh in order to appropriate the other's flesh.* This transformation (even desire itself) thus seems to be a strategy that I use in order to get a hold on the other as flesh. What then is desire, and why do I need it as a strategy?

The other is, in *Being and Nothingness* based upon the *look*, that is, the other is first and foremost someone who is *seeing* (me), and therefore *judging* me. Under his eyes my movement is arrested; I can no longer aim to be what I am not, for when the other sees me, he sees what I am. I am thus being determined as this or that, closed up in my own being like a thing.[3] Indeed, Sartre writes that my concrete relations with others "are wholly governed by my attitudes with respect to the object which I am for the Other."[4] The upsurge of desire takes place within this drama of the look.[5] My desire for the other is described as an answer to the feeling of being seen and judged; desire is, in short, born out of the vulnerability that I experience because I am in a world where there are others. And since I am nevertheless responsible for this being that the other sees, since it is *me,* my project from now on will be to recover my own being. But the only way to do this is to assimilate or somehow destroy the Other's freedom, he who sees me. One way to achieve this would be to make myself into a look, with the result that the other's freedom immediately disappears and the other is made into an *object* under my gaze. It is in reply to this failure to capture the other, and in an attempt to capture the other *in his body as well as in his consciousness*, that I choose my flesh. In other words, I aim to enchant the other with my own body as a means. Thus, if the look in Sartre's philosophy is what gives rise to desire, the result of desire is something completely different, for "it is my body as flesh which causes the Other's flesh to be born."[6]

---

3. "For the Other I am irremediably what I am [...] thus the in-itself recaptures me at the threshold of the future and fixes me wholly in my flight [...] But this fixed flight is never the flight which I am for myself; it is fixed *outside.*" BN, 363.
4. Ibid.
5. Indeed, Sartre (after a presentation of the problem and its philosophical tradition) opens the third part of *Being and Nothingness* – the *Being for-others* – with a section on *the look* [*Le regard*] which is then followed by the chapters on *The body* and *Concrete relations with others.*
6. BN, 390, "c'est mon corps de chair qui fait naître la chair d'autrui" EN, 431.

What then is this flesh? For Sartre it is born within the logic of the look, but it can obviously not come into being *by means of* the look, nor can it be maintained by it. My opening quote tells us that the flesh is something that is usually hidden when the body is moving; Sartre tells us that "nothing is less 'in the flesh' than a dancer even though she is nude." The reference to the dancer is significant, as we shall see later when Sartre contrasts this gracefully moving body with the obscene. For now, let us note that when the human body is actively involved in a situation, the body parts can be seen as meaningful constituents of this movement, whereas the flesh is the very same body deprived of its meaning and justification, existing as a pure here and now.

Sartre also tells us that only the *caress* can give birth to the flesh. "the caress is not simple stroking; it is a *shaping*. In caressing the Other I cause her flesh to be born beneath my caress, under my fingers."[7] Should I try to grab hold of the other as I grab hold of a tool, I would destroy the other's presence as flesh. But when I take the other's hand and start caressing it, I discover it as an extension of flesh and bone rather than as a hand. The caress "reveals the flesh by stripping the body of its action, by cutting it off from the possibilities which surrounds it; the caress is designed to uncover the web of inertia beneath the action – *i.e.*, the pure "being-there" – which sustains it."[8]

In order to make the other appear as flesh, I thus have to let my own body go through a transformation. Sartre's description of the desiring relation in *Being and Nothingness* is a description of a reciprocal relation (the only one, I think, that can be found in the chapter on concrete relations with others). In order to reach the other in his flesh, I have to stop trying to escape my own facticity and become presence, wholly and fully. When I, as Sartre describes it, am watching the graceful dancer, and with my look start to discover underneath the leaping legs "the curved extension of the thighs," I have not only made the dancer into flesh, but also myself. The caress, at the same time as it realizes

---

7. BN, 390, "[…] la caresse n'est pas simple effleurement : elle est *façonnement*. En carressant autrui, je fais naître sa chair par mon caresse, sous mes doigts." EN, 430.
8. BN, 390, "la caresse révèle la chair en déshabillant le corps de son action, en le scindant des possibilités qui l'entourent : elle est faite pour découvrir sous l'acte la trame d'inertie – c'est-à-dire le pur 'être-là' – qui le soutient," EN, 430.

the incarnation of the other, discloses my own incarnation to myself. The result of desire is thus a *reciprocal incarnation*.[9] If my body and my facticity are something that I usually pass beyond, then in the desiring mode *I live them*. But at the very moment that I start relating to the other as a moving consciousness with acts and goals, or if for that matter I start using him for my own purposes and thereby make him into an object for me, his fleshiness will disappear as will my own.

What seems to be characteristic for the flesh as it appears in this part of *Being and Nothingness* is thus its non-referentiality. In my ordinary dealings with other human beings, I more or less understand them with reference to their movements. In phenomenological terms, human being is normally understood in his or her dealings with the world, as "in the process of…" or "aiming at…," always on the verge of becoming something else. The same applies to the tool that I use, which is never really appreciated for its own sake, never really seen as what it is on its own unless, as Heidegger notes, the tool breaks, thus causing it to become visible.[10] When the other is experienced as flesh, he is no longer "skipped over" for the benefit of his goals, neither for my own aspirations, but present as it were, here and now. And the means to make the other visible in his flesh is my own incarnation. The ideal of desire is being here and now; *being-in-the-midst-of-the-world* (*l'être-au-milieu-du-monde*).[11]

The Obscene Flesh

But what happens then if the enchantment that desire *is*, is suddenly dispelled? Sartre shows us that when desire fades away, the attractive flesh, marked by facticity and without reason for being, is within a

9. BN, 391 / EN, 431.

10. Martin Heidegger, *Sein und Zeit* (Tübingen: Max Niemeyer Verlag, 1993 [1927]), §16.

11. BN, 392 / EN, 432f. "When I am in the desiring mode," Sartre explains, "the world transforms for me as well, and instead of taking hold of the pen as something that I can write with, what appears to me is rather its weight, its form and the cool feeling it gives me in my hand. I have ceased to transcend the things in the direction of their possibilities, and instead I sense them in their pure 'being-there,' in their flesh."

second transformed into something ridiculous. By describing this transformation, Sartre shows us how close the flesh is to the *obscene*.

> The *obscene* appears when the body adopts postures which entirely strip it of its acts and which reveal the inertia of its flesh. The sight of a naked body from behind is not obscene. But certain involuntary waddlings of the rump are obscene. This is because then it is only the legs which are acting for the walker, and the rump is like an isolated cushion which is carried by the legs and the balancing of which is a pure obedience to the laws of weight. It can not be justified by the situation; on the contrary, it is entirely destructive of any situation since it has the passivity of a thing [...] Suddenly it is revealed as an unjustifiable facticity; it is *de trop* like every contingent. It is isolated in the body for which the present meaning is walking; it is naked even if material covers it, for it no longer shares in the transcendence-transcended of the body in action.[12]

This distinction between the graceful [*gracieux*] and the disgraceful [*disgracieux*] gives us a clear picture of what the flesh can signify if desire is lost. While the graceful is something that is in accordance with its situation, like the dancer's beautifully raised arm or the athlete who stretches his body to the limit of its capacity, the disgraceful flesh is that which is "redundant," excessive or "*de trop*." Every part of the graceful body is in accordance with its movements, every movement is *called for* and has its justification in this situation.[13] But the waddling

---

12. BN, 401 "L'*obscène* apparaît lorsque le corps adopte des postures qui le déshabillent entièrement de ses actes et qui révèlent l'inertie de sa chair. La vue d'un corps nu, de dos, n'est pas obscène. Mais certaines dandinements involontaires de la croupe sont obscènep. C'est qu'alors ce sont les jambes seules qui sont en acte chez le marcheur et la croupe semble un coussin isolé qu'elles portent et dont le balancement est pure obéissance aux lois de la pesanteur. Elle ne saurait se justifier par la situation ; elle est entièrement destructrice de toute situation, au contraire, puisqu'elle a la passivité de la chose et qu'elle se fait porter comme une chose par les jambep. Du coup elle se découvre comme facticité injustifiable, elle est "*de trop*", comme tout être contingent. Elle s'isole dans ce corps dont le sens présent est la marche, elle est nue, même si quelque étoffe la voile, car elle ne participe plus à la transcendance-transcendée du corps en acte..." EN, 441f.
13. "The goal to come illuminates the act in its totality," BN, 400.

rump, on the other hand, is not justified. It just exists in its disgraceful awkwardness.

What then, one may ask again, is this flesh, this pure *"being-there"* (instead of *being for . . .* or *being for the sake of . . .* or *being on the way to . . .*), this "pure contingency of presence," this "being-in-the-midst-of-the-world," this "simple presence"? What kind of presence is it that in a moment can be turned into the obscene and the ridiculous? Is Sartre here evoking the being of plenitude, that fully positive being that Merleau-Ponty in *Le visible et l'invisible* described as "the Great Object" with which science is always preoccupied?[14] Sartre himself seems to suggest that it is indeed the other reduced to a thing that I have in front of me, a thing, that is, which has lost its meaning along with its justification. For example, he describes the world of desire as a "destructured world which has lost its meaning," a world in which things stick out "like fragments of pure matter, like brute qualities," and that to be made flesh is to be reduced to "pure matter," "stripped of meaning," that it is to be made into a "pure mucous membrane."[15] Nevertheless, Sartre's treatment of the flesh elsewhere suggests something different.

Flesh as Being for Others

It is evident that the concept of flesh plays an important role in Sartre's philosophical works as well as in his novels. But whenever it appears it is almost always marked by trouble. In *Being and Nothingness*, flesh and desire are associated with a "clogging of consciousness," with "being swallowed by the body," and with "a yeasty tumescence of fact." Similarly, in the novel *Nausea*, there is a passage where the main character is passing by a butcher shop, and while looking at the garnished pigs' trotters and sausages he sees in the window a fat girl who generously reveals her breasts and who at the same time takes a piece of dead meat [*chair*] with her fingers. And in the next sentence, Sartre tells us, "(i)n his room five minutes from there, monsieur

---

14. Maurice Merleau-Ponty, *Le visible et l'invisible* (Paris: Gallimard, 1964), 31.
15. BN, 395f / EN, 435f.

Fasquelle was lying, dead."[16] I think this passage reveals to us more than anything the trouble that the flesh marks for Sartre. The flesh is anything but a neutral inanimate "thing" in front of our eyes. On the contrary, the flesh gains its power, its nausea, from the fact that it was once graceful movement. But despite its troublesome character, the centrality and the frequency of the concept in *Being and Nothingness* shows us that it has not been chosen by coincidence.

In *Being and Nothingness*, the flesh shows up for the first time when Sartre depicts the body's different modes of being in the chapter on "The Body."[17] If this chapter as a whole can be said to establish the difference between being-for-itself and being-for-others (while at the same time showing that all of science is based on being-for-others and fails to see the being-for-itself), the flesh can be found within this difference. For if the first dimension of the body (being-for-itself) is the body as it is lived, the second dimension, Sartre explains, is the body insofar as it is *utilized and known by the other*.[18] Sartre uses the flesh to describe this latter mode of others' existence for me and equates it at the same time with facticity.[19] If the other thus shows up in my world as something that I can know and utilize, and if this aspect of the other can be termed as "flesh," is the flesh subsequently to be understood as a thing in front of me that suddenly blocks my path? At times Sartre himself seems to suggest this. In order to shed light on the concept of flesh, Sartre writes that the other's facticity is usually hidden or masked by clothes, make-up and gestures, but that there will always come a time when the mask falls and the other is exposed in the pure contingency of his presence, that is, in his flesh. The "flesh"

---

16. Jean-Paul Sartre, *Nausea* (New York: New Direction Books, 1964), 74.

17. It may be noted that this is the chapter which precedes the chapter on concrete relations with others.

18. BN, 351 /EN, 392.

19. "What for the Other is his *taste of himself* becomes for me the *Other's flesh*. The flesh is the pure contingency of presence." BN, 343, "C'est qui est *goût de soi* pour autrui devient pour moi *chair de l'autre*. La chair est contingence pure de la presence." EN, 384. Cf EN p. 388: "cette immobilité d'être toujours dépassé, jamais realisée, à laquelle je me réfère perpétuellement pour nommer ce qui est en movement, c'est la facticité pure, la pure *chair*, le pur *en-soi* comme passé perpétuellement passéfié de la transcendence-transcendée."

thus seems to be very close to a kind of everyday understanding of the concept as the naked skin, concealed by a beard or a piece of clothing that can be made to fall off at any moment, an understanding that indeed comes close to that of an inanimate thing. But the flesh, as we have already seen, is clearly a richer and more complicated concept in *Being and Nothingness*. I would now like to point to two circumstances that show the complexity of this concept.

Firstly, the other does not suddenly show up in his flesh when his thing-body intersects with my look. The other, Sartre writes, has in fact been indicated to me all along by other things in the world. When the other is absent, the chair in which he used to sit points me to him, and the letter from him gives me his "being-elsewhere-in-my-world." Consequently, when the other actually walks through the door, his presence does not alter the world's fundamental structure of revealing others to me. But then what is it that changes when the other walks through the door? Suddenly, Sartre writes, the other appears "on the ground of the world as a *this* which I can look at, apprehend, and utilize directly."[20] Sartre thus describes the other's presence as flesh, on the one hand, as an appearance on the ground of an absence, and on the other hand as facticity, that is, as characterized by a simultaneous necessity and contingency, the contingency of being here instead of someplace else and the necessity to be somewhere. More than anything therefore, the use of the term "flesh" seems to be precisely a way for Sartre to describe this indescribable "being there," this presence of something, this sudden but simple appearance of a radiant being.

This supposition is strengthened by the fact that Sartre, in the beginning of the section on the body-for-others, seems to use the term "flesh" in a less deliberate way. A common way of accounting for the other's presence in the world, Sartre writes, is by describing him or her as an object, as an instrument indicated by other things. The other is then "a point of view on which I can have a point of view, an instrument that I can use with other instruments."[21] But this way of describing the other, Sartre claims, "does not give us his being-there '*in flesh and*

---

20. BN, 342 "[...] sur fond de monde comme un *ceci* que je peux regarder, saisir, utiliser directement." EN, 382.
21. BN, 340/EN, 380.

bone'."[22] This linguistic expression, and others similar to it – such as "in the flesh" – suggests the connotations of presence and manifestation that "flesh" has in language and that Sartre is evoking by his very use of the term.

Secondly, the flesh in *Being and Nothingness* cannot be reduced to an enclosed thing since Sartre goes to great lengths to show that if the experience of the other as flesh would be that of an isolated object, we would really be experiencing a corpse.[23] The flesh cannot be compared with the dead corpse, for the flesh is alive. On the contrary, then, the other's body as flesh must be understood as the center of reference that it is, in a situation that is organized around it, and unthinkable out of this situation. The other's body as flesh must be understood in its relationship with the surrounding world, not as inserted into an already established situation, but as that which makes it possible for there to be a situation at all.[24] And at the same time, these very relationships are what constitute the facticity of the flesh.

> A body is a body as this mass of flesh which it *is* is defined by the table which the body looks at, the chair in which it sits, the pavement on which it walks, etc. [25]

Sartre concludes that the other's body, being the totality of signifying relationships to the world, "thus… is *meaningful*," and that meaning in fact "is nothing other than a fixed moment of transcendence."[26] Here it seems as though meaning is something that belongs to facticity, rather than something that is excluded from it. There is here a play

---

22. "son être-là 'de chair et d'os'." EN, 381. This is translated as "in flesh and blood" in the English version. BN, 341.
23. BN, 344, EN, 384.
24. "[…] un corps d'autrui comme chair ne saurait *s'insérer* dans une situation préalablement définie. Mais il est précisément ce à partir de quoi il y a situation." EN, 384.
25. BN, 344 "Un corps est corps en tant que cette masse de chair qu'il *est* se definit par la table qu'il regarde, la chaise qu'il prend, le trottoir sur lequel il marche, etc." EN, 384f.
26. BN, 344, "Ainsi, le corps d'autrui est-il *signifiant*. La signification n'est rien autre qu'un movement figé de transcendence." EN, 384.

between transcendence and facticity that I find to be very typical of Sartre's writings. And it is in fact our body that is the source of the paradox. As we have seen, Sartre is in the chapter on the body trying to establish the difference between the body-for-itself and the body-for-others, but when he tries to describe how I understand the other in his relationship with the world, this distinction clearly collapses, or rather, a connection is established between the two dimensions of the body. For if my body-for-itself is at the center of my meaningful relationships with the world, the world and the things in it constantly refer to this center. The fact that I, as transcendence, am the center of the world is therefore the very reason that I am there in the middle of the world, ready to be seen.[27] And in this way the body's being for-itself is transformed into the body-for-others. What is interesting in Sartre's account of the body is not so much the radical difference he establishes – a difference paralleled in all other parts of the work – between the body for-itself and the body for-others, but instead the *relationship* between these two modalities, the *transition* from one to the other. From Sartre's description it is clear that my facticity can be understood only with reference to my movement. The world and my body constitute one and the same system, organized according to a specific purpose (for example, the athlete who is jumping over the bar), and this involvement is what makes the world, and my body, meaningful. But at the same time this involvement also makes it possible for me to be seen – judged – with the world as a ground. When the body is active in the world it is in relation to everyone and everything, and the same is true when the body is seen and my facticity, instead of being the goal of my actions, moves to the foreground. The difference in this latter case, Sartre seems to suggest, is that these relationships are no longer possibilities for me but more like fettering bonds. The flesh is for Sartre a fleeing toward the world, which has been transformed into a state in the world, but where this fleeing remains in the background. The flesh must therefore not be seen in opposition to transcendence, but rather in opposition to the corpse. It seems as though what Sartre here wishes to illustrate is not the

---

27. Sartre further declares that the structure of the world thus implies that I cannot see without being visible.

alterations between an absolute nothingness and an absolute being, but rather a living body that maintains its relationship to the world also when it has coagulated into flesh. The flesh, it seems, must be described not as an object in opposition to consciousness, not as pure presence in opposition to a surveying look, but rather as a stillness that is apprehensible only with reference to the movement that preceded it, and moreover, to the movement which will follow.

"Flesh" is a concept that in French (as well as in English) arouses many associations, and Sartre plays with the whole spectra of meanings. The flesh exists as a philosophical concept in *Being and Nothingness* because of the fact that I exist in a world where there are others, and it receives its nourishment from the simultaneous exposedness and possibility, captivity and freedom, that this relationship marks. Having come this far in our investigation of the concept of flesh in Sartre's *Being and Nothingness*, we can establish that it is not very fruitful to discard this concept as a residue of Sartre's dualistic approach, seeing that this concept *in its very existence* (despite what Sartre himself might have intended[28]), gives evidence of a being that resists any type of dualistic account and that it indeed comes close to the concept that Merleau-Ponty would elaborate almost twenty years later.[29] Far from being an object exposed to an anonymous look, the flesh in *Being and Nothingness* is an ambiguous concept that arises from the difference and the movement between the being-for-itself and the being-for-others. A movement that, in its turn, is characterized by a dialectic, by a never-ending passage between background and foreground.

---

28. In this article I am not interested in what Sartre's intentions might have been in using the concept of flesh. However, one might notice that the ambiguity of the flesh shows up despite Sartre's attempts to simplify it by describing it as alternately "thing," "object," "pure matter," etc.

29. I am not trying to suggest that Merleau-Ponty was inspired by Sartre when, in *Le visible et l'invisible,* he uses the concept of flesh to describe that which "has no name in traditional philosophy." I do not even want to suggest that the two concepts are similar. The relationship between Sartre's and Merleau-Ponty's philosophical writings is far too complicated to be able to be described in a simple statement. I hope to illuminate this relationship in my coming dissertation, as well as why I think that Merleau-Ponty's concept of flesh is something entirely new in philosophy.

However, when Sartre in the chapter on "The Body" presents the flesh as a modality of the presence of the other, he is still basing this presence on the look. The other is mentioned as something to be known and utilized. And because the look is still the predominant theme in this chapter, Sartre speaks about the flesh as "immobility," as the counterpart of movement (for the characteristic of the look is precisely that it "freezes" that which it looks upon). To know the other is therefore in this context equivalent with "passing the other by," that is, to transcend him in the direction of my or his possibilities. This is shown by Sartre at the end of the section on the body-for-others when he states that the other is given to me in what he *is*, but that this existence is given only insofar as it is *surpassed*.[30] Consequently, even if the other's anger always appear to me as a free anger,

> I can always transcend it – *i.e.*, stir it up or calm it down; better yet it is by transcending it and only by transcending it that I apprehend it.[31]

Thus, Sartre concludes, the body is that object which is always more-than-a-body since it is never given to me without its surroundings, since it always points beyond itself in space and in time. Whether it is presented to me as organism, as character, or as tool, the other's body is always known – *judged* – on account of these surroundings.[32] And at the same time, the very same body is facticity – *flesh* – that is, this facticity is presented as that which is always and already passed beyond. This raises a question, for is it not precisely this passing beyond, here presented as the fundamental and unsurpassable relationship with the other, that is annulled in desire?

Flesh as Choosing the Present

Let us return once again to the point of departure for this essay, name-ly the concept of flesh as it is presented in the chapter on concrete

---

30. BN, 350/EN, 391.
31. BN, 351 "[…] je puis toujours la transcender, c'est-à-dire l'attiser ou la calmer, mieux, c'est en la transcendant et seulement ainsi que he la saisis." EN, 391.
32. "[…] il est le fait objectif que le corps – que ce soit comme organisme, comme caractère ou comme outil – ne m'apparaît jamais sans *alentours*, et doit être determiné à partir de ces alentours." EN, 391.

relationship with others, that is, the flesh that is born from desire. Sartre describes flesh and desire as an enchantment, and as a strategy used to escape from the never-ending circle of looking and being looked at that I am caught in. He declares that desire is doomed to failure (much like every other attitude which I take up in relation to the other). For, of course, I can never escape the other's look completely; as long as I live I will be in a world where there are others. Nevertheless, I think, the flesh in desire as an appeal to facticity also speaks about something else, about a possibility to live this relationship and the world in a different way, a way that is not in the first instance ruled by the look but, on the contrary, based upon the very ambiguity that emerges in the chapter on the body.

For what then is desire in this play between meaning and non-meaning, between pure facticity and transcending consciousness? When describing desire, Sartre states that the look is inadequate – if, that is, I want to make the other appear as flesh – since it makes the other into an *object*, with the result that his freedom and, with that, his fleshiness, disappear. The only way to make the other appear as flesh is to make myself into flesh. Flesh in desire is not something that is "judged" by the look, or "frozen," to use Sartrean language. But neither has it lost its situation; it is not experienced as redundant or obscene, it is simply rendered present.[33]

The goal of desire is to see the other, not in the way I usually see him, as someone on the way to something else and somewhere else, or

---

33. One may note that Merleau-Ponty in this part of *The Visible and the Invisible* criticizes Sartre's philosophy (which he names the philosophy of negativity, *philosophie du negatif*) precisely for not being able to account for the presence of the other. The only experience that I have of the other in this philosophy is, according to Merleau-Ponty, that of my own passivity, of the alienation I feel when I am being reduced to my situation by the other's look. Instead of accounting for the other's presence, negativist thought only manages to describe the other as an outer force that suddenly freezes me in my being, as an anonymous faceless phantom or as a neutral non-me in general. Merleau-Ponty thus argues that Sartre's description of the relationship with the other fails to capture the essential structure of this relationship, which is precisely that of this simple presence, of the "*il y a*". Maybe Merleau-Ponty's judgment on Sartre's philosophy would have been different had he started from the flesh in desire instead of from the flesh under the look.

even worse, as a means for my own ends, but instead to render the other as well as myself present in the same way that the tool comes into presence when it breaks.[34] It is this presence that Sartre describes as flesh, and it is obvious from his writings that the flesh is not meaningless but rather meaning*ful*. It is not a thing, but neither is it something in particular. Flesh and desire can be found, I think, in this tension between movement and rest. It is not absolute immobility, but rather a momentary rest. It is not outside time and space, but rather a here and a now that gain their intensity only in relation to a possible elsewhere. Desire is described in *Being and Nothingness* as a situation in which I no longer try to transcend the other, or use the other, for some other purpose. The other is my only purpose. In desire I do not want to be some other place or in some other time, I choose the here and the now at the same moment as I choose the other in his body. More than anything, flesh and desire as it is presented in *Being and Nothingness* speak to us about *choosing*, and one could perhaps also say, about *accepting*. (And this is where I would like to push the possibility of desire, as it is presented in *Being and Nothingness*, further than Sartre wanted to himself.)

Speaking about the choice, and learning how to choose, is of course what existential philosophy is all about. But this choosing, contrary to what is often suggested, I think, has in fact nothing to do with deciding between different options, but must on the contrary be described as an acceptance or as a *taking on* of something that is given.[35] Sartre

---

34. Again, I am here referring to how Heidegger in §16 of *Sein und Zeit* uses the example of the broken tool as a way of showing how things, and ultimately the structure of the world, come into presence.

35. This choice can therefore neither be described as fully active, nor as fully passive. To choose in this way is to accept, to simply say OK to something. This is never as clear, I think as in Simone de Beauvoir's essay *Pour une morale de l'ambiguïté* (Paris: Gallimard, 1947) where she separates two different attitudes with regard to what is given: the will to be and the will to disclose being. Where the will to be can be described as a will to embrace an identity, or a wish to engulf what is other than me, the wish to disclose being is on the contrary to assert that which is human and therefore ambiguous. To disclose being is to make being be and it can only be accomplished if I stop trying to *be* it, and instead establish a relation to it. The world can exist only in the distance or the gap that man creates in relationship to it. This last attitude, the desire to disclose being, can also be

shows us that to desire another, to make myself flesh in order to reveal the other as flesh, is a will to choose what is present, what is already there (against the background of the possibility of being somewhere else or something else). It is a commitment to what is present, or to making present. This choice could therefore also be described, I think, as a limitation. By looking at desire in this way, as that which aims for flesh, it follows that desire cannot be described as the selfish *eros* opposed to unconditioned and self-sacrificing love, *agape*. From the point of view of flesh and the choice of flesh, we must instead think of desire and love as one phenomenon, or perhaps think of this choice as one of their common characteristics. One could perhaps say that far from being a "free choice," love and desire are already there for me to choose, that they are like a "hang-up," something that gnaws within me, something which causes me to encircle this one and the same point and to ceaselessly remain in its proximity. Love is then, like desire, an obsession, but it is an obsession that is a choice. It is to get stuck, to not want to go further, to for a moment not aim toward any place.

described as to refrain from being in order to let something else, something other than me, be. This acceptance of what is given – an acceptance which nowhere in Beauvoir's essay is connected with a passivity but on the contrary with a *taking on*, with a *making mine* (it is still described as a *desire!*) is what I here mean by the term *choosing*.

Accusing the Erotic Subject
in Levinas

CARL CEDERBERG

They have used concupiscence as best they could for the general good; but it is nothing but a pretense and a false image of charity; for at bottom it is simply a form of hatred.

Blaise Pascal, *Pensées,* 404

Abstractions and Concretions

In the history of philosophy, the aim has predominantly been a universal and therefore neutral description of phenomena. The sphere of the erotic, so clearly linked to the sexual and gendered specificity and singularity of the subject, seems for this reason to be a difficult subject for philosophers. At what level of abstraction should one approach the erotic phenomenon? Phenomenology aims to treat the phenomenon as it shows itself – in itself. Yet never is it more evident than in the treatment of erotic phenomena that one needs to start from a personal experience or attitude, otherwise the phenomenon described becomes abstract and non-committal. On the other hand, it is probably never more disturbing than when a philosopher stretches personal experience too far, and claims it to be universal.[1]

I will personally seek to avoid this problem wherever possible by speaking about *Levinas'* philosophy of the erotic. By Luce Irigaray especially, Levinas was accused of universalizing a male standpoint in

---

1. One may of course say, that this is true for all philosophical topics. But this doesn't show the problem to be void; rather underlines that the erotic is a field where this problem can be approached in an interesting way.

his description of the erotic phenomenon, thereby silencing the feminine voice. And of lacking in love – Irigaray writes: "he knows nothing
of communion in pleasure. Levinas does not ever seem to have experienced the transcendence of the other which becomes immediate ecstasy in me and with him – or her."[2] This kind of accusation is interesting, because it shows that the erotic is a very particular field of philosophy. What status must the utterances of an erotic philosophy have
so that the field does not become a nasty quarrel about who is and who
is not capable of a healthy or transcendental, a progressive or a politically correct, erotic experience? I do not want to deny the validity of
Irigaray's remarks or try to disqualify the philosophical position of
which they are a part. Nonetheless, it seems to me that when choosing
these wordings, she is also opening up for the possibility of comparing
her position to that of the dissatisfied and/or disappointed lover. One
could even claim that accusation is her philosophical style.

One seemingly safe way out of this kind of argument (note the
double meaning of this word) would of course be to avoid the subject
altogether, or to talk at such an abstract distance from it that the problem of particular experience does not occur. We could then find ourselves on the level of the transcendental ego or of a neutral *Dasein*, not
yet belonging to either sex, who, as Levinas teasingly says, is never
hungry. This term, a neutral *Dasein*, was of course primarily used by
Heidegger in order to emphasize that his transcendental philosophy
should not be confused with an anthropology. In this sense this neutrality is not abstract, but, as Hegel also said, the most concrete.[3] There
is an intricate dialectic between abstract universality and singular concreteness in the descriptive notion of a neutral *Dasein*. But interest-
ingly, "this neutrality also indicates that *Dasein* is neither of the two
sexes."[4] This does not mean that *Dasein* is indifference, rather "it is the
original positivity and powerfulness [*Mächtigkeit*] of essence."[5] Its neu-

2. Luce Irigaray, "Questions to Emmanuel Levinas. On the Divinity of Love" in
Re-reading Levinas, eds. Robert Bernasconi and Simon Critchley (Bloomington:
Indiana University Press, 1991).
3. Martin Heidegger, *Die Metaphysik des Satzes vom Grunde* (Vittorio Klostermann,
Frankfurt am Main, 1990 [1928]), 176.
4. Ibid, 172.
5. Ibid.

trality lies in it not yet being applied to the description of the factical existence it always is: "*Dasein* bears the inner possibility for the factical dispersion in corporeality and therefore in sexuality."[6] The original source of this "inner possibility" is the neutral *Dasein*, which as neutral does not exist (172). Thus, corporeality and sexuality are referred to as a force neither posited in nor exposed to the world.

Levinas sees this claim of neutrality as symptomatic for the entire tradition of philosophy. His critique of this claim is based on the idea that it distorts the representation of human existence in general, which he understands always from intrinsicly non-neutral interhuman relations. When Levinas turns to the description of pleasure, love and ethics, it is because he is convinced that one must seek to describe the *concrete* human being – hungry, happy, sexually aroused, in pain, etc. From the point of view of a philosophy of a neutral *Dasein*, this aversion to the neutral could be seen as a version of the fear of the conceptual systematic philosophy, typical for a philosophy of life.[7] And that epithet has something to it. The abstraction to a "neutral level" is in Levinas' eyes a silent affirmation of one position in the non-neutral life world. The insistence on the concrete and the embodied is also the main reason, I think, that in his description of the erotic phenomenon, Levinas writes from an explicitly male heterosexual perspective, or at the very least, from an interpretation of one version of this perspective. His aversion to neutral abstractions makes him refuse or avoid to speak about either sex or gender in a more abstract sense, as if one could write from a non-gendered point of view. Still, even if Irigaray is wrong to claim that he universalizes the male perspective, it is clear that he associates it without question to the subject's perspective, a position which of course has implications for his views on the feminine other. In *Time and the Other*,[8] he represents the feminine as the exemplary modality of the other, whereas twenty-five years later in *Totality and Infinity*[9] he describes it as a more intimate and in that sense "less"

---

6. Ibid.
7. Ibid.
8. Emmanuel Levinas, *Le temps et l'autre* (Paris: Fata Morgana, 1979 [1946/1947]).
9. Levinas, *Totalité et infini* (Le livre de poche, 1990 [1961]), henceforth TI, trans. Alphonso Lingis *Totality and Infinity. An Essay on Exteriority* (Pittsburgh: Duquesne,

other than the absolute other. That this provides a highly problem-atic essentialization of the feminine and the masculine is obvious. When, in work subsequent to *Totality and Infinity*, Levinas would dis-tance himself from both this gendered language and from the ontolo-gising language of *Totality and Infinity*, he would make reference to his earlier text in the following way: "[. . .] I thought twenty years ago that the feminine is another Gender (Germ. *Genus*) in the full meaning of the word: it is not the same Genus as the ego [. . .] What now remains from this is the thought of being-otherwise not only formally but with a certain content."[10] But this step away from gendered thinking would lead to a very marginalized discussion of the erotic in his later work. Here, I would like to show what systematic content we can retain from Levinas' philosophy of the erotic in *Totality and Infinity*. For Levinas, the erotic occupies a kind of middle ground between enjoyment and ethics. In order to describe the phenomenon, we must therefore start out in a description of these modes of existence.

Enjoyment vs. Ethics

All work and no play makes Jack a dull boy
All play and no work makes Jack a mere toy
(Irish proverb)

According to Levinas, one of the most basic conditions of human life is the search for happiness and pleasure. This is not just an accidental or isolated fact about human existence; enjoyment has a primary on-tological status: human beings do not primarily encounter objects in the world, but they enjoy the world in its elements. Here Levinas partakes in the common, and possibly simplistic, criticism directed towards Husserl, namely that Husserl conceived the object too much from the viewpoint of mental representation, as well as extending his criticism toward Heidegger's conception of the object as tool/*Zeug* or

---

2004 [1969]), henceforth TaI.

10. "Intention, Ereignis und das Andere, Gespräch zwischen Emmanuel Levinas und Christoph von Wolzogen am 20. Dezember 1985 in Paris" in Levinas, *Huma-nismus des anderen Menschen* (Hamburg, Felix Meiner, 1989), 135.

Ready-at-hand (*Zuhandenheit*), deemed to be equally inadequate. Instead Levinas tries to show how taking pleasure in the elements of the world is more fundamental than encountering them as objects of representation or tools to use. The fresh air we breathe and the loaf of bread I eat – are these to be viewed as tools in any other world but one extremely marked by a protestant work ethic, in a technocratic, industrialist society? Enjoyment is never a specimen of work; rather I work in order to be able to enjoy, and I can even take pleasure in working. Enjoyment is our primary relation to life, our primary way of living. Life is understood as enjoying in the sense of living from... (*vivre de...*). I live from that which I enjoy. So needs are not understood as lacks, the human being is "happy for his needs" (TI 118 / TaI 114).

The ethical is described as running counter to, or as a rupture with, this happy enjoyment of the world. Suddenly, I can no longer allow myself to enjoy – someone else needs me. This does not mean that Levinas is endorsing an ethics calling upon us to forsake enjoyment. Rather, he is trying to *describe* ethics as a rupture with enjoyment, a possibility of an ethics irreducible to the search for happiness and pleasure.

In relating to the other ethically, the other is treated *kath'auto,* as his or herself. This is precisely not an action based on a pre-conceived notion of who he or she is. What, for Levinas, is foremost emphasized is the very alterity of the other. In the manifestation of *kath' auto* the other expresses him or herself; he or she appears before us as a living presence. But this presence is also an absence: it unmakes every form-presented. The other introduces a language in which she produces meaning *by him- or herself*, without fitting into my schemes. Not only does she not fit, she produces meaning *by virtue of* not fitting into my schemes, by destroying them. The encounter with the other is here described through the face. The other faces me, looks at me. The gaze of the other speaks to me, forces me to respond, and thus calls upon me to be responsive and responsible. This is a source of meaning, and of rationality; the other provides a measure for my actions, and impels me to justify them.

This relation defines the subject as subject. A subject is someone to whom one can ascribe actions. Subjectivity therefore implies responsibility, someone who can say "I did it. It was me. I hurt you," and who can say "I'll do it. I'll help you." Both in the sense of guilt of what has happened and of taking charge of what must be done. So in this sense, it is the ethical relation that defines the subject *qua* subject, and the other *qua* other. When Levinas says: the other accuses me (*autrui m'accuse*), this bears a double meaning: on the one hand, the other holds me responsible, forcing me to justify myself; on the other hand, the other causes me to appear more clearly, bringing me acutely forth.[11] But if, according to Levinas, I am brought forth as a responsible subject by the other, who or what was I before? What is there that can be accused and brought forth as subject, what is this previous subjectivity and what is its relation to the other?

The Erotic Subjectivity

Even if the ethical relation is understood as the defining relation, it is not the only way in which one relates to the other. It is contrasted to all other relations to the other; typically those described in terms of conflict or war, where one will try to subdue the other, or in terms of the relation of commerce, where both parties act in their own interest to gain advantage from trading with each other, or the erotic relation where both lovers take pleasure in the other and in the other's pleasure. Of systematic importance for Levinas, however, is the erotic relation, which, via Pascal's dictum of ethics as love without concupiscence, Levinas has sometimes explicitly contrasted to the ethical relation.

The only book where the erotic relation is extensively investigated by Levinas is *Totality and Infinity*. And even here it appears at the end, after both the sphere of enjoyment and the ethical relation have already been described. In the introduction to the section labeled phenomenology of Eros, Levinas starts out by saying that the erotic phenomenon belongs to a plane that both presupposes and transcends

---

11. For this meaning of the word, Larousse, dictionnaire de la langue française, 1999, provides: "Mettre en relief. Faire ressortir par rapport à ce qui entoure : *La lumière rasante accuse les reliefs.* (syn. accentuer) *Je vous ferai ici un petit conte pour bien accuser la pensée que je vous propose* (*Valéry*) (syn. souligner). *Les rides accusent son age* (syn. indiquer)." In all of these examples the essential features of something already there are brought forward.

the face. Here he is not suggesting a transcendent metaphysics, which would reintroduce an underlying substance as an explanation for our world here. But it is still "a plane where the I bears itself beyond death and recovers also from its return to itself. This plane is that of love and fecundity, where subjectivity is posited in function of these movements" (TI 284 / TaI 253).

So what is Levinas looking for in his description of the erotic? By saying that the erotic phenomenon lies beyond the face, Levinas is announcing the search for a layer of subjectivity, which is not the ethical, but a layer in which the ethical can appear. This layer of life, behind and beyond the ethical, must meet some requirements:

1. It must allow for the ethical to appear as interpersonal, it must therefore provide separate terms which relate to each other as different.

1 a). It can therefore be just an instance of im- or subpersonal reason (TI 283 / TaI 252) – in order for the Other to appear for me, I must already be a person. The language introduced by the other is fundamentally interpersonal, and can never be totally impersonal. The impersonal language presupposes the interpersonal language, not the other way round. He will seek a dimension of the subject allowing for the impact of the other.

b). Nor can it be a mere animal partiality, a force fulfilling its needs (TI 283/ TaI 253). It must be already human, already treating the other as a human being.

2. The subject must be situated in a time that is not only constituted by its own death, but reaches beyond death; the subject must transcend itself.

So what Levinas is looking for is a dimension of subjectivity opening up to infinity, to transcendence, to the interpersonal, to a relation to what is not me, that is not enveloped in my projects. This will be a relation where I am neither in power or overpowered.

Love manifests itself through an ambiguity. On the one hand the relationship to the other goes beyond the relation to the face. This relation to the other is not best described in terms of responsibility, respect. These borders are crossed. But they are still essential for the erotic relation – "disrespect presupposes the face" (TI 294 / TaI 262). This means that only if I recognize the transcendence of the other can the intimate immanence be erotic; the erotic is constituted by "a

simultaneity [...] of concupiscence and transcendence" (TI 285 / TaI
255). But the erotic goes beyond the face; in voluptuosness the caress
is not stopped by the nudity of the face.

The caress searches – it is not searching for something, in the sense
that there is a definite object for its search. It seeks something in
communication with the will of the other. Not in the sense that it
wants to establish a fact about the other's desire, or dominate the
desire of the other. It seeks what is not yet there (TI 288 / TaI 258).
The discovery does not entail an increase of power or knowledge. This
"not yet" is not something that will appear as apart of my scheme or
plan. In fact, my having plans, my very position as a subject is swept
away. The erotic subject delights in being moved. This does not mean
that a caress cannot be part of a plan – but if that is so the caress as
such will threaten to move the subject wanting to be the absolute
mover: "Eros is not accomplished as a subject that fixes an object, nor
as a pro-jection, toward a possible. Its movement doesn't expand the
realm of possibilities, but consists in going beyond the possible" (TI
292 / TaI 261); i.e. beyond the "I can."

Seen from the viewpoint of the ethical relation, the discovery of the
erotic other entails a certain violation, a certain disrespect toward the
other as transcendent. This means that it presupposes the ethical. It
does not violate the face by necessarily being unethical, rather it
removes the ethical standard. Seriousness becomes play. Where the
ethical relation leads toward universalization, rationality, the erotic
relationship in contrast is intimate, a closed society of the here and
now. The lovers are alone in the world, in a community of the sentient
and the sensed. The other is sensed as sentient, desired as desiring. In
the ethical relationship I can never disclaim responsibility, whereas in
the erotic relationship it is often unclear and unimportant if you or I
did whatever it is we are doing.

In this sense it is an inward relation, relating "to a community of
feeling." It is inward in the sense of referring to a community in which
the community in which the subject itself takes part. Still it is inter-
subjectively structured. The other is not desired as other *kath'auto*, but
as desiring me. "In voluptuosity the Other is me and separate from
me" (TI 297 / TaI 265). The meeting of desires is nothing like possession, reification or domination; as usual, Levinas wants to contrast his

ACCUSING THE EROTIC SUBJECT IN LEVINAS

own account with the dialectics of master and slave. Far from reification or domination, the erotic desire delights in the desire of the other. With this background, Irigaray is hardly fair to claim that "the
description of pleasure given by Levinas is unacceptable to the extent
that it presents man as the sole subject exercising his desire and his
appetite upon the woman who is deprived of subjectivity except to
seduce him."[12] Irigaray is right insofar as Levinas strongly associates
subjectivity to masculinity. But the beloved isn't deprived of subjectivity, she is always loved as loving. If one were to look for something like
a proto-feminism in Levinas' eroticism, it would consist in not uni-
versalising the masculine desire, but in describing a masculine desire
in the encounter with a feminine, without saying how far they are
universal. Even if there is a distinct classical masculine and feminine
position described by Levinas, there is also an overturning of them in
the very description of the erotic. Otherwise, when describing the
lonely subject, the subject to be approached by the other, Levinas
writes about the classical autonomous subject with its projects as a
virility – and here, it becomes obvious that this subject undergoes a
change. This virile I is in some sense "feminized," and it proves to be
a blessing, because it releases me from being me (TI 302–305, TaI
270–272).

Irigaray also says: "To caress, for Levinas, consists [...] not in ap-
proaching the other in its most vital dimension, the touch, but in the
reduction of that vital dimension of the other's body to the elaboration of a future for himself."[13] This seems a positioning of Levinas that
makes sense only from the point of view of Irigaray's own philosophical project. For Levinas the erotic is never a personal project, fulfilling
the ego. On the contrary, it is a future that releases me from being me
in the sense of my projects, while the caress is a shared experience
which releases us. Maybe one could say with Irigaray's own words that
it gives us rebirth as others.

"If love is to love the love the Beloved bears me, to love is also to
love oneself in love, and thus to return to oneself"(TI 298 / TaI 266).
But at the same time it is a movement away from oneself. My identity

---

12. Irigaray, 115.
13. Ibid, 110.

with myself is altered, as is the difference to the Other. But we are not engulfed in a unity; instead says Levinas, we engender a child.

This is where he causes some bewilderment. Surely he is aware that the erotic does not necessarily generate a child, or necessarily aim for a child? On the contrary, the erotic is as such per definition independent of the natural goal of reproduction. Is this then a concealed concession to biologism? Is the erotic all about the reproduction, preservation and the prolongation of the species? Perhaps it is a veiled religious commandment to procreate? Or is Levinas just losing himself in metaphors? In order for this to make sense, I suggest we read this as a statement about a similarity of the structures of the erotic and the structure of reproduction. We can find some helpful remarks on this relation in Bataille's introduction to *Eroticism*:

> while it is true that eroticism is defined by the mutual independence of erotic pleasure and reproduction as an end, the fundamental meaning of reproduction is none the less the key to eroticism. Reproduction implies the existence of discontinuous being. [...] Reproduction leads to the discontinuity of beings, but brings into play their continuity.[14]

The erotic phenomenon as well as reproduction blurs the distinction between continuity of the ego and discontinuity in my relation to another, and suggests a continuity of the discontinuous, a discontinuity of the continuous. We can transpose this onto Levinas: just as the erotic moment carries a certain separated unity and a united separation, so does the parent-child relationship.

The child is in my interpretation neither a metaphor, nor a biological category. I would like to see it more as an example, demonstrating a subjectivity that goes beyond itself as subject. The possibility of a child entails the evidence of a future beyond projects, a future that is me without being mine. Levinas writes: "By a total transcendence [...] the I is, in the child, an other" (TI 299 / TaI 267). The child is not mine, *but me as an other*. So, the description of the erotic phenomena does not instrumentalize the sexual relation for the purpose of

---

14. Georges Bataille, *Eroticism* (London: Penguin, 2001), 12–13.

reproduction. The two are instead, linked but parallel phenomena, with a similar structure.

This relationship to the future Levinas calls fecundity. It is in a sense a possibility, but not in the sense of a project that I set out for myself. It is a possibility for me, but for a me complicated by the erotic structure. This is an attempt to allow for a different kind of possibility than that of a logical possibility, which is less than being. But it is also different from his understanding of the Heideggerian possibility "which transforms the relation of the future into a power of the subject" (TI 299 / TaI 267).

This implies a complication of the subject's finitude. The subject thus transcends the tedium of repetition and is no longer riveted to itself. Levinas also refers to this phenomenon as *youth*. The subject is at its origin, but is not tied to this origin, not encumbered with itself.[15] Philosophy also lives from this kind of youth, making it possible to reach out anew to the others and continue philosophical dialogue. The erotic is beyond the meaning created by projects, but this does not entail the meaninglessness that causes anxiety. "Fecundity continues history without producing old age" (TI 301 / TaI 268).

It is in this way that Levinas can criticize the notion of an ego as the origin of everything, without having to resort to a neutral entity behind the ego. Both in the erotic and in the parental relation with the other, the I is itself and becomes other. This means that I am not locked into my fate, for "a being capable of another fate than its own is a fecund being" (TI 314 / TaI 282).

This is described as a starting point for a critique of the privilege of unity over multiplicity. Even when thinking multiplicity, one has traditionally envisaged it as many of a kind, a multiplicity of monads. Levinas' analysis of fecundity seeks to show how transcendence of the I is possible without being self-refuting, without obliterating the I. He acknowledges Heidegger's philosophy as an attempt to break with this fixation with unity. *Dasein* is not only its actual here and now, it is first and foremost its possibilities, its future. But this is always described in terms of power: *Dasein* is either master of its situation or subdued

---

15. This was an important problem in early texts such as *Reflections on the Philosophy of Hitlerism* and *On escape;* in the latter text erotic pleasure was treated as an escape that fails, since it leads back to the self in the moment of satisfaction.

under *das Man*. In his later texts Heidegger strongly emphasized that there is always a powerlessness in power. But Levinas means that Heidegger still thinks the subject too much in terms of mastery. Powerlessness is still only a negation of power, thus dependent upon power. The erotic relation, however, is before the powerful or powerless subject. It is thus also liberation from the subject-as-power (or *Dasein* as *Mächtigkeit*). Fecundity offers a proof of the plurality of being, in the form of an I and an other that are not just separate monads, separate versions ("avatars") of the I. In the next step, it is imtimated that this structure is responsible for structuring the subject itself. It shows another way of being a subject than being a power center. This is paralleled by the erotic encounter. As we saw, the caress searches for an unknown future that is not controlled by the subject in the taking place of the encounter. The longing that is a part of the caress can be described as a longing to break the chains of the I seen only as the subject of projects. I live the other and am lived by the other. This kind of attachment is both subpersonal and superpersonal.

In a further step, fecundity is used as a sort of explanation of the possibility of ethics. Through my relation with the child, filiality and paternity, I am linked to all human beings; all human beings are my brothers. This is what allows the face to appear: "The human I is posited in fraternity: that all men are brothers is not added to man as a moral conquest, but constitutes his ipseity. Because my position as an I is *effectuated* already in fraternity the face can present itself to me as a face" (TI 312–313 / TaI 279–280). By this filial link between all human beings, the I is opened up to an understanding of infinite time that does not make goodness something empty and unapparent.

So, now it seems that the erotic and the ethical spheres are mutually dependent on each other. On the one hand, without the face of the other, there would be no erotic phenomenon, only lust. On the other hand, the key erotic concept of fecundity is the condition of possibility for the fraternity that makes the appearance of the face possible.

Levinas' descriptions of the erotic and of fecundity are attempts to show some related ways in which human beings can share in other people's lives without there being a common neutral entity that they share in, such as a transcendental subject. They are in some sense each other.

But on the other hand, one could think that the ethical phenomenon must contradict this view. The other as absolutely other would not allow for a shared starting point in concupiscent love or in family, rather it is the stranger with a disturbing gaze. If the charity shown to the stranger would be somehow justified through the concept of fecundity and fraternity (my being the other), won't the very idea of the absolute gratuity of the ethical be lost? The concept of fraternity blurs the sharp distinction between the erotic and the ethical. But how can Levinas then understand ethics as love *without* concupiscence?

One way to avoid this paradox is to view the ethical only as a different aspect of a reality that it has in common with concupiscent or otherwise reciprocal love. The ethical would be love not necessarily *without* concupiscence or even reciprocity, but in disregard of concupiscence and reciprocity. So while the erotic phenomenon and fecundity serve as examples of a real or possible community with all human beings, in my truly ethical relation, this community is not something I can fall back on. I am called to re-enact it in my actions, rather than hope that I will do the right thing just because of a feeling that we all belong together anyway. Rather, this feeling is always under suspicion in Levinas' texts. The ethical stamp is rather given only to an an-archic disturbance, assenting to actions that are carried out in spite of oneself.

The story of the caress, fecundity, paternity and fraternity comes at the end of *Totality and Infinity* and serves as a kind of hindsight, or an ad hoc explanation, which tries to mediate between, on the one hand, the "virile" autonomous, autarchic, self-sufficient subject and, on the other, one's encounter with the other. The account is questionable for many reasons, the emphasis on the masculine only being the most obvious problem. The biggest problem is that it first seems that the ethical encounter needs the contrast with the seemingly autonomous subject in order to be described, whereas later the autonomous subject must be softened by the description of its erotic origin in order to rationalize the possibility of ethics.

Firstly: was there ever the autonomous subject? Indeed, even in Levinas' description in the period of *Totality and Infinity*, there never was – rather, it is described as a sort of fiction necessary for the whole ethical intrigue. This puts the focus on the interhuman as living in the encounter with the other, in the (non-)experience of the other. Levinas was trapped in a phenomenological language that he was trying to avoid. But in his later works, Levinas was to tell this intrigue differently. Or perhaps we should say that he gives up on the idea of the ethical intrigue, i.e. the possibility to describe the ethical in the mode of an experience for the otherwise autonomous subject. Rather, what is now being described is the subject as pre-originally determined as susceptibility, i.e. responsibility. Here, instead of describing the ethical (non-)experience as almost a miracle turning the otherwise predetermined egoistic tide of the subject, the description of the human subjectivity is now focused on being the condition of possibility for the ethical. As Robert Bernasconi puts it: "Levinas reframes the question of the possibility of ethics by turning from the other to the ethical subject so as to ask about the possibility of such a subject... [H]e goes behind the back of the consciousness of the I, so that there is no longer any danger that Levinas will be read as if the ethical first arose as a concrete event in the life of an already constituted ego."[16]

To this we can add that the same goes for the erotic. Levinas is now clearly conceiving subjectivity as sensibility – the presupposition for the ethical and the erotic, as well as for the classical idealist ego of consciousness. In *Otherwise than Being*,[17] the subject is not described as being divided between an erotic and an ethic relation to the other. Rather sensibility is described as a more fundamental concept, a category that aims to account for not only ethical and erotic relations, but for subjectivity as such. Now, he no longer needs the erotic as a background for an egosphere in which the other supposedly breaks through. There is now "a possibility of a libido in the most elementary and most 'rich' signification of proximity" (proximity being one of the many synonyms encircling the key concept of pre-original responsibility). Responsibility is however still "before Eros" (AE 143n /

---

16. "To what question is substitution the answer?" in *The Cambridge companion to Levinas*, eds. Simon Critchley and Robert Bernasconi (Cambridge: Cambridge University Press, 2002), 245–246.

17. Emmanuel Levinas, *Autrement qu'être ou au-délà de l'essence* (Livre de poche 1990 [1974]), *Otherwise than Being or Beyond Essence*, trans. Alphonso Lingis (Duquesne, Pittsburgh, 1998). Henceforth AE / OB.

OB 192n). But "before" is a very difficult word in all philosophy, and especially so in *Otherwise than Being*, which questions the language of primacy at the same time as it seems to reintroduce it in another way. In this statement of responsibility being before *eros*, I understand it thus: we can question *eros* from the point of view of responsibility, for responsibility is closer to the order of a question and an answer.

But still, the conflict between the ethical and the erotic might seem to reappear in a new guise – after all, the erotic often seems to be interpreted as a version of the subject's conatus, the subject's drive to be in the world. This is exemplified by one of the opening mottos for *Otherwise than Being*, a quote from Pascal's *Pensées*:

> They have used concupiscence as best as they could for the general good; but is nothing but a pretense and a false image of charity; for at bottom it is simply a form of hatred (*Pensées*, 404; OB vii).

Is concupiscence thus the antonym of the Good? In fact, for Levinas it cannot be its antonym, for the Good has none:

> The Good invests freedom – it loves me before I love it. Love is love in this antecedence. The Good could not be the term of a need susceptible of being satisfied, it is not the term of an erotic need, a relationship with the seductive which resembles the Good to the point of being indistinguishable from it, but which is not its other, but its imitator. The Good as the infinite has no other, not because it would be the whole, but because it is Good and nothing escapes its goodness (AE 25n / OB 186n).

This makes a few central points clear. The Good does not have an opposite, but an "imitator." Concupiscence is questioned insofar as it, as Pascal says in the above quote, claims lust not to be only good, but *the* Good. One way in which this has been claimed is the common view that lust is a need, the most central human need, which has to be fulfilled. Levinas sees it rather as part of a force of life, which also always produces a surplus, allowing it to give to the other, even to the point where it is itself destructive for this particular life. Levinas is not attacking the lustful per se; the word "concupiscence" here comes to stand for the view that the erotic and the lustful are "the whole" and "the Good," and where impossibility for a view on the Good goes against the grain of caring for oneself.

Another question might still be plaguing us, however. If the description of one's relation to the other shifts from being couched in terms of an experience (which is never an experience) to the quasi-transcendental questions on the very possibility of ethical and erotic relations, are we not led back to the very "neutrality," which Levinas had been trying to avoid? Is the an-archic subject, depicted in *Otherwise than Being,* perhaps not so far from the idea of the neutral *Dasein,* after all? Yes, maybe not. Though an important difference remains: its originary *Mächtigkeit* is accused, it is being made and held responsible, and brought forth (remember the wider meaning of *accuser*) as already responsible. In this sense, Levinas already practised the art that Irigaray continued: philosophy bears its fruits not only in dialogue but also in accusation.

Erotic Perception:
Operative Intentionality as Exposure

LISA FOLKMARSON KÄLL

Let us try to see how a thing or being begins to exist for us through desire or love and we shall thereby come to understand better how things and beings can exist in general.

Maurice Merleau-Ponty

I

Luchino Visconti's cinematic portrayal of Thomas Mann's novella *Death in Venice* is, to quote its New York Times review, something of "an elegant bore."[1] The film, which was awarded the 25th Anniversary Prize at the 1971 Cannes Film Festival, is a quite melodramatic affair of over two hours in which a series of loosely connected scenes tells the story of avant-garde composer Gustav von Aschenbach's exposure to desire, to himself and to the deadly pestilence that threatens Venice and that finally takes his life.[2] The protagonist, who has come to Venice

---

1. Canby, "Movie Review: *Death in Venice.*"
2. Visconti's film differs in significant ways from Mann's novella and the transformation of the protagonist Gustav von Aschenbach from a writer in the novella to a composer in the film is one of the most explicit departures. Here I am not interested in comparing the two works or in raising issues of how well or how poorly the film manages to capture elements of the novella. My interest here is with the film and how the film displays a specific understanding of erotic perception and exposure. Also this interest is quite limited and there is of course much more to be said about the film's portrayal of erotic perception than I will accomplish here. Especially the display of homoerotic perception and of the performative constitution of bodies, identity and sexuality deserves much further investigation.

on doctor's orders after having exhausted his health to the point of physical breakdown, appears distracted, tense and full of conflict. Almost immediately after settling into the extravagantly elegant Grand Hôtel des Bains on the Lido, he fixates on the beautiful blond adolescent boy Tadzio who is vacationing with his mother, sister and governess. His attraction to Tadzio develops into a full-blown obsession and von Aschenbach spends much of his time in Venice gazing after the young boy and following him around. Jeopardizing his own life to be near the object of his desire, he stays on too long in Venice and falls victim to the lethal pestilence that has secretly been spreading throughout the city. He dies gazing out at the sea where Tadzio is seen on the horizon.

The film contains very little dialogue and is carried through as a series of beautiful and haunting images of the time in Venice with flashbacks from von Aschenbach's history. The character of Tadzio is strikingly uninteresting. He performs one function in the film and that is to be the object of von Aschenbach's gaze, turning slowly, smiling with sweet allure and returning the gaze without a word. Gustav von Aschenbach on the other hand is interesting and as troubling as he seems troubled. He is intensely private and yet on full display, he is pathetic and tragic but at the same time endearing and quite amiable. He is drawn into a world of desire where his relation to the world literally becomes a matter of life and death. What interest me in the portrayal of von Aschenbach is his exposure and the way in which his relation to the world both exposes him but also rests on the exposure of his being.

Here I will read the portrayal of erotic perception and exposure in Visconti's *Death in Venice* together with some of Maurice Merleau-Ponty's writings, letting both speak to each other. I will turn to Merleau-Ponty's account of erotic perception and sexuality in *Phenomenology of Perception*, suggesting that the operative intentionality made manifest in Merleau-Ponty's description of erotic perception is unveiled as through and through exposure. This corporeal intentionality is what constitutes our attachment to the world as a bond that unbinds in binding. Following Merleau-Ponty's claim that erotic experience is that which most manifestly brings to light the attachment between the self and the world, I want to claim that erotic experience is also a privileged area for bringing out this attachment as one of exposure. I will turn to Visconti's portrayal of von Aschenbach in *Death in Venice* to show how the portrayal illuminates this attachment as exposure in exaggerated form. While the story, as Visconti tells it, is quite banal and lacking in originality in the sense of being fully predictable and obvious, there is at the very same time nothing banal about it. The portrayal displays in all of its exaggeration, heavy ornamentation and melodrama how erotic perception lays bare human subjectivity as exposure to itself and to the world of which it forms part.

II

In his account of the body in its sexual being, Merleau-Ponty argues that sexuality and erotic experience demonstrate in *the most manifest way* the bond between the embodied self and the world. He brings to light the embodied, affective aspect of the advent of meaning showing how something begins to exist for us precisely to the extent that the body is a power of transcendence towards it. The intentional structure of erotic perception can for Merleau-Ponty not be described in terms of a "*cogitatio* which aims at a *cogitatum*" and cannot be located on the level of consciousness or in the order of reflection or understanding. Instead he famously identifies sexuality and erotic experience as one form of original intentionality which through one body aims at another body and takes place in the world of lived experience. There is, he writes, "an erotic 'comprehension' not of the order of understanding, since understanding subsumes an experience, once perceived, under some idea." Desire, on the other hand "comprehends blindly by linking body to body."[3] As is well-known, the body Merleau-Ponty has in mind here is quite clearly not the body of any natural or material science, but rather the body as it is (inter)subjectively lived, experienced and expressed in its surrounding world and in relation to others. This understanding of the body is crucial for understanding his account as a rejection of any attempts at naturalizing sexuality. Instead,

---

3. Maurice Merleau-Ponty, *Phenomenology of Perception*, trans. Colin Smith (London & New York: Routledge, 1962), 157; *Phénoménologie de la perception* (Paris: Gallimard, 1945).

Merleau-Ponty wants to reintegrate sexuality into human existence and resist simple biological accounts.[4] In fact reducing sexuality or any other aspect of existence to a mere biological function is impossible within a phenomenological framework that takes seriously the situatedness of embodied subjectivity as well as of scientific thinking and of the sciences. Merleau-Ponty writes explicitly and repeatedly that sexuality is not "a peripheral involuntary action" but rather a form of original operative intentionality "which follows the general flow of existence and yields to its movements."[5]

But what does it mean to say that desire comprehends blindly by linking body to body? How should we make sense of this intentionality that Merleau-Ponty says follows the general flow of existence and yields to its movements? Operative intentionality that is unveiled in erotic perception is described as the very foundation of the noesis-noema structure of object directed intentionality and the task, or one of the tasks, of the phenomenologist is to disclose and describe the structures of this foundation. True to this task, Merleau-Ponty spends a great deal of his philosophical oeuvre describing how this operative intentionality functions and how it is by its own making, through its very structure, transformed into different forms of object directed intentionality.[6] While the very term intentionality carries connotations

---

4. This ambition is much in line with insights of psychoanalysis on which Merleau-Ponty draws in his own account. However, in his engagement with psychoanalysis, he also challenges the view of sexuality as a bodily expression of repressed memories or unconscious representations.

5. Merleau-Ponty, *Phenomenology of Perception*, 157.

6. As Merleau-Ponty says, the relationship between the embodied subject and its world is generally transformed into an epistemological problem of how the subject knows a world that seems to exist in itself independently of the subject. Subject and world, consciousness and body, fall apart into irreconcilable opposites and all too easily these opposites are given ontological status as two essentially different forms of existence. The human lived body, however, belonging simultaneously "to the order of the 'object' and to the order of the 'subject' reveals to us quite unexpected relations between the two orders [and] teaches us that each calls for the other." See Merleau-Ponty, *Phenomenology of Perception*, 154, 198; *The Visible and the Invisible. Followed by Working Notes*, ed. Claude Lefort, trans. Alphonso Lingis (Evanston: Northwestern University Press, 1968), 137; *Le visible et l'invisible* (Paris: Gallimard, 1964), 137. In the elaboration of this non-representational

to volition, autonomy and independent detachment, the foundation of any object directed intentionality lays bare its structure as one of attachment and co-dependence (or even co-conditioning). The two relata of intentionality exist in a symbiotic relation of mutual co-constitution and as consciousness bestows meaning on the world, the world is also given to consciousness as a world of meaning. The attachment between consciousness and the world is brought out beautifully in Merleau-Ponty's description of the reflection. With reference to Eugen Fink's account of the phenomenological reduction in terms of wonder in the face of the world, Merleau-Ponty famously and poetically writes,

> Reflection does not withdraw from the world towards the unity of consciousness as the world's basis; it steps back to watch the forms of transcendence fly up like sparks from a fire; it slackens the intentional threads which attach us to the world and thus brings them to our notice[7]

What appears in reflection is thus, on Merleau-Ponty's account, first and foremost our attachment to the world; the world stands out as the foundational ground for our being rather than as a detached object world. When we let go of our habitual tendency of objectifying the world, a shift of focus occurs from *what* the world is to *how* the world and our relation to the world is given and our being is exposed as intimately interrelated with and embedded in the world.

In this shift, not only a transformation of our attitude towards the world occurs but also a disclosure of our own being. The phenomenological suspension of knowledge of the world as an object world and of the truths of the natural and human sciences unveils the embodied self as being-in-the world and intentionally directed towards the world in which it is embedded. It brings to light the lifeworld and is for

---

operative intentionality is also where Merleau-Ponty famously locates the originality of Husserl's thinking. It is to be found, he writes, "beyond the notion of intentionality [...] in the discovery, beneath the intentionality of representations, of a deeper intentionality, which others have called existence" (*Phenomenology of Perception*, 140, note 54).

7. Merleau-Ponty, *Phenomenology of Perception*, xiii.

Merleau-Ponty the phenomenological return to the things themselves, to the world as it is experienced and lived prior to scientific descriptions and judgments. The suspension of knowledge also involves unveiling the exposure of existence as the event in which the meaning of the lived world and of the self continuously originates anew. As the world comes into being for the self, the self also comes into being in relation to the world, as a reaching out of itself and, in that reaching, as exposure to the world, to others and to its own exterior. What reflection brings to light is thus an intimate bond and interrelation between the embodied self and its world in which both are continuously given birth in relation to one another.

It is this intimate interrelation of continuous becoming that erotic perception, according to Merleau-Ponty, lays bare for us in the most manifest way. As one form of original intentionality through which the body is directed towards its world, sexuality and erotic experience bring to light "the vital origins of perception, motility and representation by basing all these 'processes' on an 'intentional arc'."[8] Erotic experience is thus not itself the origin of perception, motility and representation but is rather the beam (or one possible beam) through which this origin is illuminated and brought into focus. This is also for Merleau-Ponty the reason why sexuality plays such an important role in human life. It provides an opportunity "vouchsafed to all and al-

---

8. Merleau-Ponty, *Phenomenology of Perception*, 157. What Merleau-Ponty calls an "intentional arc" founds perception and experience and results in our being situated in a specific cultural, ideological, historical, moral and physical setting. It "endows experience with its degree of vitality and fruitfulness." The intentional arc is on the one hand that which carries the body into the world, as it is the general power I have of putting myself in a situation. It thereby results in the situatedness of the embodied self and ultimately refers to the facticity of human subjectivity. But, on the other hand, the intentional arc can in some sense even be equated with the living, experiencing body, which in a fundamental dialectic between itself and the world projects and understands meanings. Merleau-Ponty's ambiguous characterization of what he calls the intentional arc is not only symptomatic of his ambiguous, alluring style of writing but also serves to illustrate the hazy meeting point and ambiguous intertwinement of on the one hand a generality and anonymity and on the other hand the individual particularity through which anonymity is brought to articulation. See Merleau-Ponty, *Phenomenology of Perception*, 158, 161f, 174, 210.

ways available" to acquaint oneself with the ambiguity of existence of both autonomy and dependence, connectedness and distance, of being both subject and object, coinciding with oneself and being other to oneself.[9] So, while erotic perception colors the world in the same manner as perception in general, it also colors the world quite differently by offering a privileged way of experiencing our being-in-the-world and the ambiguity of our existence.

This ambiguity of our existence is further doubled in Merleau-Ponty's account of erotic perception in so far as the very relation between existence and sexuality is characterized as thoroughly ambiguous and impossible to determine. Rejecting both the idea that all existence has a sexual significance in which existence would merely be another name for sexual life, and the notion that sexual life is "an expression of our general manner of projecting our setting," Merleau-Ponty claims that sexuality is always present in human life like an ambiguous atmosphere and as such it is "co-extensive with life." There is, he continues, "interfusion between sexuality and existence, which means that existence permeates sexuality and *vice versa*, so that it is impossible to determine, in a given decision or action, the proportion of sexual to other motivations."[10] What precisely makes perception erotic is thus impossible to tell and cannot be determined through a set of clearly defined criteria. However, it is clear from Merleau-Ponty's writings on the constitution and emergence of meaning, that perception, whether erotic or not, is not in any way neutral or untainted but is rather already infused with sense and signification of the situation in which it emerges and is formed.[11]

---

9. Merleau-Ponty, *Phenomenology of Perception*, 167. This is also what Simone de Beauvoir expresses in *The Second Sex* when writing that erotic experience is that which most vividly lays bare the ambiguity of the human condition. See de Beauvoir, *The Second Sex*, trans. Constance Borde & Sheila Malovny-Chevallier (New York: Alfred A. Knopf/Random House, 2010), 416. Merleau-Ponty further argues that it is *only* in the sphere of ambiguity that we come to achieve contact with ourselves. See *Phenomenology of Perception*, 381.

10. Merleau-Ponty, *Phenomenology of Perception*, 159, 169 (italics in original).

11. Merleau-Ponty puts it aptly in the preface to *Phenomenology of Perception* where he writes "we are *condemned to meaning*" simply by virtue of being embodied beings embedded in the world "and we cannot do or say anything without its

The area of sexuality and eroticism is unquestionably soaked with conflicting and ambiguous meaning embodied in prohibitions, social conventions, trends and fashions that contribute to forming the horizon of erotic perception and to establishing whether or not a site has erotic significance. While eroticism and sexuality are often viewed as belonging to a realm where affectivity, as Diprose writes, "either puts the self most at risk" or "might secure the self's liberation from social constraints," this view rests on the flawed assumption that the realm of eroticism and sexuality can be detached from social, cultural and historical meanings and values.[12] Perception, erotic or not, is always given birth in and of a social, cultural, material, historical situation and is thoroughly intersubjective across temporal and spatial dimensions. Singular articulations of meaning are composed of the borrowed, habituated, continuously transformed and established conducts, gestures and expressions that haunt and inhabit embodiment by virtue of its intercorporeality. When Merleau-Ponty writes that erotic perception in the most manifest way lays bare our relation to the world, this also involves our relation to its social, cultural and historical dimensions and does not refer to some "pure" and socially undistorted immediate corporeal attachment to the materiality of the world. There is no such pure attachment. Rather the fleshy sense I have of the world and of myself as part of the world is in equal measure a social, cultural and historical sense. And, meaning must be understood as through and through embodied and material prior to any detachment or abstraction. Meaning is sense and involves, as the word suggests, the feeling, sensing, sentient, and sensible dimensions of embodied material existence.[13] The body's relation to the social world is, to borrow words from Diprose, "inseparable from, and of the same order as, its relation to the world, not a relation of objectification but of carnal intertwining prior to any reflexive judgment."[14]

acquiring a name in history." See *Phenomenology of Perception*, xix (italics in original).

12. Rosalyn Diprose, *Corporeal Generosity: On Giving with Nietzsche, Merleau-Ponty, and Levinas* (Albany: SUNY Press, 2002), 76.
13. See Alphonso Lingis, *Libido: The French Existential Theories* (Bloomington: Indiana University Press, 1986), 104f.
14. Diprose, *Corporeal Generosity*, 104.

It is thus the total situation of my embodied existence, in all of its overflowing ambiguity that will determine whether or not perception has an erotic significance for me. And in so far as erotic perception is the lens through which the structure of operative intentionality and our attachment to the world most clearly is made manifest, this also marks erotic perception as a privileged lens for bringing to light how operative intentionality as a foundational structure cannot be understood as separate from and untainted by that which it founds. Quite to the contrary, all objectifications, reflections and abstract meanings seep through down to their foundation and contribute, without any possibility of determining how or in what measure, to forming the way they are founded. The total situation of my embodied existence includes all of my history, cultural and social context, all of my sedimented knowledge and habituated prejudice.

As is clear from the above, it would be a mistake to locate the bond between the self and its world, as well as erotic experience through which it is made manifest, in a realm entirely separate from reflection and objectifying thought. Rather, this bond is always present also in the most abstract of reflections. As is also clear above, it would equally be a mistake to make this bond a relation between two stable entities. Rather, the bond between self and world is one of transformation and continuous becoming in which both the self and its world (and self and other) as well as the specific relation between them emerge in movements of intertwinement and unraveling, identification and differentiation, approach and withdrawal. Merleau-Ponty demonstrates how this attachment has the structure of an intentional movement and directionality on a corporeal level through perception and motility. To move one's body, he writes (and shows), "is to aim at things through it." As the body is operatively-intentionally directed towards the world and in that direction separates itself from the world (to which it still nevertheless remains attached in detachment) it is at the same time exposed to the world and to itself. Merleau-Ponty continues the quote just above by saying that to move one's body "is to allow oneself to respond to their [things'] call, which is made upon it independently of any representation."[15] In its intentional movement and direction

---

15. Merleau-Ponty, *Phenomenology of Perception*, 139.

towards the world, the body also exposes a direction towards itself as it is called upon by things in the world. The operative intentionality that comes to light through the lens of erotic experience is brought to the fore as exposure of existence as the event in which the meaning of the lived world and of the self continuously originates anew. As the world comes into being for the self, the self also comes into being in relation to the world, as a reaching out of itself and, in that reaching, as exposure to the world, to others and to its own exterior.

III

What then is this exposure that I want to locate at the very core or our being as that operative intentionality through which we are attached to the world? What is it to expose and to be exposed? Etymologically the word indicates a putting of something outside of and out from itself. To expose something is to make it manifest or visible and thereby also to delineate its boundaries (and often give the illusion of these boundaries as stable, fixed, original and true). To be exposed carries the meaning of being uncovered or unprotected without shelter or defense. Skin is exposed to a burning sun or a glacial wind. Eyes are exposed to light. One can be exposed to hostility, violence or danger. To be exposed indicates defenselessness and vulnerability. The word exposure is also heavily laden with connotations of the real, truth and authenticity and it suggests that there is something underneath appearances that can be uncovered or unmasked and brought to light. Exposure is in one sense after all the unveiling of *aletheia*.

While exposing oneself, the putting of oneself out from oneself, may obviously be entirely voluntary, it must also on a different level and in a different sense be understood as involuntary, or rather as falling outside any framework operating in terms of volition. The non-volitional exposure of oneself to others is also a simultaneous exposure of oneself to oneself, an exposure that may strike unexpectedly and with some measure of surprise or shock. One may willfully want to expose oneself through the posing of something in a specific form outside of itself, such as a persona or recognizable identity with which one identifies or wants to identify, and this willful ex-posure (or ex-posing) may in fact also involve the exposure of something entirely different.

Taking on a specific tone of voice before an audience may be an attempt to ex-pose a sense of authority and command but may appear
forced and instead expose that very authority and command as belonging to a sheltering persona. Too good of a performance may expose it
for the performance it is while also exposing the performer, or exposing an emptiness or void in the midst of and flooding the performance.
In such cases we should be careful not to locate a substantial and
autonomous inner subject behind the performance. While there may
indeed be an experiential dimension of being distanced or even detached from a certain way of acting, this dimension cannot easily be
located inside of an external shell or behind, beyond, beside or in front
of what is seen. This dimension cannot be localized and even saying
that it is in the midst of that which is seen is misleading for it is at once
an overflowing and recoiling that defies any objective determination
even as that which is seen is objectively determined.

Visconti's portrayal of Gustav von Aschenbach in *Death in Venice* is
a telling and tragic portrait of precisely this ambiguity between exposure (ex-posing) and exposure. Tormented by his obsessive attraction to Tadzio and by his newly confirmed knowledge that Venice is
indeed gripped by pestilence, von Aschenbach finally does not follow
the advice to leave the city but instead attempts to escape having to
face his own mortality in more ways than one. Several dimensions and
meanings of exposure and concealment emerge and are brought into
play here. As von Aschenbach is exposed to the truth of the concealed
plague that is threatening the city and with that also to his own exposure to the deadly threat, he places himself in the hands of a coiffeur
who reassures him that he will take away his grey hair and restore the
natural color that belongs to him. He is told that he is far too important a person to be slave to conventions about nature and artifice.[16]
Not willing to escape the threat of the deadly plague and the threat of

---

16. The reference to nature and the natural in this interchange between von
Aschenbach and his coiffeur is interesting. On the one hand the coiffeur appeals
to von Aschenbach's sophistication and importance as the raison d'être for not
buying into conventions about nature and culture, on the other hand, in offering
to remove the grey hair he appeals precisely to an underlying nature that should
be restored. The idea of what is natural is thus both something to be overcome
and something to be reinforced.

his own impending death, von Aschenbach covers up the signs of aging and transforms himself into a clown-like figure with all the tragedy embodied by it. With his transformation he also unintentionally and ironically turns himself into an image of the old man in full make-up who greets him with well-wishes upon his arrival in Venice as well as of the haunting toothless street musician who sticks out like a sore thumb in the exclusive sphere of the Grand Hôtel des Bains. Both of these figures stir up repulsion and disgust displayed with no uncertainty in von Aschenbach's facial expression and in his drawing away at their encounter. In both of them the decay of the flesh is exposed in all of its ghastly horror through excessive make-up laying bare the vulnerability that it is intended to cover up. Gustav von Aschenbach's own transformation into another one of these scripted figures masked in make-up seems to seal his already foreseen doom.

The ex-posure of von Aschenbach takes place in and is accentuated by the world of posing in which he finds himself and of which he is part. The sheltered and threatened milieu of the Grand Hôtel des Bains is a world of posing, of enormous hats with extravagant plumage, of parasols, of velvet, satin, silk and long pearl necklaces, of cigars and leather sofas, of palm trees in oversized vases on pedestals, of linen suits and straw hats, of elegant decadence. It is a world in which von Aschenbach fits perfectly prior to his transformation, in spite of appearing utterly uncomfortable. After his transformation however, he no longer seems to belong quite as easily in these surroundings and there is something inappropriate and indiscreet in the unintentional intrusion of his new appearance. There is a vulgarity in the display of von Aschenbach that threatens the privileged and secluded milieu of the Grand Hôtel des Bains and that serves to expose this milieu in a rather unforgiving way. Through the manifestation of von Aschenbach's exaggerated pose after his transformation, both the artificiality of the milieu of the Grand Hôtel and its guests as well as the seemingly unquestionable naturalness with which this artificiality is performed stand out with clarity.[17]

_____

17. Further, through exposing himself in ex-posing the mask of his artificially made up appearance, he directs an uncomfortably sharp light on the vulnerability of this sheltered milieu and seem to not only seal his own doom but also the fate

Also concealed and exposed is von Aschenbach's own vulnerability in the face of his threatening desire for Tadzio. He leaves the coiffeur with new confidence and the encouraging words that now, after the re-fabrication of his youth and restoration of his nature, he may fall in love. While his desire puts him outside of himself and exposes him in more ways than one, leaving him uncovered and without protection, von Aschenbach at the same time attempts to expose himself in a different way than being without shelter, namely to put himself outside of himself, to make himself manifest and delineate his identity through the masks of make-up and dyed hair. He recalls of Alphonso Lingis' description of the "sparked and streaked coral fish" that "school and scatter as a surge of life dominated by a compulsion for exhibition, spectacle, parade."[18] He is exposing a pose, finding and creating a role for his exposure. He is ex-posing himself through the pose of an ideal of youth, embodied in red lips, whitened face and darkened hair. This exposure of his being, the very identity of his being, comes to be through and *as* the ex-posure designed both to protect and lay bare. There is thus a double dimension to the exposure on display in the portrayal of von Aschenbach. His own willful exposure of himself as an object exposes his vulnerability that is brought out throughout and that he attempts to control by a masked return to a fabricated ideal of a past that never was. Through his ex-posure his being is brought out as exposure. There are slippages of desire in his ex-posure through which he reaches out and passively lays himself open to experience simply by virtue of being in and of the world.

The very basic sense of exposure as openness to experience and to the world impressing and imposing itself on us points us right to that original form of bodily operative intentionality that Merleau-Ponty makes manifest in his descriptions of sexuality and erotic perception. When seeing how beings begin to exist for us through desire or love and thereby coming to understand corporeally how things and beings can exist in general, we are confronted with the desire for existence as exposure to existence. This sense of exposure also carries an element of direction inherent in the meaning of intentionality in so far as

---

of an entire way of life.

18. Alphonso Lingis, *Excesses: Eros and Culture* (Albany: SUNY Press, 1983), 9.

exposure is exposure directed in specific ways towards an outside. The corporeal operative intentionality which is my basic and necessary attachment to the world and which lies as the foundation for all object-directed intentionality, detachment, distancing and forms of reflection is at the same time a basic exposure to the world in terms of an openness to experience. Intentionality which is a directedness from an inside or a stretching (from *tendere*) out of and from itself is at the same time exposure of itself as an outside. Interiority is made open in the exterior and exteriority is at the same time found at the very heart of interiority. Inside and outside are, as Merleau-Ponty insists, "wholly inseparable. The world is wholly inside and I am wholly outside myself."[19]

Understanding operative intentionality in terms of exposure thus has the advantage of displacing the interiority of the self and rethinking its relation to exteriority and to that which is transcendent to it. Such an understanding offers the possibility of disrupting the problematic vocabulary of inside and outside, inner and outer, interiority and exteriority that is burdened by dichotomous thinking and all too often reduced to a schematic structure of exclusionary terms. The interiority of subjectivity is no longer shut off from the world towards which it is intentionally directed but rather is to be found in the midst of and exposed to this world and to itself.[20] The disclosure of the inner world of intentionality as exposure is recognition of the impossibility of pinning down subjectivity by giving it a spatial designation and locking it up on the inside of a physical body. Subjectivity "haunts space," as Lingis writes, "it is nowhere localizable, and most evident in the distances." Attempts at positing subjectivity in "the here-and-now of a palpable body" are bound for certain failure and will only demonstrate its absence in that body and the impossibility of making

---

19. Merleau-Ponty, *Phenomenology of Perception*, 401.
20. Already in the preface to *Phenomenology of Perception* Merleau-Ponty dismisses philosophies that argue for an inner self as the sole and absolute constituting force. He writes, "there is no inner man, man is in the world, and only in the world does he know himself"; "there is no 'inner' life that is not a first attempt to relate to another person." See *Phenomenology of Perception*, xi; *The World of Perception*, trans. Oliver Davis (London & New York: Routledge, 2004), 88; *Causeries 1948* (Paris: Editions du Seuil, 2002).

that absence present.[21] Instead of being posited within the boundaries of the skin, subjectivity is everywhere present but nowhere to be grasped.

The original form of intentionality that Merleau-Ponty brings out in his account of erotic perception and through which my body aims at another on a level of blind comprehension does not originate in my body as a self-enclosed entity with distinct boundaries but rather in my body as it is extended out into the world and receiving its boundaries as it encounters the world's resistance and thereby also itself and its own exterior.[22] As I am intentionally directed towards the world and others I am at the same time perpetual exposure to the world and others and I continuously become who I am in and as this exposure. It is important here to bear in mind that this radical disruption of the distinction between inner and outer through operative intentionality as exposure in no way does away with a sense of interiority vital to experience. We do experience a sense of interiority or own-ness that is untouchable and untouched by the outside and this experiential dimension cannot be dismissed in favor of a complete collapse between interiority and exteriority. While what is traditionally located on the inside and outside respectively cannot be easily distinguished but are rather revealed as being one and the same, it is nevertheless of imperative importance to recognize the immediate presence of self to self as a sense of intimate interiority. However, recognizing this sense of intimate interiority as vital to experience does not entail reducing interiority to a self-enclosed entity. Quite to the contrary, the very experiential dimension of this intimate sense of self exteriorizes it and

---

21. Lingis, *Libido*, 104.

22. In the same way as my body cannot be understood as a mere vessel for the mind, the world cannot be understood simply as a container for the lived body. And, it is equally misguided to view the mind as a vessel for either body or world. To speak with Merleau-Ponty, "We have to reject the age-old assumptions that put the body in the world and the seer in the body, or, conversely, the world and the body in the seer as in a box" (*The Visible and the Invisible*, 138). Rather, he writes, being embodied "is to be tied to a certain world, [...] our body is not primarily *in* space: it is of it" (*Phenomenology of Perception*, 148). In the later writings, he famously deepens this understanding of the relation between the embodied self and its world as one of intertwinement and mutual becoming.

exposes me to the other and to the world of which I form part. The lived body is brought out as the exterior of my most intimate interiority and at the same time the interior experience of an exteriority that is only present through continuous escape and absence.

IV

The operative intentionality of erotic perception that "comprehends blindly by linking body to body" is, as we have seen, not directed towards the world or bodies as objects. According to Merleau-Ponty, "a sight has sexual significance for me, not when I consider, even confusedly, its possible relationship to the sexual organs or to pleasurable states but when it exists for my body" as a power of transcendence towards it.[23] Erotic significance, situated and emerging in a cultural, social and historical context, forms and marks the identifiable boundaries of its object. There is, as Lingis puts it, "no contour disengaging a figure from the ground without a significance." Rather, "it is the significance that delineates the contour."[24] Identity comes to being and becomes identifiable as a specific identity through intentional relations of sense in which it is continuously exposed to itself in its delineation of itself. In Visconti's *Death in Venice* it is clear that von Aschenbach's desire is not directed towards Tadzio as an object. Tadzio's erotic significance does not stem from any objectively recognizable features of his being and cannot be caught by representational descriptions. Rather, his identity as an object (which may or may not be sexualized) rests on the significance he receives in his encounter with von Aschenbach on the level of corporeal intentionality and exposure.

Drawn by desire, blinded by desire even, von Aschenbach follows Tadzio's every move as if his own existence depended on his exposure to Tadzio's presence. The boy comes to embody an ideal of beauty that he has long sought and Tadzio's carnal presence, to speak with Diprose, strikes von Aschenbach's "carnality as a variation, as a resonating

---

23. Merleau-Ponty, *Phenomenology of Perception*, 157.
24. Lingis, *Libido*, 104f.

echo" of a manner he himself possesses in his incarnate self-awareness.[25] Through Tadzio's presence the world for von Aschenbach comes to be in an entirely new way full of wonder, torment, pleasure, pain, excitement and anxiety. As Tadzio begins to exist for him through the corporeal intentionality of desire, he also begins to exist for himself as desiring and as exposed to the world and to Tadzio. What is it then that von Aschenbach desires? If it is not directed towards Tadzio as an object, what is the aim of his desire? What is the operative corporeal intentionality of erotic perception directed towards? What is the animating force of exposure?

Portraying an experience of diving and encountering the world under the surface of the sea, Alphonso Lingis describes how the "eye adrift in the deep finds itself in a cosmos of phenomena and not of noumena" where it "is not penetrating, examining, interrogating, surveying, gauging" but "passes over surface effects, caresses."[26] For the caressing eye "moved by the thalassa complex," he continues, "the deep is an erotogenic zone."[27] This eroticized and voluptuous eye "that no longer pilots or estimates, that moves, or rather is moved" does not seek "the substances, the principles, the causes of the alien" but instead seeks for "the look of the other."[28] It is this look of the other, the look of Tadzio that von Aschenbach desires; through his caressing eye, he aims (aimlessly) at being caressed and being seen. The caressing eye, writes Lingis, is moved by the movement it provokes in the other.[29] But, following Merleau-Ponty, we are lead to say that the caressing eye is more than moved by how it incites the other. It depends on the look of the other for its own look and the desire to be seen is a desire also to see and to become seer-seen. Erotic perception, as well as perception in general, does not for Merleau-Ponty originate in a detached perceiver but is instead given birth in the midst of the perceivable. He illustrates the birth of vision and the emergence of visible bodies in terms of a reflexive folding and turning back: "a cer-

25. Diprose, *Corporeal Generosity*, 103.
26. Lingis, *Excesses*, 9f.
27. Ibid., 10.
28. Ibid., xi, 10, 13.
29. Ibid., 10.

tain visible, a certain tangible," he writes, "turns back upon the whole of the visible, the whole of the tangible, of which it is a part."[30] Vision comes to be only when it is situated in a certain visible, which appears in this chiasmic movement of what Merleau-Ponty terms flesh.[31] It is thus not I as seer who constitute the other as seen, nor the other as seer who constitutes me as seen. Rather, we both emerge as seers-seens, as visible seers in the midst of the visible of which we form part.

In this description of the emergence of perception our bond with the world and with others is brought out with clarity. Poetically, Merleau-Ponty writes that there is a human body "when the spark is lit between sensing and sensible."[32] This birth of human embodied existence as visible to others is also the birth of sensation, of vision and touch experienced and embodied by human subjectivity in continuous emergence. While this attachment quite easily recedes from view in the experience of perception in general in which we take a perspective

30. Merleau-Ponty, *The Visible and the Invisible*, 139.
31. Merleau-Ponty describes the notion of flesh as "an ultimate notion" and a prototype of being, for which there is "no name in traditional philosophy." It is intended to move beyond and overcome the absolute dualisms between mind and body, subject and object, consciousness and world. The flesh, Merleau-Ponty writes, "is not matter, is not mind, is not substance." Instead, he describes it as "a sort of incarnate principle that brings a style of being wherever there is a fragment of being" (*The Visible and the Invisible*, 139). In this description of the flesh as an incarnate principle, which is also termed an "anonymity innate to Myself," Merleau-Ponty indicates its formative force and function, and he writes further that the flesh is "the formative medium of the object and the subject" (*The Visible and the Invisible*, 139, 147). The notion of flesh is somewhat enigmatic as it resists definition and reduction into either of its manifestations. The flesh is that underlying element which through a chiasm or intertwining breaks down the walls and bridges the gaps which are inherent to and constitutive of binary oppositions. The notion of flesh provides the resources for dichotomizing but the notion is at the same time beyond all attempts of analysis through the categories of subject and object, or any other dualisms. Subject and object, touching and touched, self and world, emerge as specific configurations of flesh and as they are of flesh, they are reversible and in constant movement, constant configuration and reconfiguration.
32. Merleau-Ponty, "Eye and Mind," trans. Carleton Dallery in *The Primacy of Perception*, ed. James M. Edie (Evanston: Northwestern University Press, 1964), 159–190, 163; *L'Œil et l'Esprit* (Paris: Gallimard, 1964).

on that which we perceive and experience detachment and distance rather than attachment, erotic perception makes this bond between self and world and self and other stand out as a bond which unbinds in binding. In erotic perception it becomes clear that operative intentionality is not immediately geared towards any objectifying function. As we know, perception carries the seed to reflection and objectifying operations and the original relationship between the embodied subject and its world is transformed by its own activity. In erotic perception as one form of operative intentionality, this transformative movement is arrested and my bond to the world and the other remains evident while also revealing a fracture or moment of unbinding within itself.[33]

The desire of erotic perception is the desire of the other which sustains my own desire and always escapes my grasp as radically other to me. In Visconti's portrayal of Gustav von Aschenbach it is brought out beautifully how the figure of Tadzio draws von Aschenbach out of himself in the reaching out of his exposure. This force of Tadzio's presence is equally a force by which Tadzio is drawn towards von Aschenbach meeting his operative intentionality and exposure. The film of course does not portray Tadzio as anything but the background and object of von Aschenbach's desire and we only see Tadzio through the perspective of von Aschenbach. Exposing himself to Tadzio in shaping him as an object of desire through his caressing eye, von Aschenbach solicits the awareness and attention of Tadzio as that off of which he feeds for the becoming of his own being and sense of self. As much as Tadzio comes to signify, he nevertheless remains the background for von Aschenbach's own exposure to himself. Von Aschenbach's desire for Tadzio has little to do with Tadzio himself but with the significance that outlines his contour. The caress of the eye, as Lingis writes, "makes contact only to expose itself" and "does not know what it wants." It struggles "to expose exposure itself."[34] In this

---

33. This is of course not to say that sexual and erotic objectification is not possible. Quite to the contrary. And, as argued above, the different ways in which bodies are and have been sexually objectified and in which different conduct and characteristics are and have been signified as sexual inform the corporeal intentionality of erotic perception.

34. Lingis, *Excesses*, 10f.

view, erotic perception as the caress of the eye seeks to uncover the very uncovering of its own movement. Following Merleau-Ponty's claim that erotic experience is what most manifestly brings to light our attachment to the world in exposing our operative intentionality as the directedness of our being towards the world of which we are part, the caress of the eye as erotic perception does expose exposure itself as that original and constant attachment which unbinds in binding.

V

I have suggested that Merleau-Ponty in his account of sexuality and erotic perception brings out an operative intentionality that is through and through exposure. Through this original form of intentionality which links body to body I am immediately related to the world of which I am part and which is part of me. The exposure of myself to the world and to others is thus at the same time a radical exposure of myself to myself through which I continuously become who I am. Merleau-Ponty argues that sexuality is the area in human existence that most manifestly brings to light our attachment to the world and he shows how this attachment is a bond that unbinds in binding. While I continuously become who I am in intimate interrelation with the world of which I form part, my becoming is at the same time one of separation and imminent loss. In being operatively-intentionally directed towards the world I am torn from the world and from myself still bound to the world. The attachment between self and world is a bond that is unbreakable but that nevertheless carries a moment of differentiation within itself in continuously binding self and world together as they emerge and receive significance in relation to one another.[35]

As I have attempted to show above, Luchino Visconti's portrayal of Gustav von Aschenbach in *Death in Venice* brings out with clarity how erotic perception makes exposure and vulnerability manifest in force-

---

35. In other writing I have referred to this mutual becoming of self and other, as well as self and world, as an expressive process of "selving" and "othering." See Käll, "Expression Between Self and Other" (in *Idealistic Studies* 39:1–3, 2009), 71–86.

ful ways. As exposed to the world and to his own desire, von Aschenbach is put outside of and out from himself in a way which propels his
becoming in new directions. The portrayal displays, through the explicit manifestation of risk in the threat of the lethal pestilence, the
ever-present risk involved in the intercorporeal becoming that constitutes the very foundation of human existence.[36] Von Aschenbach, in
more ways than one, risks himself through desire and only becomes
who he is in the continuous possibility of his own loss as he is exposed
outside of himself. In his energetic flow of life, he loses himself and
through the loss is revealed to himself in unexpected ways. He finds
himself as he feels himself alive without anything to guard him against
the threats to his exposed vulnerability. This movement of becoming
is a movement of return without origin, a movement in which the
identity of the self is fractured and becomes itself through alteration.
The return of self to self is no return to a sameness that remains unal-
tered and in the return reemerges intact as it was. Instead the return
is the very moment of alteration within identity and constitutive of
identity.

This intimate interrelation of continuous becoming is what on Merleau-Ponty's account is brought to light with such clarity in erotic
experience. He makes manifest how our bodily operative intentionality is exposure of our existence in terms of a corporeal openness to
experience and to the world impressing itself upon us. As we experience the birth of being through desire or love, we at the same time
experience our desire for existence as exposure to existence. The desire
that draws us toward the other is equally a desire for oneself, as it is a
desire for the other. This desire is the longing of the self for itself in
relation to the other, reaching out from itself in order to become itself.

---

36. As Rosalyn Diprose writes, no "project involving a generosity of flesh, that
carnal giving and transformation of oneself through the other's flesh" is ever safe
in terms of securing one's body integrity. I always risk myself in becoming myself
and the integrity and boundaries of my body are continuously reconfigured and
renegotiated in the process of intercorporeal becoming. See Diprose, *Corporeal
Generosity*, 92.

The Erotic as Limit-Experience: A Sexual Fantasy

JONNA BORNEMARK

1. *Introduction*

It is difficult to write about eroticism; it is at once too personal and too common. Phenomenology is supposed to start out from experience, making the task even more difficult. We can try to hide under the cover of eidos or under what is general, without giving away our own relation to this burning question, but this risks only to show the blindness of our own specificity, our own personal desires, as one of (at least) two sexes. In the phenomenological attempts to address this issue – such as in the work of Levinas, Marion and Sartre – one could argue that this endeavor has been carried out by a certain kind of (French) man.[1] Their specificity might be more pronounced here than when they broach other subjects. They are, so to say, caught with their pants down, where we often gain an insight into how their own sexual life is structured. All their intellectualism tends to be seen as a façade, behind which lay a male-centric, heterosexist, patriarchal variant of sexuality, the kind of which we are all too familiar. They are, after all, "only men." So writing on the erotic risks degrading the intellectual to mere drives. To write on the erotic is to go to a place

---

1. Jean-Paul Sartre, *Being and Nothingness*, trans. Hazel E. Barnes (New York: Washington Square Press, 1966), part 3, chapter 3, Jean-Luc Marion, *The Erotic Phenomenon*, trans. Stephen E. Lewis (Chicago and London: University of Chicago Press, 2007); *Le phénomène érotique: six méditations* (Paris: B. Grasset, 2003), Emanuel Levinas, *Totality and Infinity*, section IV, trans. Alphonso Lingis (The Hague: Martinus Nijhoff, 1969). See also Cederberg's and Dahlberg's articles in this volume.

where the intellectual task unavoidably becomes personal, and where the personal goes beyond every person. But even if I complain about the chauvinism exhibited by those above mentioned philosophers, praise must nonetheless be given to those who dare to take the subject on.

One reason for this tension within the erotic phenomena might be its problematic relation to what is interior and what is exterior and how these are interrelated. The erotic is in my opinion not only an ontic region that should be described but a phenomena through which some central tenets of phenomenology come into play. In the following I shall attempt to show how this subject can provide us with philosophical material for thinking the relation between interiority and the exterior, between immanence and transcendence. In order to do so I would like to start by presenting a problem in phenomenology that has its starting-point in Edmund Husserl, namely the problem regarding objectifying intentionality and its limits. This problem receives a special kind of solution in the philosophy of Michel Henry who resolves it by distinguishing between two very different kinds of intentionality. Also Jean-Luc Marion undertakes a similar separation where it plays a specific role in his analysis of the erotic phenomenon. I shall argue that both Henry and Marion resolve this problem in a similar way, but that the solutions they offer are problematic. Nonetheless, I will find in their theories certain themes that are worth developing further. By trying to give an alternative interpretation of the erotic experience I would like to give another kind of solution to the problem discussed. And I will finally try to use this analysis of the erotic to understand why eros is such a problematic theme within philosophy.

2. A Phenomenological Problem

Husserl describes intentionality as directed and as such involving an object that it is directed towards. The aim of Husserlian phenomenology is to analyze intentionality itself and to uncover its structure. The intentionality of the phenomenologist is thus directed towards the structure of intentionality and turns in this way back to itself, making itself into an object. It is in this movement that a problem arises: once

THE EROTIC AS LIMIT-EXPERIENCE

intentionality is turned into an object, is it still intentionality? Intentionality is per se what experiences and when the experien*cing* capacity itself is changed into something experien*ced*, it could be argued that its central features or eidos is lost. It is no longer the movement of lived subjectivity but rather it is turned into an object within the stream of intentionality. What is supposed to be studied is thus slipping away, it is what *performs* the study, instead of staying in place as the *object* for the study.

Husserl stumbles upon this problem in his analyses of inner time consciousness. Such analyses are supposed to give the base for his phenomenological investigation.[2] He formulates it as an infinite regress where each analysis of intentionality opens up for a new one. In Husserl (as well as after Husserl) there have been two major interpretations of how to understand this infinite regress. One way is to understand it as a chimera and to claim that there is no difference between intentionality as thematized and intentionality as thematizing. To become an object for thematization does not change anything, nothing is lost in the transformation.[3] But in his later texts Husserl gives an opposing interpretation, according to which this problem is understood as instituting an irreducible gap between subjectivity and objectivity – a gap that can never be overcome. Something central to intentionality is thus lost once it becomes an object.[4]

---

2. Edmund Husserl, *Ideen zu einer reinen Phänomenologie und phänomenologischen Philosophie, Buch 2*, Hua IV, ed. Marly Biemel (Haag: Martinus Nijhoff, 1969) §22, 102f

3. Husserl himself wants to make such an interpretation in for example *Die Bernauer Manuskripte über das Zeitbewusstsein (1917/18)*, Hua XXXIII, eds. Rudolf Bernet och Dieter Lohmar (Dordrecht : Kluwer, 2001), text 10, 201f and in *Zur Phänomenologie des inneren Zeitbewusstseins*, Hua X, ed. Rudolf Boehm (Haag: Martinus Nijhoff, 1966), text 54, 382.

4. The problematic is discussed not least through the concept *Nachträglichkeit*, i.e. through what can only be understood afterwards, and as something that always transcends consciousness. See for example *Späte Texte über Zeitkonstitution (1929– 1934). Die C-manuskripte.* Hua, Materialien band VII, utg. Dieter Lohmar (Dordrecht: Springer, 2006), text 32, 130f and *Die Bernauer Manuskripte über das Zeitbewusstsein (1917/18)* text 15, 287. See also Smith's contribution in this volume. Klaus Held is one of the first to use this character of the infinite regress in a positive way. He claims that the living stream (*Lebendige Gegenwart* or *Nunc stans*) cannot be

The first of these interpretations has resulted in a phenomenology proximal to Husserl's own explicit project whereas the second has been central in a reformulation of phenomenology, not least among French phenomenologists. This latter interpretation has been formative in the development of a phenomenology interested in questions regarding passivity, transcendence/immanence, along with other kinds of intentionality besides an objectifying one. Michel Henry belongs to those afflicted with this second tendency.

3. Michel Henry's Solution

Michel Henry takes this problem as the starting-point of his philosophy. The main features are given in *Essence of Manifestation* from 1963.[5] For Henry the problem with phenomenology is its too narrow understanding of intentionality. He claims that understanding oneself, as an intentionality directed towards itself, is not an act of an object-creating consciousness but a radically different kind of intentionality, the intentionality of self-affection or self-knowledge. And he understands this kind of intentionality as foundational to object-intentionality. We can thus differ between two kinds of intentionality:

Object-directed intentionality through which we relate to transcendent beings. i.e. beings that are other than the one who experiences them and which are known through a mediated and outer knowledge. Since there is a gap between intentionality and its object such knowledge is always uncertain.

Self-affection on the other side is a kind of knowledge through which our own being is given to us directly. This means that such knowledge is given immediately, it is a reflection that does not involve any distance. It is an action, an effort, and a movement. It is therefore

---

reformulated as an object without losing its central tenets, but that it nevertheless is given in a positive way. Klaus Held, *Lebendige Gegenwart – Die Frage nach der Seinsweise des transzendentalen Ich bei Edmund Husserl, entwickelt am Leitfaden der Zeitproblematik*, (The Hauge: Martinus Nijhoff, 1966).

5. *Essence of Manifestation*, trans. by Girard Etzkorn, (The Hauge: Martinus Nijhoff, 1973). *L'essence de la manifestation*, (Paris: PUF, 1960). He poses the question for example at page 28. The following references are made to the English translation.

not mediating or objectifying knowledge, which demands distance. Henry identifies this knowledge with the active and knowing productive force, that is, the ego which does not see itself as an object but receives itself in self-affection (233). For Henry this means an inner, and absolute, knowledge upon which all outer knowledge is dependent. In contrast to all transcendent experiencing, this knowledge is understood as immanent. Here there is a perfect coincidence between the act of experiencing and the content that is experienced. Both are related to the same essence. Henry understands this as the unity of presence (72).

The first kind of intentionality – the objectifying intentionality – is dependent upon the second self-affective intentionality, since this is the living, experiencing force of every intentionality. What Husserl was seeking – namely, a basis for all knowledge that we have direct access to – is what Henry claims to have found. But it is at the cost of the possibility to formulate a content of this intentionality. Language needs the distance between intentionality and its object and in an intentionality without such distance, there can be no room for words. Henry disagrees with both Husserl and Heidegger when he challenges an understanding of consciousness as giving representations (51, 81). Instead he emphasizes that this distanceless immanence is the essence of manifestation and functions as a foundation for every experience. Before the split, where consciousness becomes transcendent to itself and turns itself into an object, it is immanent (228).

This self-consciousness is, though, not a consciousness of *a* self, but a consciousness of the self in the experience of the object. A self-consciousness that makes it possible for objects to come forth. Henry's point is that this self-consciousness, which makes all consciousness possible, is characterized neither by a split nor an internal division. Henry therefore accuses most phenomenology for being an ontological monism, having too narrow an understanding of intentionality. He rejects the idea that there is only one kind of phenomenality and that the given can only be given as an object. By this, he means that this mistake has led phenomenology to the paradigm of intentionality, which also understands self-consciousness as objectified. Henry wants instead to understand self-manifestation as an immediate, non-objectified, passive phenomenon of self-affection. As such there is no distance between the feeling of pain and the consciousness of it. This immanent being is very different from the transcendent being: it is a non-horizontal, non-ecstatic, atemporal and acosmic immanence. Its unique form of immediate, non-ecstatic manifestation cannot be grasped by any categories that are adjusted for objectified phenomenality; rather, he claims that this immanence is what always escapes reflexive thematization. This immanence has therefore been called invisible and obscure. Its appearance is invisible, but it is not non-appearance; on the contrary, it is the most foundational kind of manifestation. It is not unknown, but known in a radically different way. It is not non-being, rather a radically different being.

This self-affection is formulated as self-sufficient and it gives rise to the following question (which has been pointed out by many phenomenologists, for example Rudolf Bernet and Dan Zahavi): how could reflection, spatiality, difference and alterity ever come into being?[6] In one of his last works *I am the Truth* this gap becomes even more problematic. Here, Henry even understands the transcendent world of exteriority as untrue in relation to the true world of immanence. In a similar way he distinguishes between the living and Life itself, prioritizing Life at the cost of the living – a dangerous strategy, not least politically.[7]

Henry develops a slightly different, and to my mind more fruitful, position in *Philosophy and Phenomenology of the Body*.[8] Here he connects the theme of self-affection to an investigation of the body. The body is here not understood as Cartesian extension, nor is it regarded as the biological body. (5ff) Rather, what Henry is interested in is described

---

6. See for example Rudolf Bernet, "Christianity and Philosophy" (in *Continental Review*, nr 32, 1999), 25–42, Dan Zahavi, "Michel Henry and the Phenomenology of the Invisible" (in ibid), 223–40.

7. *C'est moi la vérité: pour une philosophie du christianisme* (Paris: Editions du Seuil, 1996); English translation S. Emanuel, *I am the Truth* (Stanford, California: Stanford University Press, 2003), xx.

8. *Philosophie et phénoménologie du corps: essais sur l'ontologie biranienn* (Paris: PUF, 1965); *Philosophy and phenomenology of the body*, trans. by Girard Etzkorn (Haag: Martinus Nijhoff, 1975). Henry is here offering a reading of Maine de Biran – but I will, in this short discussion of the text, neglect Biran and only describe Henry's position. The following references are made to the English translation.

as a transcendental body. This body is as fundamental as the ego and fuses with the self. To define the human being as body therefore results not in a materialism but, instead, in an undermining of materialism (11).

Henry focuses on the ability of the body, or rather the body as ability. The body is the hand that strokes and thus the ability to strike. The movement is not something that is mediated by a body as something between an ego and a world, rather this action is understood as the direct knowledge of self-affection. The action, the movement, *is* the ego and it *produces* a world. The body is therefore not an instrument that someone is using, rather, the movement of the body produces both a transcendent world and a transcendent self as an object for itself. Before the body becomes objectified it is a force. To understand the body as an immanent, transcendental, direct and distance-less being and, moreover, to understand this body as foundational for subjectivity, means to accept another way of understanding both being and knowledge. As discussed above it is a distanceless knowledge which entails no division in being. In this way, Henry can claim that the ego *is* the categories that *have* transcendent knowledge (73ff).

In *Phenomenology and Philosophy of the Body*, Henry thus emphasizes the relation between self-affection and an objectifying intentionality. The body, as the place of self-affection, is thus called *transcendental* – and not *immanent* as self-affection, as it will come to be named in *Essence of Manifestation*. The point of calling it transcendental is to focus on its relation to what is transcendent. He understands this relation in the following way: when my hand meets resistance, transcendent extension is created. Transcendent extension is thereby a formulation of the limits of my effort. We find the transcendent world as a necessary consequence of the body as transcendental movement. Transcendent and transcendental share a conceptual root because they belong together; the transcendental is the necessity of the movement and the transcendent is what resists this movement. The necessity and certainty of the movement, the transcendental, therefore also includes the certainty of the transcendent, that which resists. The existence of the outer world is as necessary as the existence of the inner. In the development of Henry's argument we could even say that "inside" and "outside" are given shape and contours in the meeting, that is, from out of the transcendental movement. The unity of the world – between two kinds of being (transcendental and transcendent) – is given by the unity of this movement. In this way Henry means that the transcendent as resistance escapes the phenomenological reduction and thereby makes transcendent being both possible and necessary as the immanence of self-affection (89ff).

Body is here primarily immediate knowledge of the self, and secondarily knowledge of the self as an object to this immediate experiencing. It is at the same time transcendental and transcendent knowledge, and therefore primarily not a knowledge *about* the self but *about* the transcendent. Bodily knowledge is therefore not exactly a knowledge but rather a power to knowledge. (125f)

The phenomenological paradox of the impossibility of seeing the seeing – that is to say, the paradox of the empirical self that at the same time is a transcendental body – is understood by Henry by a twofold usage of sign: the words "to see," i.e. the sign for seeing, is used as a reflection of this experience of seeing. Seeing moves from being a transcendental, internal, experience and becomes an object for a new experience in reflection. "To see" becomes thereby a transcendent correlate to the immanent body. It is no longer the seeing that is seen, but a representation of the seeing. Thus a split arises which is necessary for the naturalized attitude, and through this split we understand the eye as an object which sees. The body splits thereby into an original, transcendental body and a physiological body (111ff). This is all very close to Husserl's distinction between "Leib" and "Körper," which, at the same time, are one.

In *Philosophy and Phenomenology of the Body* Henry thus focuses on how immanence – here symptomatically called transcendental – is connected to transcendent being. But in texts such as *Essence of Manifestation* and *I am the Truth*, the difference and incompatibility of immanence and transcendence is emphasized. Generally speaking, Henry's philosophy is always at the border of becoming a dualism where an objectifying intentionality is secondary and is on the morally bad side (especially in *I am the Truth*). This sharp division between immanence and transcendence is, however, balanced in the best way in his analysis of the transcendental body.

4. Jean-Luc Marion and the Erotic: the Problem Reappears

A theory of intersubjectivity and of the other person does not play any important role in Henry's philosophy. From this perspective Marion's phenomenological analysis of the erotic can be understood as a development of Henry's philosophy of the body. As we will see, the immanence of self-affection is here reached in the erotic phenomena, but only through a total dependence upon the other person. Even so, in the end Marion's philosophy of the erotic inherits a set of problems from Henry's philosophy of immanence.

In *The Erotic Phenomenon* Marion argues for what he calls an erotic reduction, this means that the self is given not mainly through doubt (as in Descartes' *Cogito ergo sum*) but through the fact that one is loved by someone else: only through this love from the outside can the existence of the self be justified.[9] The I finds itself whenever the question "Am I loved?" arises. Like others in the phenomenological tradition Marion also claims that I can think myself only since I can feel myself, but through the question of whether I am loved he claims that I experience how I am given from an outside. Me loving myself is not enough, I need to borrow the loving gaze of the other person to understand myself as one among many in a world. However, the starting-point for Marion is not only the love of the other person, but equally the love that the self feels toward the other person. This love is without why – or rather it is the place where every "Why?" is born. Love starts out without knowing what love is, who the loved one is or who me that is loving is, all this can only come after love (90).

It is in loving that Marion finds a self-affection, where I affirm myself, since I have to go along with my own feeling. I find myself as loving and as already affirming my own desires (94, 97). And this is a self that always stands in relation to another, open to alterity. The self-affection is here, in contrast to Henry, only possible within a network of otherness. Marion also gives the flesh and the impossibility to feel the feeling a central role in his argument. In contrast to Henry's

---

9. *The Erotic Phenomenon*, 22 ff. Following references are made to the English translation.

understanding of immanence, Marion claims that the self can not fully know itself since it can only know itself as felt and not as feeling. It is not firstly an ego that knows the other, but the ego is rather loving and structured around the other, and where the other is only second-arily an object. Primarily we are loved and loving. It is also through desire we are individualized: I am the loved one of the other and thus am different from all other. To summarize it is in love that I receive myself through a threefold passivity: the first passivity is the dependence upon the other who loves me; the second is the receiving of one-self as loving, even before the love has a specific content and this second passivity also shows the third one, namely that in loving I put myself at risk and in risking myself I realize that there is a self to risk (109f). The individual is thus given passively through both the love of the other and the love of the self. Love as a structure before knowledge is an old phenomenological theme, developed not least by Max Scheler (even though Scheler emphasizes loving as giving the person its direction, whereas Marion emphasizes the love of the other as the possibility for my existence).[10] This analysis of love gives us a different understanding of intentionality, which is important to phenomenology since intentionality is no longer only a knowledge-structure. In Marion's writings it is developed further into an understanding of the erotic encounter but, as we will see, I think a certain problematic returns at this point.

Having a self that can be put at risk also includes being flesh – a body among many in the world. This body is exposed to a world that affects me and includes within me a certain passivity. The world affects me but the things of the world are characterized as something that can be experienced but they are themselves not experiencing. The world is in this way only given as body and as full of "things," i.e. of transcendent beings (in Henry's vocabulary), rather than of flesh (or transcendental body in Henry's terminology) as that which produces both an immanence of self-affection and a world of transcendent beings. But the erotic experience changes exactly this state of affairs. In the

---

10. I discuss this in my *Kunskapens gräns, gränsens vetande: en fenomenologisk undersökning av transcendens och kroppslighet* (Huddinge: Södertörn Philosophical Studies, 2009), 131ff.

erotic encounter the other person is suddenly given as giving, i.e. as experiencing flesh. It is thus not only a thing but another flesh. I can feel the other person as *feeling* at the same time as he or she is also a body that remains inaccessible to me (114ff).

So Marion claims that the erotic encounter is an experience of pure experiencing flesh – beyond every experience of the body as an object. How is the experiencing flesh of the other person experienced? In the world it is only the I that is given as flesh, and not the other person. My flesh alone has the doubleness of feeling and being felt, and I can only feel the world since I can feel myself. The world is given only through my flesh. I can only take the experience of the other person seriously through turning it into an experience of mine. The experiencing flesh of the other is only supposed, and never experienced. Neither is the object of desire something that can be reached as a worldly object to be possessed and consumed. The erotic object is simply not an object among many in the world. Rather, flesh and the denuding of flesh would not entail an uncovering of an object. That no flesh can appear as object suggest that, in Marion's philosophy, there is an irreversible gap between the flesh and the body.

In the erotic, Marion continues, I feel the other, I feel the other feel and I feel the other feel me. An intertwining between me and the other take place. Nevertheless, there are still two different subjects who feel. What changes this, Marion argues, is that the flesh of the other does not resist me as other bodies do. Bodies of the world expel me from their space – which makes me find myself as this body that is expelled. But in the erotic encounter an inaccessible body suddenly invites me and makes room for me. Precisely, it is this phenomena that characterizes the erotic experience in Marion's philosophy. He claims that in the erotic encounter the flesh of the other makes room for him; the other lets herself be penetrated so that he can stretch out for the first time. Her flesh is "allowing me to come in, by letting itself be penetrated." (118) The other does not want to resist him, and lets him invade her without defending herself. His flesh, thus, no longer touches *some-thing*, since the flesh of the other person no longer is a thing, but the place where he can become flesh in her flesh (119f). Here the straight male perspective is evident, particularly in the resignatory role accorded to his female counterpart. When Marion states that the woman gives place and does not resist, it almost sounds like a rape-victim who has admitted defeat. This inactivity of Marion's woman is further reinforced when he adds that it is her passivity, which increases an arousal "more powerful than every activity" (119).

There is consequently in Marion's analyses never anything erotic to see – what is seen immediately becomes ridiculous as it is thrown out of the immanent experience of the flesh. Thus there is no place for fantasy or any play of the body as an object. Neither are there any erotic organs in the erotic flesh. The role of the other is also so central that Marion claims that auto-erotization has no meaning. He argues that since one's own flesh is only given through this opening in the flesh of the other person, only sex with the other person provides pure flesh and therefore any auto-erotic experience is meaningless. I cannot give flesh to myself (122). An orgasm on one's own and an orgasmic experience with another person are thus two completely different things. Here it is easy to suspect it is the Catholic in Marion that is speaking. I would rather claim that the experience of orgasm on one's own and with another person does not show such essential difference (even if it differs on a social level). Marion means that the auto-erotic experience only involves the body, whereas only the sexual encounter with another person provides us with pure experiencing flesh.

In Marion's description the erotic is the transformation of the body as pure flesh, i.e. pure experiencing, where it is only through this experience that one can become pure flesh. He formulates this as that which she gives him what she does not have and what he does not have on his own. As flesh, no longer any difference exists between different parts of the body. The whole body is eroticized – becoming flesh. As we have seen Marion fixates on the erotic experience as a relation with one other person. The other person is more inner to me than myself, so that he does not have her flesh and his own flesh is given to him when he gives her, her flesh. It is a journey beyond intentionality when he enjoys her enjoyment. Marion even writes that the body becomes "almost immaterial" (135).

The gap between body and flesh also culminates in the climax of this journey, but not in terms of an ascent to the apogee of a mountain-face but in terms of a descent into the emptiness of a ravine within which one hastily falls. Suddenly nothing remains and the lovers are back in a world of things as if nothing had happened. The flesh disappears and the lover is once again part of the world where he finds himself as a naked body. The experience of pure flesh is now understood as a meeting with nothingness. In the return to the world the lover can only formulate his experience in terms of there nothing to see. The orgasm leaves nothing to see and nothing to say. It even takes the memory of the flesh with it. He thus calls the orgasm an erased phenomenon and not a saturated phenomena that would intend more than what is signified[11] (135ff).

The flesh is thus essentially erotic and as such moves towards the flesh of the other. But the erotic must itself also have a limit since, it would otherwise extinguish the world with its bodies in time and space. It is in light of this that Marion claims that we have no common world, only a common flesh: the engagement with the other person brings me beyond the world, and we have nothing to say to one another since language belongs to the world. The erotic encounter only gives a negative language since language only can be about things. This negativity even makes the lover in Marion's philosophy uncertain whether there ever was the flesh of the other person or only her body. It even gives him a suspicion about his own flesh. The erotic thus never fully leads to either the alterity of the other or of the self (143 ff).

Marion's concept "flesh" bears a closer resemblance to Henry's concept of immanence in *Essence of Manifestation*, rather than to his concept of transcendental body in *Phenomenology and Philosophy of the Body*. Both flesh and immanence are pure experiencing beyond any*thing* experienced. The greatest point of difference between them is that in Henry this flesh/immanence is self-donated, whereas Marion claims that this giving takes place in relation only to another person. Despite this, both have the tendency to separate the immanence of the flesh from the exteriority of the body. Marion states that there is no bridge between these two areas: after the orgasm there is nothing to say since the experience of being pure flesh is not possible to take with us to the

---

11. Marion defines the saturated phenomena as a phenomena where the given is experienced as more than what is given directly and more than what is contained in any ideas about the given. See *Etant donné: essai d'une phénoménologie de la donation* (Paris: Presses Universitaires de France, 1997), 280ff.

world of objects. In this way Marion comes closer to Henry's concept of immanence and the problem of two orders of fact that can never come into contact with one another.

Instead of this strict separation between body and flesh (in Marion's terminology) and transcendence and immanence (in Henry's terminology) I want to investigate the erotic as an in between. In the following I will both criticize Marion's and Henry's theories and discuss certain themes that I find fruitful. With Marion, I will uphold the claim that the erotic provides us with a phenomena of central importance to phenomenology. With Henry, I will develop his theory of the transcendental body, understanding it as a springwell for thinking both the interiority of immanence and the objectivity of transcendence. What I want to try to understand is how the gap between the feeling and the felt is constructed in the erotic experience of the transcendental body. I am interested in how images and erotic objects are related to the experience of the flesh. With this aim in mind, there are two phenomena I would like to give specific consideration to, namely the role of fantasy and the erotic body as a limit-experience.

5. Another Phenomenological Analysis of the Erotic

Marion has nothing to say about the role of fantasy in the erotic experience, and I would like to claim that to bring fantasy into the analysis results in a different understanding of the relation between interiority and objectivity. This changed relation between interiority and objectivity can also be developed from the erotic experience understood as the bodily experience of destruction and creation of borders between the inside and the outside. It is, just as Marion writes, an experience where one's own body as well as the body of the other are no longer characterized in terms of a border between an exterior and an interiority. But Marion still understands eroticized flesh in strict separation from the world. Contrariwise, I would like to focus on the connection between the eroticized flesh and objects of the world and try to focus on this experience as entering into the very drawing of a limit that takes place "before" an inside and outside –and that creates thereby an inside and outside.

But let us begin with an analysis of the role of fantasy in the erotic. Fantasy has often been understood as a freedom from the here and now, as the very possibility for the movement of thought.[12] This is true to a certain extent, i.e. insofar as you understand "here and now" as the sense-impressions of a here and now. But if "here and now" instead is understood as a living presence, we can think fantasy as an intensification of the here and now, rather than taking us away from it. This intensification is engendered through the creation of objects or images. Fantasy is the capacity to *make* images present. The erotic fantasy is maybe the most intense kind of fantasy, and its images can really function as an intensification of the living present. The erotic feeling is thus a certain intensification of the feeling of being alive. The fantasy makes the presence fully directed towards one thing: increasing the erotic feeling. Objects – for example the body of the other person – takes part in the fantasy and becomes permeated by the erotic fantasy. The erotic is thus not, as Marion says, to leave the world of objects, but rather to deepen the experience of them and make them permeated with significance. In this intensification we can experience a relation between object and subject – or between the transcendent and the transcendental in Henry's vocabulary – where each is not yet fully separated and where their origin in the living stream is experienced. In this way the erotic fantasy, in permeating the object with significance, draws it into a close connection with the living stream.

It is also through fantasy that we can come close to the erotic experience and that affords thereby the possibility of taking a closer look. So in order to approach this connection between objectivity and interiority and the erotic as a point where they meet and where, for a second, they even fuse, let us enter an erotic fantasy. As is the case with any erotic fantasy, or real encounter, we must lay stress on its singularity, so that we are not describing some universal phenomena. It can thus never be described in the third person; it always takes place between you and me.

So, what attracts me in you is a strong feeling of you being other

---

12. See for example Edith Stein, *Zum Problem der Einfühlung* (Halle: Buchdruckerei des Waisenhauses, 1917), 6ff.

than me, but in this alterity there is also a sense of belonging together, of recognition. Or rather, it is something in that otherness of you that I want to bring closer to me, something that I want to "have." But since I know that I want to have it, it is already in me. You wanting me creates a field of tension between us, playing on alterity and recognition. I want you, and more specifically, I want your body, I want what I can objectify, and I want to experience my own body as a beautiful "thing" that you want. I desire to objectify as much as I desire to be objectified, but this does not turn us into neutral "things" with mere extension. Not even things are things with mere extension, they are filled with meanings that are also redrawn from my experience, meanings that through fantasy can make them burn with significance. They remind me, promise me and, at the same time, hide from me. The other person as an erotic object has everything to do with vision, a vision of a promise. Erotic objectification does not deny the living force of the body, but it celebrates our exteriority, the manifestation of our difference and specificity, i.e., our specific traits. I want to get close to these "specific traits," to have them, to make this specific person mine. How do I do it?

A simple touch, skin that meets skin, would make something happen, it would change things. It would draw my attention to this and nothing else. I would have a very clear direction, and I would long for another touch. I would *feel* the distance between us, a distance that would no longer be made of air, but rather materialized. To be outside of you, other than you, would mean to be directed towards you; it would give me another position, no longer being "inside" a body, controlling a body. But *on, in and of* the skin, I would be only the limit between you and me. You would force me towards my own borders. And this limit between you and me would be on fire, such a fire would mean that the limit, the border between us, no longer only separates us, but also connects us. Every limit, or border, has this double function: it separates and it connects. The limit is what we share.[13]

---

13. The Swedish word for "sharing" is "dela" and, as is the case with the German word "teilen,," it has a double meaning. The sentence: "Vi delar något" / "Wir teilen etwas," means both that we share something or have something in common, "something" would then bind us together, and it could also mean that we take

Right now we could experience how this surface between us connects us and separates us, but there is more than that, since we do not observe this, I do not distance myself from this shared limit, rather I experience it, I am in it. Neither do I experience it as a stable or static phenomenon; on the contrary it is only its own movement, its urge, its attempt to reach and its desire that brings me forth into the "here and now".

In this experience the exteriority and interiority of the body would be one and the same, since it would be my limit, I would be only my limit. And if you were to touch me again, that touch would mean that your skin, where you are, your limit, would join mine in that fire. But only because you can take your skin away again. I would want to violate your borders. Consume you and incorporate what you thought was yours into me. There has to be friction – not only acceptance. I want at the same time to erase your borders *and* to keep them in order to feel them. I want both body and flesh. Destruction of a limit is no clean operation, it is messy and sticky, intertwining and exchanging. Trying so desperately to erase the difference between my own sensitivity and your sensitivity.

In touching me you would not only touch my skin, my border towards an outer world, you would be even closer, touching those places where I normally only touch myself, where the skin becomes membrane, the inside of my mouth in the kiss, the membrane of the vagina in the encounter of the genitals. You break my borders and you dislocate my own self-encounter when wet perforated parts meet. And if we would start to move we could play with the materialized space between us and within us, we could play within the meetings of these limit-drawings, creating difference through annihilating it. Motility would activate all of the body. In the beginning the body would have parts, but when the "I" comes to the limit of the skin, temporality would start to show itself without spatiality and the movement of the circumscription of these limits would be intensified, no longer producing different parts. Instead the different parts of the body would start to dissolve into one another and into an intensified now. It would all be membrane, between you and I.

---

something apart, "something" would then be split up.

You would be my only alterity, the only non-me. Your alterity is intensified, but since you as well as me are nothing but this difference in relation to each other we *exist* only in relation to each other. And when exteriority and interiority melt together or become membrane, we are left with nothing but the event of drawing a line. Membrane resolves the clear distinction of the skin. Through the membrane things gets messy and smooth. Liquids are exchanged and bodies are open.

In orgasm finally the distinct person of "you" and of "me" would be erased, but life and the now would not. In orgasm "I" am no one, I am anonymous, but the "am" is very much present, existence is not erased. This "am" or "sum" is not something of the world, not distinct from something else – it is in this sense a "nothing" and not a worldly experience among many. But even so, I would not say that it is an experience *beyond* the world, rather it goes *into* the world. It only erases differences by intensifying them, intensifying the border itself into its limit-drawing origin, the creation of the border, the powerful energy of annihilating difference, creating difference. It explores pure experiencing beyond you and me – but immediately defined as "my" orgasm – immediately creates a limit between the two of us. Henry's concept of an immediate, non-ecstatic, self-affection and Marion's concept of pure experiencing flesh are born. But these areas are not a lost paradise, they are only created in relation to the simultaneous birth of transcendence and an objectifiable body.

The orgasm is not the end of the world and it does not separate us from the world of extension. Rather, it is the beginning of the world. Through annihilation we experience the creation of the world in two ways, the annihilation is the process of creation seen in reverse. After the orgasm we also experience how the differentiated world returns, how the borders of my and your body re-emerge. How I am once again a separate body and you are another body next to mine. There is also a special connection between our bodies after this, the world re-appears for "us." Our borders are re-constituted, and we are through that separated and able to meet each other in a plural world. After the orgasm, there is not "nothing to say" – as Marion would have it – but everything to say. It is from here that we can speak and allow a world to emerge.

That the other welcomes me and does not resist me is not specific to the erotic phenomenon, as Marion claims; so does a hot bath. What is specific for the erotic encounter is instead its specific kind of meeting in which I am no longer an interiority that tries to communicate with another. I am the limit – not departing from the exteriority of the body to an experience of pure immanence. Pure experiencing is not an interiority separated from the exteriority of the world as both Henry and Marion suggest it to be. Erotic experiencing annihilates and creates the world in one and the same breath and gives birth to the world and the body. The extension of the erotic encounter is to "talk the world," describing it anew – as it arises between us. Experiencing the limit of myself and meeting you there, meeting you as experiencing me. Experiencing beyond you and me – an experience that is a pure limit. The body is a limit in this experience in three ways: first, it is a limit as the maximum of bodily experience; second it is the border of my body as a field next to yours, and finally it is a limit that both divides us and binds us together. This limit shows the possible annihilation of me as a person – and thus also shows the limit constitutive of me and you.

6. Conclusion: On the Limit

Let us go back to the initial question of the relation between transcendent phenomenality and immanent, self-affective flesh. What does the above analysis of the erotic encounter add to an understanding of the relation between these two phenomenalities? My analysis shows in what way these two are intimately bound in a mutual interdependence, more in line with Henry's theory of the transcendental body than with his discussions on immanence. Or, rather immanence turns out to be the *drawing* of the line, the separating movement itself. This drawing of a line (immanence, flesh or transcendental) can thus never have a value on its own, but only in relation to the transcendent world that it constructs and deconstructs. Orgasm might be a true limit-experience in which the limit-drawing is most apparent. Maybe this limit-drawing could even be formulated as a "living wellspring of experience," to borrow an expression of Jan Patočka.[14]

---

14. Jan Patočka, *Body, Community, Language, World*, trans. Erazim Kohák (Chicago and la Salle, Illinois: Open Court, 1998), 3.

Through this differentiating and separating movement, gaps are created. This limit-drawing always results in the identification of one side as "mine" and primary, and the other side as "other" and secondary. It thus draws a line between you and me, manifesting "me" as known and primary and you as partly unknown and secondary. But it also draws a line within this "me" separating the operating, primary, limit-drawing operation, from the empirical, objectified, secondary self, and the flesh, identified with the "inner self," from the body, as a constructed exteriority. The movement and living force in the limit-drawing thus immediately identifies itself as one side of the differentiation.

The erotic coheres around the experience of destruction of the border between body and flesh, immanence and transcendence, between you and me. Through these destructions the mutual dependency of the two sides also shows itself. It is also a unique experience of an intensification of a life-force, of the here and now, of a creative life.

Maybe this also gives us a hint about why the erotic is such a problematic theme within phenomenology. If phenomenology starts out from experience and "first-person-perspective," the erotic encounter is dangerous since it risks this perspective. It cannot, as other theories, keep the phenomena at a safe distance, discussing it as if it did not affect me. Instead it puts the phenomenologist in an awkward position: we are stripped of all our defenses, showing ourselves as most un-sophisticated bodily impulses, in its bluntness as exactly *this* life. At the same time the erotic in its specific way touches upon something common, and maybe even universal: limit-drawing as both a creative and separating movement. But this creative movement immediately casts me aside as but a contingency, which could have been drawn quite differently, and the theories of which could have been constructed otherwise.

Bibliography

Agamben, Giorgio, *L'ombre de l'amour. Le concept d'amour chez Heidegger*, Paris: Payot et Rivages, 2003

Arendt, Hannah, *Der Liebesbegriff bei Augustinus. Versuch einer philosophischen Interpretation*, Berlin: Philo-Verlagsgesellschaft, 2005; Berlin: Springer, 1929

Arendt, Hannah, *The Human Condition*, Chicago: The University of Chicago Press, 1998

Arendt, Hannah, *The Life of the Mind*, New York: Harvest Book, 1971

Arendt, Hannah, *The Origins of Totalitarianism*, New York: Harcourt, 1994 [1951]

Arendt, Hannah, "What is Existenz Philosophy?" in *The Phenomenology Reader*, eds. Dermot Moran and Timothy Mooney, London: Routldge, 2002

Arendt, Hannah and Heidegger, Martin, *Briefe 1925–1975*, Frankfurt am Main: Vittorio Klostermann, 1998

Arnou, René, *Le désir de Dieu dans la philosophie plotinienne*, Paris: F Alcan, 1921

Bataille, Georges, *Inner experience*, trans. Leslie Anne Boldt, Albany: State University of New York Press, 1988

Bataille, Georges, *La part maudite*, Paris: Les Éditions de Minuit, 1967; *The accursed share*, trans. Robert Hurley, New York: Zone Books, 1991; 1993

Bataille, Georges, *L'érotisme*, Paris: Les Éditions de Minuit, 1957; *Eroticism: Death and Sensuality*, San Francisco: City Lights Books, 1986 [1962]; 2001

Bataille, Georges, *The absence of myth: Writings on surrealism*, ed. and trans. Michael Richardson, London and New York: Verso, 1994

Bataille, Georges, *Theory of religion*, trans. Robert Hurley, New York: Zone Books, 1989

Bataille, Georges, "The passage from animal to man" in *The cradle of humanity: Prehistoric art and culture*, ed. Stuart Kendall, trans. Michelle Kendall and Stuart Kendall, New York: Zone Books, 2005

Bataille, Georges, *The tears of Eros*, San Francisco: City Lights Books 1989

Beauvoir, Simone de, *Le deuxième Sexe*, Paris: Gallimard, 1949; *The Second Sex*, trans. Constance Borde and Sheila Malovny-Chevallier, New York: Alfred Knopf / Random House, 2010

Beauvoir, Simone de, *Pour une morale de l'ambiguïté*, Paris: Gallimard, 1947

Bernasconi, Robert and Critchley, Simon (eds.), *Re-reading Levinas*, Bloomington: Indiana University Press, 1991

Bernasconi, Robert and Critchley, Simon (eds.), *The Cambridge companion to Levinas*, Cambridge: Cambridge University Press, 2002

Bernet, Rudolf, "Christianity and Philosophy" in *Continental Review*, nr 32, 1999, 25-42

Binswanger, Ludwig, *Grundformen und Erkenntnis menschlichen Daseins*, Zürich: Max Niehans, 1942; Ausgewählte Werke, Bd 2, Heidelberg: Asanger, 1993

Bittrich, Ursula, *Eros und Aphrodite in der antiken Tragödie. Mit Ausblicken auf motivgeschichtlich verwandte Dichtungen*, Berlin: De Gryuter, 2005

Bornemark, Jonna, *Kunskapens gräns, gränsens vetande; en fenomenologisk transcendens och kroppslighet*, Huddinge: Södertörn Philosophical Studies, 2009

Broch, Hermann, "Evil in the value-system of art" in *Geist and Zeitgeist: The spiritual in an unspiritual age*, ed. and trans. John Hargraves, New York: Counterpoint, 2002

Broch, Hermann, *The death of Virgil*, trans. Jean Starr Untermeyer, New York: Pantheon, 1945

Cairns, Dorion, *Conversations with Husserl and Fink*, The Hague, 1976

Calasso, Roberto, *The Marriage of Cadmus and Harmony*, trans. Tim Parks, New York: Vintage International, 1994

Canby, Vincent, "Movie Review: *Death in Venice*" in *The New York Times*, June 18, 1971

Cicero, *Tusculan meditations*, trans. C. D. Yonge, New York: Harper, 1877

Coulanges, Fustel de, *The Ancient City*, New York: Anchor Books, 1956

Couloubaritsis, Lambros, *Aux origines de la philosophie eruopéenne. De la pensée archaïque au néoplatonisme*, Bruxelles; de Boeck, 1992

Dastur, Françoise, "Amore, noità e cura. Note a proposito della Grundformen di Lundwig Binswanger" in *Ludwig Binswanger. Esperienza della soggetività e transcendenza dell'altro*, A cura di Stefano Besoli, Quodlibet; Macerata, 2007, 519-534

Deleuze, Gilles, *Difference and repetition*, trans. Paul Patton, New York: Columbia University Press, 1994 [1968]

Deleuze, Gilles and Guattari, Félix, *Anti-Oedipus: Capitalism and schizophrenia*, trans. Robert Hurley, Mark Seem, and Helen Lane, Minneapolis: University of Minnesota Press, 1983 [1972]

Deleuze, Gilles and Guattari, Félix, *What is philosophy?*, trans. Hugh Tomlinson and Graham Burchell, New York: Columbia University Press, 1994

Depraz, Natalie, *Transcendance et incarnation. Le statut de l'intersubjectivité comme altérité à soi chez Husserl*, Paris: Vrin, 1995

Derrida, Jaques, *De la grammatologie*, Paris: Minuit, 1967

Derrida, Jaques, "Freud and the scene of writing" [1966] in *Writing and Difference*, London: Routledge, 1997

Derrida, Jaques, *La voix et le phénomène*, Paris: PUF, 1967

Diprose, Rosalyn, *Corporeal Generosity: On Giving with Nietzsche, Merleau-Ponty, and Levinas*, Albany: SUNY Press, 2002

Dōgen, *Shushōgi* in *Zen master Dōgen: An introduction with selected writings*, trans. and ed. Yūhō Yokoi and Daizen Victoria, New York: Weatherhill, 1976

Fanon, Frantz, *Black skin, white masks*, trans. Charles Lam Markmann, New York: Grove Press, 1967

Farber, Marvin (ed.), *Philosophical Essays in Memory of Edmund Husserl*, Cambridge MA: Harvard University Press, 1940

Farrell Krell, David, *Lunar voices: Of tragedy, poetry, fiction, and thought*, Chicago: The University of Chicago Press, 1995

Fink, Eugen, "Eros und Selbstverständigung – Seinssinn des Eros" in *Grundphänomene des menschlichen Daseins*, Freiburg:Karl Alber Verlag, 1995

Franck, Dider, *Chair et corps. Sur la phénoménologie de Husserl*, Paris: Minuit, 1981

Freud, Sigmund, *Penguin Freud Library*, 15 volumes, eds. Angela Richards and Albert Dickson, Hammondsworth: Penguin Books, 1973-1986

Freud, Sigmund, *Project for a Scientific Psychology* [1895] in *Standard Edition*, vol. I, London: The Hogarth Press and the Institute of Psychoanalysis, 1953-1974

Freud, Sigmund, *Studienausgabe*, 11 volumes, eds. Alexander Mitscherlich, Angela Richards and James Strachey, Frankfurt am Main: Fischer Verlag, 1969–1975 with *Ergänzungs Band*, Frankfurt am Main: Fischer Verlag, 1975

Freud, Sigmund, Gadamer, Hans-Georg, *Wahrheit und Methode: Grundzüge einer philosophischen Hermeneutik*, Tübingen: Mohr, 1960; *Truth and Method*, New York: Crossroad, 1989

Geiger, Moritz, "Fragment über den Begriff des Unbewußten und die psychische Realität" in *Jahrbuch für Philosophie und phänomenologische Forschung* IV, 1921

Gram, Moltke, "Intellectual Intuition: The Continuity Thesis" in *Journal of the History of Ideas*, 42 1981: 287–304

Hadot, Pierre, *Plotin. Traité 50 (III, 5). Introduction, traduction, commentaire et notes*, Paris: Cerf, 1990

Haraway, Donna, *When species meet*, Minneapolis: University of Minnesota Press, 2008

Hegel, G W F, *The Phenomoenolgy of Spirit*, Cambridge: Oxford University Press, 1979

Heidegger, Martin, *Basic writings*, trans. David Farrell Krell, Harper, San Franscico, 1992

Heidegger, Martin, *Besinnung*, Gesamtausgabe 66, Frankfurt am Main: Klostermann, 1997; *Mindfullness*, New York: Continuum, 2006

Heidegger, Martin, "Das Ding" in *Vorträge und Aufsätzte*, Stuttgart: Verlag Günther Neske, 1954

Heidegger, Martin, *Das Ende der Philosophie und die Aufgabe des Denkens*, Tübingen: Max Niemeyer Verlag, 1976

Heidegger, Martin, *Die Metaphysik des deutschen Idealismus: zur erneuten Auslegung von Schelling: philosophische Untersuchungen über das Wesen der menschlichen Freiheit und die damit zusammenhängenden Gegenstände (1809)*, Gesamtausgabe 49, Frankfurt am Main: Klostermann, 1991

Heidegger, Martin, *Die Metaphysik des Satzes vom Grunde*, Frankfurt am Main: Klostermann, 1990 [1928]

Heidegger, Martin, "Ereignis" in *Gedachtes*, Gesamtausgabe 81, Frankfurt am Main: Klostermann, 2007

Heidegger, Martin, *Erläuterungen zu Hölderlin's Dichtung*, Gesamtausgabe 4, Frankfurt am Main: Klostermann, 1981

Heidegger, Martin, *Grundprobleme der Phänomenologie*, Gesamtausgabe 58, Frankfurt am Main: Klostermann, 1993

Heidegger, Martin, *Heraklit: 1. Der Anfang des abendländischen Denkens; 2. Logik, Heraklits Lehre vom Logos*, Gesamtausgabe 55, Frankfurt am Main: Klostermann, 1979

Heidegger, Martin, *Metaphysische Anfangsgründe der Logik*, Gesamtausgabe 26, Frankfurt am Main: Klostermann, 1978

Heidegger, Martin, *Reden und andere Zeugnisse eines Lebensweges*, Gesamtausgabe 16, ed. Hermann Heidegger, Frankfurt am Main: Klostermann, 2000

Heidegger, Martin, *Sein und Zeit*, Tübingen: Max Niemeyer Verlag, 1993 [1927]; *Being and time*, trans. Joan Stambaugh, Albany: State University of New York Press, 1996

Heidegger, Martin, "Was ist Metaphysik?" in *Wegmarken*, Frankfurt am Main: Klostermann, 1967; "What is metaphysics?" in *Basic Writings*, ed. David Farell Krell, Routledge, London, 1993

Heidegger, Martin, *Zollikoner Seminare*, ed. Medard Boss, Frankfurt am Main: Klostermann, 1987; *Zollikon Seminars*, Evanston, Il: Northwestern University Press, 2001

Heidegger, Martin, *Zu Hölderlin,* Gesamtausgabe 75, Frankfurt am Main: Klostermann, 2000

Heidegger, Martin and Blochmannn, Elisabeth, *Briefwechsel 1928-1969*, Marbach am Neckar, 1990

Held, Klaus, *Lebendige Gegenwart – Die Frage nach der Seinsweise des transzendentalen Ich bei Edmund Husserl, entwickelt am Leitfaden der Zeitproblematik*, The Hauge: Martinus Nijhoff, 1966

Henry, Michel, *C'est moi la vérité: pour une philosophie du christianisme*, Paris: Editions du Seuil, 1996; *I am the Truth*, trans. Susan Emanuel, Stanford, California: Stanford University Press, 2003

Henry, Michel, *Généalogie de la psychanalyse. Le commencement perdu*, Paris: PUF, 1985; *The genealogy of psychoanalysis*, trans. Douglas Brick, Stanford: Stanford University Press, Stanford, 1993

Henry, Michel, *L'essence de la manifestation*, Paris: PUF, 1960; *Essence of Manifestation*, trans. Girard Etzkorn, The Hauge: Martinus Nijhoff, 1973

Henry, Michel, *Phénoménologie matérielle*, Paris: PUF, 1990; *Material phenomenology*, trans. Scott Davidson, New York: Fordham University Press, 2008

Henry, Michel, *Philosophie et phénoménologie du corps: essais sur l'ontologie biranienn*, Paris: PUF, 1965; *Philosophy and phenomenology of the body*, trans. Girard Etzkorn, Haag: Martinus Nijhoff, 1975

Hesiods, *Theogony*, Harvard: Loeb Classical Library, 1914

Husserl, Edmund, *Analysen zur passiven Synthesis. Aus Vorlesungs- und Forschungsmanuskripten (1918–1926)*, Husserliana XI, ed. Margot Fleischer, Den Haag: Nijhoff, 1966

Husserl, Edmund, *Die Bernauer Manuskripte über das Zeitbewusstsein (1917/18)*, Husserliana XXXIII, eds. Rudolf Bernet and Dieter Lohmar, Dordrecht : Kluwer, 2001

Husserl, Edmund, *Erste Philosophie (1923/4). Zweiter Teil: Theorie der phänomenologischen Reduktion*, Husserliana VIII, ed. Rudolf Boehm, Den Haag: Nijhoff, 1959

Husserl, Edmund, *Ideen zu einer reinen Phänomenologie und phänomenologischen Philosophie, Buch 2*, Husserliana IV, ed. Marly Biemel, Haag: Martinus Nijhoff, 1969

Husserl, Edmund, *Logische Untersuchungen*, Husserliana XIX/1, ed. Ursula Panzer, Den Haag: Nijhoff, 1984

Husserl, Edmund, *Philosophie der Arithmetik. Mit ergänzenden Texte (1890–1901)*, Husserliana XII, ed. Lothar Eley, Den Haag: Nijhoff, 1970

Husserl, Edmund, *Späte Texte über Zeitkonstitution (1929–1934): Die C-Manuskripte*, Husserliana Materialen 8, ed. Dieter Lohmar, Dordrecht: Springer, 2006

Husserl, Edmund, *Zur Phänomenologie des inneren Zeitbewusstseins (1893–1917)*, Husserliana X, ed. Rudolf Boehm, Den Haag: Nijhoff, 1966

Husserl, Edmund, *Zur Phänomenologie der Intersubjektivität. Texte aus dem Nach-lass. (1905–1920)*, Husserliana XIII, ed. Iso Kern, Den Haag: Nijhoff, 1973

Husserl, Edmund, *Zur Phänomenologie der Intersubjektivität (1928–1935)*, Husserliana XV, Den Haag: Nijhoff, 1973

Hölderlin, Friedrich, *Poems and fragments*, trans. Michael Hamburger, London: Anvil Press Poetry Ltd., 1994

Hölderlin, Friedrich, *Sämtliche Werke und Briefe*, 3 volumes, ed. Jochen Schmidt, Frankfurt am Main: Deutscher Klassiker Verlag, 1992

Hölderlin, Friedrich, *Sämtliche Werke und Briefe*, 3 volumes, ed. Michael Knaupp, München: Carl Hanser Verlag, 1992

Irigaray, Luce, "Questions to Emmanuel Levinas. On the Divinity of Love" in *Re-reading Levinas*, eds. Robert Bernasconi and Simon Critchley, Bloomington: Indiana University Press, 1991

Jaspers, Karl, *Way to wisdom: An introduction to philosophy*, second edition, trans. Ralph Manheim, New Haven, Yale University Press, 2003 [1951]

Kane, Sarah, "Phaedra's Love" in *Complete Plays*, London: Methuen Publishing Ltd, 2001

Kéléssidou-Galanos, A., "Le voyage érotique de l'âme dans la mystique plotinienne" in *Platon*, 24, 1972, 88–100

Kundera, Milan, *The book of laughter and forgetting*, trans. Aaron Asher, New York: Harper Collins, 1996 [1978]

Kundera, Milan, *The unbearable lightness of being*, trans. Michael Heim, New York: Harper and Row, 1984

Kurz, Gerhard, "Aus linkischem Gesichtspunkt: Zu Hölderlins Ansicht der Antike" in *Antiquitates Renatae: Deutsche und französische Beiträge zur Wirkung der Antike in der europäischen Literatur. Festschrift für Renate Böschenstein zum 65. Geburtstage*, eds. Verena Ehrich-Haefeli, Hans-Jürgen Schrader and Martin Stern, Würzburg: Königshausen & Neumann, 1998

Kurz, Gerhard, *Mittelbarkeit und Vereinigung: Zum Verhältnis von Poesie, Reflexion und Revolution bei Hölderlin*, Stuttgart: J. B. Metzlersche Verlagsbuchhandlung, 1975

Käll, Lisa Folkmarson, "Expression Between Self and Other" in *Idealistic Studies*, 39:1–3, 2009, 71–86

Lacoue-Labarthe, Phillipe, "Typography" in *Typography: Mimesis, philosophy, politics*, ed. Christopher Fynsk, Stanford: Stanford University Press, 1989

Laplanche, Jean and Pontalis and Jean-Bertrand *The Language of Psychoanalysis*, London: Karnac Books, 1988

Levinas, Emmanuel, *Autrement qu'être ou au-delà de l'essence*, Paris: Le livre de poche, 1990; 2004 [1974]; *Otherwise than Being or Beyond Essence*, trans. Alphonso Lingis, Pittsburgh: Duquesne, 1998

Levinas, Emmanuel, *Humanismus des anderen Menschen*, Hamburg: Felix Meiner, 1989

Levinas, Emmanuel, *Le temps et l'autre*, Paris: Fata Morgana, 1979 [1946/1947]

Levinas, Emmanuel, *Totalité et Infini. Essai sur l'extériorité*, The Hague: Martinus Nijhoff, 1961; Paris: Kluwer, 1971; Le Livre de Poche, 1990; *Totality and infinity: An essay on exteriority*, trans. Alphonso Lingis, Pittsburgh: Duquesne University Press, 1969

Liddel, Henry George and Scott, Robert, *A Greek-English Dictionary*, The Perseus Project, http://perseus.mpiwg-berlin.mpg.de

Lingis, Alphonso, *Excesses: Eros and Culture*, Albany: SUNY Press, 1983

Lingis, Alphonso, *Libido: The French Existential Theories*, Bloomington: Indiana University Press, 1986

Marion, Jean-Luc, *Etant donné: essai d'une phénoménologie de la donation*, Paris: Presses Universitaires de France, 1997

Marion, Jean-Luc, *Le phénomène érotique*, Paris: Bernard Grasset, 2003; *The erotic phenomenon*, trans. Stephen Lewis, Chicago: University of Chicago Press, 2007

Merleau-Ponty, Maurice, *Causeries 1948*, Paris: Editions du Seuil, 2002; *The World of Perception*, trans. Oliver Davis, London & New York: Routledge, 2004

Merleau-Ponty, Maurice, *La Prose du monde* (Paris: Gallimard, 1969) trans. John O'Neill, *The Prose of the World* (Evanston: Northwestern University Press, 1973), 143.

Merleau-Ponty, Maurice, *Le visible et l'invisible, suivi de notes de travail*, ed. Claude Lefort, Paris: Gallimard, 1964; 1999; *The Visible and the Invisible. Followed by Working Notes*, ed. Claude Lefort, trans. Alphonso Lingis, Evanston: Northwestern University Press, 1968

Merleau-Ponty, Maurice, *Phénoménologie de la perception*, Paris: Gallimard, 1945; *Phenomenology of Perception*, trans. Colin Smith, London & New York: Routledge, 1962

Merleau-Ponty, Maurice, *Signs,* trans. Richard Mc Cleary, Evanston: Northwestern University Press, 1964

Mishima, Yukio, *Confessions of a Mask*, trans. Meredith Weatherby, New York: New Directions, 1958

Mondolfo, Rodolfo, *El pensamiento antiguo. Historia de la filosofía greco-romana*, Buenos Aires: Ed Losada, 1983

Montaigne, Michel de, "That to philosophize is to learn to die" in *The complete works of Montaigne*, trans. Donald Frame, Stanford, California: Stanford University Press, 1967

Moutsopoulos, Evanghelos, *La musique dans l'oeuvre de Platon*, Paris: Presses universitaires de France, 1959

Nancy, Jean-Luc, *Being singular plural*, trans. Robert D. Richardson and Anne E. O'Byrne, Stanford: Stanford University Press, 2000

Nancy, Jean-Luc, "L'amour en éclats" in *Une pensée finie*, Paris: Galillé, 1991

Nietzsche, Friedrich, *Also sprach Zarathustra. Vorrede. Kritische Studieausgabe*, München: de Gruyter, 1988

Nietzsche, Friedrich, *The Birth of Tragedy*, trans. W. Kaufmann, New York: Random House, 1967

Nietzsche, Friedrich, *Werke in drei Bänden*, ed. Karl Schlechta, München: Carl Hanser Verlag, 1956

Nishida, Kitarō, *Last writings: Nothingness and the religious worldview*, trans. David Dilworth, Honolulu; University of Hawaii Press, 1987 [1945]

Nishida, Kitarō, "The unity of opposites" in *Intelligibility and the philosophy of nothingness*, trans. Robert Schinzinger, Honolulu: East-West Center Press, 1966

Nonnus, *Dionysiaca*, trans. William Henry Denham Rouse, Loeb Classical Library 344, Cambridge: Harvard University Press, 1940

Nygren, Anders, *Eros och ágape*, Stockholm: AB Tryckmans, 1930

Ortega y Gasset, José, *Estudios sobre el Amor*, Madrid: Salvat, 1971 [1939]; *On Love: Aspects of a Single Theme*, trans. Toby Talbot, New York: Meridian Books, 1957

Ortega y Gasset, José, *What is philosophy?*, trans. Mildred Adams, New York: Norton, 1960 [1929]

Pankseep, Jaak and Burgdorf, Jeff, "'Laughing' rats and the evolutionary antecedents of human joy?" in *Physiology & Behavior* 79, 2003, 533–547

Patočka, Jan, *Body, Community, Language, World*, trans. Erazim Kohák, Chicago and la Salle, Illinois: Open Court, 1998

Pépin, Jean, "La dernière parole de Plotin" in *Porphyre. La vie de Plotin*, vol. II, 355–383

Pigler, Agnès, "La réception plotinienne de la notion stoïcienne de sympathie universelle" in *Revue de Philosophie Ancienne*, 19, 1, 2001, 45–78

Pigler, Agnès, *Plotin: une métaphysique de l'amour. L'amour comme structure du monde intelligible*, Paris: Vrin, 2002

Plato, "Phaedo" in *Five dialogues*, second ed., trans. George Maximilian Anthony Grube, rev. John Cooper, Indianapolis: Hackett, 2002

Plato, "Republic" in *Complete Works*, trans. George Maximilian Anthony Grube, rev. C. D. C. Reeve, ed. John Cooper, Indianapolis: Hackett Publishing Company 1997

Plato, *Symposium*, trans. Alexander Nehamas and Paul Woodruff, Indianapolis: Hackett Publishing, 1989

Porphyrius, *La vie de Plotin*, Paris: Vrin, 1992

Reinhardt, Karl, "Hölderlin und Sophokles" in *Tradition und Geist: Gesammelte Essays zur Dichtung*, Göttingen: Vandenhoeck and Ruprecht, 1960

Ricœur, Paul, *De l'interprétation. Essai sur Freud*, Paris: Seuil, 1965

Sappho, *Alcée Sapho*, Paris: Les Belles Lettres, 1966

Sartre, Jean-Paul, *L'être et le néant. Essai d'ontologie phénoménologique*, Paris: Gallimard, 1943; 2003; *Being and Nothingness: A Phenomenological Essay on Ontology*, trans. Hazel Barnes, New York: Washington Square Press, 1992, 1956; Routledge, 1958; 1966

Sartre, Jean-Paul, *Nausea*, New York: New Direction Books, 1964

Scheler, Max, *Liebe und Erkenntnis*, Bern: Francke Verlag, 1955

Scheler, Max, "Ordo amoris" in *Schriften aus dem Nachlass, Band I, Zur Ethik und Erkenntnislehre*, Bern: Der neue Geist Verlag, 1933

Scheler, Max, *Schriften aus dem Nachlass, Band III, Philosophische Anthropologie*, Bonn: Bouvier Verlag Herbert Grundmann, 1987

Scheler, Max, *Vom Umsturz der Werte*, Bern: Francke Verlag, 1955

Scheler, Max, *Wesen und Formen der Sympathie*, Bern: Francke Verlag, 1974

Scheler, Max, *Zur Phänomenologie und Theorie der Sympathiegefühl und von Liebe und Haß*, Halle: Verlag von Max Niemeyer, 1913

Schelling, F W J, *Aphorismen über die Naturphilosophie*, 1806

Schelling, F W J, *Philosophie der Mythologie*, 1842

Schelling, F W J, *The ages of the world*, 1815 draft, trans. Jason Worth, Albany: The State University of New York Press, 2000

Singer, Peter, *Animal liberation: A new ethics for our treatment of animals*, New York: New York Review Books, 1975

Smith, Nicholas, *Towards a Phenomenology of Repression. A Husserlian Reply to the Freudian Challenge*, Stockholm: Acta Universitatis Stockholmiensis, 2010

Stein, Edith, *Zum Problem der Einfühlung*, Halle: Buchdruckerei des Waisenhauses, 1917

Stendhal, *De l'amour*, Paris: Hypérion, 1936

Tani, Toru, "Transzendentales Ich und Gewalt" in *Phänomenologie und Gewalt*, eds. Harun Maye and Hans Rainer Sepp, Würzburg: Königshausen and Neumann, 2005

Taylor, Thomas, *Eleusinian and Bacchic Mysteries*, Lighting Source Publishers, 1997

Wirth, Jason, "Nietzsche's joy: On laughter's truth" in *Epochē: A Journal for the history of philosophy*, 10 (1), 117–139, 2005

Wirth, Jason, "The dark night is also a sun: Bataille's thanotic mendacity in Red America" in *International studies in philosophy*, 40.1, 2008, 129–142

Zahavi, Dan, "Michel Henry and the Phenomenology of the Invisible" in *Continental Review*, nr 32, 1999, 223–40

Index of Names

Index of Concepts

Authors

Jonna Bornemark

Jonna Bornemark is a philosopher and director of the Centre for Studies in Practical Knowledge at Södertörn University (Sweden). Her publications include *Kunskapens gräns, gränsens vetande: en fenomenologisk undersökning av transcendens och kroppslighet* (Södertörn Philosophical Studies, 2010), ""Ambiguities of the human body in phenomenology and Christian mysticism" in *The Body Unbound: Philosophical Perspectives on Religion, Embodiment, and Politics*, eds. Ola Sigurdson, Marius Timmann Mjaaland, and Sigridur Torgeirsdottir (CSP, 2010) and "Max Scheler and Edith Stein as Precursors to the 'Turn to Religion' within Phenomenology" in *Phenomenology and Religion: New Frontiers* (Södertörn Philosophical Studies, 2010), a volume she also co-edited. Her current research interests are philosophy of religion, theory of practical knowledge, the concept of "Bildung," animal–human relations, and phenomenology of eros and pregnancy.

Marcia Sá Cavalcante Schuback

Marcia Sá Cavalcante Schuback is professor of philosophy at Södertörn University (Sweden). She has also worked as associate professor at the Universidade Federal do Rio de Janeiro (UFRJ) in Brazil. Her field of research is continental philosophy, with focus on phenomenology, hermeneutics, German idealism, and hermeneutical readings of ancient philosophy. She is the author of *O começo de deus: A filosofia do devir no pensamento tardio de Schelling* (Vozes, 1998), *A doutrina dos sons de Goethe a caminho da música nova de Webern* (UFRJ, 1999), *Para ler os medievais: Ensaio de hermenêutica imaginativa* (Vozes, 2000), *Lovtal till intet: essäer om filosofisk hermeneutik* (Glänta, 2006), *Olho a olho: ensaios de longe* (7 Letras, 2010), *Att tänka i skisser* (Glänta, 2011). She has also translated several works of philosophy into Portuguese, among others *Being and Time* by Heidegger.

Carl Cederberg

Carl Cederberg is a philosopher working at Södertörn University (Sweden). He has previously published *Resaying the Human*: *Levinas Beyond Humanism and Antihumanism* (Södertörn Doctoral Dissertations, 2010), *Att läsa Platon* (Symposion, ed. 2007), and *En annan humaniora: en annan tid* (Södertörn Philosophical Studies, co-ed., with Hans Ruin, 2008). He teaches at the Centre for Studies in Practical Knowledge, the Philosophy Department, and the Department for Teacher Training and Education Studies. His research interests lie in the intersections of ethics, metaphysics, and politics.

Helena Dahlberg

Helena Dahlberg is a philosopher and dancer who works at the Department of Literature, History of Ideas and Religion at the University of Gothenburg. Her dissertation from 2011 in the field of history of ideas is entitled *Vikten av kropp: Frågan om kött och människa i Maurice Merleau-Pontys Le visible et l'invisible* (Gothenburg University, 2011) and deals with the concept of the flesh in Merleau-Ponty's philosophy and it's relationship to French humanism in the 1940s. She has also published *Reflective Lifeworld Research* together with Karin Dahlberg and Maria Nyström (Studentlitteratur, 2008). Her research concerns questions about the body and human embodiment from a phenomenological point of view, and it specifically focuses on questions about the at once familiar and alien character of the body. She is also interested in the intersection between dance and philosophy.

Françoise Dastur

Françoise Dastur taught philosophy in the University of Paris I from 1969 to 1995, in the University of Paris XII from 1995 to 1999, and in the University of Nice-Sophia Antipolis from 1999 to 2003. She taught also as visiting professor in the Universities of Warwick, Essex,

De Paul (Chicago) and Boston College. She is now, as Honorary Professor of Philosophy, attached to the Husserl Archives of Paris (ENS Ulm), a research unit affiliated to the French National Center for Research (CNRS). She was one of the founding members in 1993 and the President until 2003 of the École Française de Daseinsanalyse, of which she is now honorary President. She has published many articles in French, English and German on Husserl, Heidegger, Merleau-Ponty, Ricoeur, Derrida, etc. and is the author of several books in French, three of which have been translated into English: *Heidegger and the Question of Time* (Humanities Press, 1998), *Telling Time, Sketch of a Phenomenological Chrono-logy* (Athlone Press, 2000), and *Death, An Essay on Finitude* (Athlone Press, 1996).

Lisa Folkmarson Käll

Lisa Folkmarson Käll holds a Ph.D. in women's studies and in philosophy. She is currently a researcher at the Center for Gender Research, Uppsala University, where she serves as coordinator of the research profile area Body/Embodiment. Her publications include "Fashioned in Nakedness, Sculptured and Caused to Be Born: Bodies in Light of the Sartrean Gaze" (*Continental Philosophy Review*, 2010) and "Expression Between Self and Other" (*Idealistic Studies*, 2009). She is editor of *Normality/Normativity* (2009) and co-editor of *Body Claims* (2009) and *Stil, Kön, Andrahet: Tolv Essäer i Feministisk Filosofi* (2010). Her research brings together philosophy, primarily from the French existential-phenomenological tradition, with current gender research and feminist theory, and bears on questions of embodied subjectivity, bodily constitution of sexual difference and sexual identity, intersubjectivity, and the relation between selfhood and otherness.

Agnès Pigler

Agnès Pigler is doctor of philosophy and teaches ancient philosophy at the University of Dijon. Her main research is on Plotinus and she is the author of *Plotin. Une métaphysique de l'amour. L'amour comme structure du monde intelligible* (Vrin, 2002) and *Le vocabulaire de Plotin* (Ellipses, 2003). She translated and wrote the introduction, commentaires, and notes to *Ennéade III,7 (45), De l'éternité et du temps* (Ellipses, 1999) and translated and wrote the introduction to *Plotin: Traité 54* (Les Editions du Cerf, 2004). Her other publications include "De la nature chez la surabondance du Premier chez Plotin" in *Dialogue XLIII*, Canadian Philosophical Association (2004). She also directs the Culture Department of the state of Dijon.

Anna-Lena Renqvist

Anna-Lena Renqvist holds a Ph.D. in philosophy and is currently connected to the reaserch program FSL at Royal Institute of Art (Sweden). She is the author of *Eros, Kronos y Kairos: Hacia una doctrina de tiempo de F.W.J.Schelling* (Universidad de Pompeu Fabra, Barcelona, 2005). Among recent publications can be mentioned "Schellings begynnelser" in Lychnos (2012), "Apology of pain" in *Dimensions of Pain* (ed. Lisa Käll, Routledge, UP), "Gränsfall" in *Kritiker* (2011), "Den skapande tiden i tidens skugga" in *Kritiker* (2010) and *Tid i kvadrat* (Ariel, UP). She has also translated works of philosophy and poetry into Swedish, among others *Att tänka det religiösa* by Eugenio Trías (Thales, 2004) and *Ferias* by Federico García Lorca (eds. Ramon Soley & Museo de Papel de Capileira, 2000).

Nicholas Smith

Nicholas Smith teaches history of philosophy, contemporary philosophy, and psychoanalytical theory at Södertörn University. His has recently publiched *Towards a Phenomenology of Repression: A Husserlian Reply to the Freudian Challenge* (Acta Universitatis Stockholmiensis, 2010). He is also the co-editor of *Hermeneutik och tradition: Gadamer och den grekiska filosofin* (Södertörn Philosophical Studies 2003). He has written extensively on contemporary philosophy, psychoanalysis, and art. He also translated Ricoeur, Nietzsche, Derrida, and Husserl, and has participated in several art projects.

Elizabeth B. Sikes

Elizabeth Sikes is a senior lecturer in philosophy at Seattle University. Her interests revolve around German idealism, ecological philosophy, and aesthetics. She is especially interested in the kinds of experiences and practices – aesthetic and religious ones, for example – that connect the human being more intrinsically with nature and thus facilitate the possibility of deep change in thought patterns destructive of the earth and self. Her published works includes "Sacred Syllogisms and Song for the Ecology of Mind," in *Comparative and Continental Philosophy*, vol. 1, nr. 1 (Equinox: 2009); "The Decline (and Fall?) of the Fatherland: The Problem of Historical Memory in Hölderlin's Poetics of Tragedy," in *International Studies in Philosophy*, vol. 40, nr. 1, 2008; and "The Enigmatic Burden of Metaphor in Hölderlin's Poetics of Tragedy," in *"Es bleibet aber eine Spur / Doch eines Wortes": zur späten Hymnik und Tragödientheorie Friedrich Hölderlins*, ed. Christoph Jamme and Anja Lemke (Paderborn: Wilhelm Fink Verlag, 2004). She is currently working on a manuscript called, "The Ecological Task of the Poet and Other Artists of Life."

Peter Trawny

Peter Trawny is a philosopher who teaches at the Department of Philosophy at the University of Wuppertal. He works in the fields of phenomenology, political philosophy, globalization, cosmopolitics, ethics, and philosophy of Christianity. He has been a visiting professor at the University of Vienna, the Tongji University in Shanghai, and Södertörn University in Sweden. He is the author of several books, including *Martin Heidegger: Einführung* (Campus Verlag, 2003), *Heidegger und Hölderlin oder Der Europäische Morgen* (Königshausen & Neumann, 2004), *Denkbarer Holocaust: Die politische Ethik Hannah Arendts* (Königshausen & Neumann, 2005), *Sokrates oder Die Geburt der Politischen Philosophie* (Königshausen & Neumann, 2007), *"Adyton": Heideggers esotherische Philosophie* (Matthes und Seitz, 2010), and *Medium und Revolution* (Matthes und Seitz, 2011). Trawny has also edited several volumes of the Martin Heidegger *Gesamtausgabe*.

Jason Wirth

Jason Wirth is professor of philosophy at Seattle University, and works and teaches in the areas of continental philosophy, Buddhist philosophy, aesthetics, and African philosophy. His recent books include *The Conspiracy of Life: Meditations on Schelling and His Time* (SUNY, 2003), a translation of the third draft of Schelling's *The Ages of the World* (SUNY, 2000), the edited volume *Schelling Now* (Indiana, 2004), the co-edited volume (with Bret Davis and Brian Schroeder) *Japanese and Continental Philosophy: Conversations with the Kyoto School* (Indiana, 2011), and *The Barbarian Principle: Merleau-Ponty, Schelling, and the Question of Nature* (forthcoming). He is the associate editor and book review editor of the journal *Comparative and Continental Philosophy* (and its attendant book series, published by Northwestern University Press).

Södertörn Philosophical Studies

Södertörn Philosophical Studies is a book series published under the direction of the Department of Philosophy at Södertörn University. The series consists of monographs and anthologies in philosophy, with a special focus on the Continental-European tradition. It seeks to provide a platform for innovative contemporary philosophical research. The volumes are published mainly in English and Swedish. The series is edited by Marcia Sá Cavalcante Schuback and Hans Ruin.